For
Richard W. Wilson
whose uncertainties as a fledgling teacher
moved the editor to assemble this book
and
for all of the thousands of industrious English
teachers whose imaginative efforts bring a bit of
magical inspiration to their
students.

REVIEW COPY

Title: CREATIVE APPROACHES TO THE
TEACHING OF ENGLISH: SECONDARY
Published: March 1974
Price: $4.95 paper

Please send copies of the review when it is published.

F. E. PEACOCK PUBLISHERS, INC.
401 W. IRVING PARK ROAD
ITASCA, ILLINOIS 60143

Creative Approaches to the TEACHING of ENGLISH: Secondary

Edited by
R. Baird Shuman
Duke University

F. E. Peacock Publishers, Inc. ITASCA, ILLINOIS 60143

RILEY LIBRARY
OUACHITA BAPTIST UNIVERSITY

Copyright © 1974
F. E. Peacock Publishers, Inc.
All Rights Reserved
Library of Congress
Catalog Card No. 73-85766
Printed in the United States of America

Contents

Preface	vii
Contributors	xiii
1 Literature *Robert E. Probst*	1
2 Drama *Charles R. Duke*	39
3 Grammar *R. W. Reising*	101
4 Writing *Jan A. Guffin*	133
5 Spelling, Punctuation, and Vocabulary *Bertrand F. Richards*	186
6 Reading *R. Baird Shuman*	221
Index	263

Preface

In his recent *Teaching English in Secondary Schools* (The Macmillan Company, 1973), Theodore W. Hipple tells his readers, "Gone forever are the days when language instruction meant only traditional grammar, when literature teaching consisted of Shakespeare and *Silas Marner* with a few poems tossed in for good measure, when composition training was a September theme on 'My Summer Vacation.' Today's English teacher has far greater responsibilities." In a sense, it is with these "greater responsibilities" — how to meet them more successfully and effectively, how to recognize both their limits and limitations, how to project them to the point that the student comes to realize and assume his own "greater responsibilities" — that this book is concerned.

No one is so overworked as the average English teacher. Even in Mr. Conant's ideal world which calls for English teachers to deal with no more than 100 students a day, the reading load is staggering; but more staggering still is the diversity of what the English teacher is expected to teach: grammar, composition, creative writing, literature, dramatics, public speaking, reading — you name it, and probably somewhere not too far from where you are sitting, an English teacher will be trying to teach it. This same English teacher will probably be running a debating society, a school newspaper, a school yearbook, or some other combination of extracurricular activities as well. And in his spare time, this paragon is expected to be actively engaged in community affairs; in taking courses to keep current in his field; in seeing plays; in keeping abreast of recent writing; possibly in doing some writing of his own; and in thinking up creative ways to teach the whole gamut of topics which come into the purview of a typical high school English program, even though he has perhaps had specific training in only a third of them.

This book has grown out of a conviction that English teachers *want* to be creative, exciting people, giving their students the very best they have to give, drawing from them the very highest level of response each student is capable of attaining. But in the face of the monumental job that English teaching turns out to be, many teachers, particularly those who are just entering the profession, can do little more than plan from day to day, work themselves to death on weekends and holidays, and count the days until summer, the period that many first- and second-year teachers reserve for doing the kind of long-term planning that is a necessary concomitant of confident teaching.

Creative Approaches to the Teaching of English: Secondary is meant to be the sort of book which harried English teachers can keep on their shelves or bedside tables to turn to when they are up to their eyeballs in work and have little inspiration for the four or five classes they are scheduled to meet the following day. It is also meant to be the sort of book that can be of substantial assistance to them in their long-range planning. Just as the really inspired cook reads cookbooks but does not follow them doggedly, so the really inspired teacher will not doggedly follow the suggestions in this book. What works spectacularly well for a teacher in Bird-in-Hand, Pennsylvania, may fail utterly for an equally dedicated teacher in Truth or Consequences, New Mexico. But there are valuable suggestions in this book for anyone who teaches English. The teacher should try what he thinks might work in his school and dismiss what he thinks will not work.

Had the range of this book been broader, as some may argue it should have been, the volume would have been unwieldy. The editor would have liked to include chapters on listening and speaking, for example, but these chapters will have to wait until a future book. This book is meant to be basic and to address from as practical a standpoint as possible some of the most common problems that face the beginning teacher.

Everyone who has contributed to the volume has had substantial teaching experience and is still actively involved in working with high

PREFACE

school youngsters and teachers in the field.

An attempt was made to keep each chapter about equal in length; however, the chapter on Drama is considerably longer than the rest because it is, in reality, two chapters. Charles Duke deals both with the teaching of drama as a literary genre and with the teaching of creative dramatics. In his chapter, he notes quite aptly that, "First, drama is Shakespeare in the minds of many students; frequently the only exposure to drama which students receive is centered on the reading of a Shakespearean play each of the four years a student is in high school. His other impression of drama usually is associated with the yearly senior play, often produced strictly as a money-raising venture; whatever dramatic appreciation occurs is a secondary and very minor consideration." In his chapter, Duke establishes realistic bases for broadening the scope of drama teaching in the school and for making it a school activity rather than merely an activity of the English class.

Duke's suggestions about the teaching of Shakespearean drama, the teaching of black drama, approaches to the Theater of the Absurd, and the uses of television drama in the school will be of particular help to teachers as will his extensive suggestions for introducing creative dramatics into the classroom.

In his chapter on the teaching of literature, Robert E. Probst concludes with the words, "The student must be free, in writing as well as in reading, to examine his own responses, to attempt to learn more about both himself and the literature." The whole thrust of Probst's suggestions is that the student must come to enjoy reading before he can grow into a sophisticated reader. Probst urges the teacher to view literature "not as a substitute for the real experience, but rather, an alternative experience, characterized by the opportunity for reflection and thought." He cautions that despite the literary scholar's predilection for knowledge about literature, "the high school student is still most likely to prefer literature as a source of experience. If that preference is ignored, it seems probable that the student's natural interest in literature will decline."

Probst feels that teachers might adopt "as an operating principle, that the model of cooperation shall prevail over the model of competition." He insists that "There should be no penalty for mistakes in the classroom—mistakes are, after all, a natural part of any learning process and they should be accepted as such, without embarrassment or condemnation." In talking about having students make films in the literature class, Probst contends that to do so is a healthy experience because "most teachers who attempt it know very little about it at the start. They are thus required to learn with the students a process that can do much to improve communication in the classroom."

The English teacher, usually a literature major more nearly than what ordinarily is broadly encompassed by the term "English major," often finds himself at sea in the teaching of those parts of the English curriculum in which his training has been sparse—grammar, writing, spelling, vocabulary building, punctuation, and reading. Yet in the average secondary school more teaching is done in these areas than in the teaching of literature. Therefore, many teachers will find concrete and immediately useful suggestions in the chapters by Robert Reising, Jan Guffin, Bertrand Richards, and R. Baird Shuman.

Robert Reising points out the need for the teacher to know something about dialects and particularly about black English. He also warns the teacher not to expect miracles in the teaching of grammar. Grammar is a respectable and interesting discipline unto itself. No real evidence exists to suggest that knowledge of grammar is related to perfection in one's speaking or writing; indeed, the weight of evidence suggests the opposite. Reising says that teachers "have good reason for teaching grammar, especially linguistically based grammar, but they should not do so in hopes of improving student writing." He shrewdly observes that "Grammar and aspirin have one feature in common: they cannot do all that people expect of them." Yet it is important that one understand language because it is "man's most important resource, the basis for his knowledge and the key to his power; and grammar study helps to explain why and how it works."

Reising outlines exciting means of teaching grammar in ways that involve students directly and actively in its study, supplying themselves many of the data to be explored in the grammar course. He points the way to the discovery method in the teaching and learning of grammar. He brings the reader to the threshold of approaches to the subject which will be not only instructive but beguiling to the high school student, particularly to the one with language problems.

Jan Guffin is concerned in his chapter both with expository and creative writing, and at times he suggests the two might be merged: "It is ironic that in our country we take such pride in our record of experimentation and creativity in science, yet persist in believing when we get around to writing about such things, that we must necessarily develop a prose style which is both unexperimental and unimaginative. Wouldn't an occasional 'whoosh,' 'zoom,' or 'splash' be refreshing in such literature?" Guffin contends that unless the teacher "clearly understands the factors which both inhibit and encourage creative expression, the teacher himself can become one of the greatest barriers to creative growth in his students." If this situation is to be avoided, teachers must learn "to value the ideas of students for their quality first, and worry about the correctness of their expression second."

Guffin is particularly vehement in feeling that fluency is the greatest problem in many students, and he suggests very practical ways of encouraging and improving fluency. He tells teachers how to spot fluency problems, warning that "Too often teachers mistake a problem in fluency for ignorance or inability." Writing must be disciplined, but it must also be fun. Guffin does not lose sight of either fact, but he chides the English teacher with the statement that "Writers of billboard advertisements probably have more fun with language than any English teacher in the country," and he suggests ways in which English teachers can make the whole writing process much more alive than it often is in today's secondary schools. Mostly, Guffin encourages teacher optimism: "Miracles happen when we expect them most."

Writing about spelling, punctuation, and vocabulary, Bertrand F. Richards differentiates between studying language and "languaging." Only the latter is likely to bring the student to the point of being able to spell decently, punctuate sensibly, and have a sufficient working vocabulary to make him fluent in expressing himself. Richards never loses sight of the fact that "language is made up of two systems, the *phonemic* and the *graphemic,* and that the graphemic system is only an attempt to give permanence to the phonemic system." He is disturbed by the fact that "As teachers we too frequently demand that our students conform to a standard which does not actually exist in their real world—the standard of textbook English"—and he urges teachers to be more realistic in their approaches than many have been in the past. He reminds teachers that "It is indeed our salvation that kids *know* far more than they *don't know.*"

Realistic in his own approach, Richards asserts that "perhaps phonetic spelling is the best spelling, but to be effective it requires a phonetic alphabet, and that the English alphabet is not." He then shows teachers how English spelling may best be learned and understood. He honestly states that there are no creative approaches to the teaching of spelling: "Spelling is a discipline and a difficult one at that. The teaching of spelling has engrossed pedagogues and classroom teachers alike for generations. Probably every method conceivable has been explored and re-explored. What can be presented are some creative approaches to the *learning* of spelling."

Richards' journeys into the history of the English language turn up some surprises for the average English teacher and serve to illustrate how spelling, punctuation, and vocabulary can best be presented to students whose interest in these topics may have been killed by years of boring drill.

Finally, there is some question about whether a chapter on reading should be a part of a book like this. Reading teachers are, ideally, specifically trained in reading, and most English teachers today are by no means reading experts. However, R. Baird Shuman asserts, quite realistically, that "Just as some administrators think that anyone who can speak English should be able to teach it, so do many administrators think that every secondary school English teacher is able to teach reading. And the administrator who has no teachers trained specifically in reading is probably correct in assuming that the English teacher is better able to help students with reading difficulties than most of his other teachers." So, for better or worse, most English teachers spend some of their time functioning either formally or informally as teachers of reading.

Shuman has not presented a quickie course in reading for the nonexpert in this chapter. Rather, he has proffered to the beginning teacher, whose tattered ego may be bleeding, a tourniquet to use judiciously to keep from bleeding to death before trained help arrives. This chapter is intended only as a first-aid kit. Our schools need more reading teachers and must eventually have them. The teacher who masters this chapter and uses its suggestions well will do a better job in the teaching of reading than would have been possible had he not read the chapter at all. But, for the most part, he must either go back to school to turn himself into a reading teacher or bring every pressure to bear in his community to get more reading experts into the schools if the reading program is to be maximally effective.

The editor and contributors to *Creative Approaches to the Teaching of English: Secondary* wish their readers well as they seek to broaden their horizons and find means of helping their students achieve growth through English. They urge teachers to grow with their students, learn with them about new approaches to learning, and not be teachers about whom a student can say, "Yeah, I had this teacher who taught me grammar through the whole tenth grade. I can't remember his name."

R. Baird Shuman

Durham, North Carolina

Contributors

CHARLES R. DUKE is Associate Professor of English at Plymouth State College in New Hampshire. He holds the Ph.D. in English education from Duke University and is a specialist in the teaching of drama and in creative dramatics. A frequent contributor to major professional journals, Professor Duke is also the editor of *Resources for the Teaching of English: Grades 8-12*, a two volume curriculum guide published by ERIC in 1973.

JAN GUFFIN has taught for ten years at the high school level and is presently on the faculty at North Central High School in Indianapolis. He is a candidate for the Ph.D. in English education at Duke University and is experienced in the teaching of writing, having offered courses in it both at North Central High School and at the Indianapolis Campus of the University of Indiana. He is on the Board of Directors of the National Council of Teachers of English and has been a Reader in English for the Advanced Placement Tests of the Educational Testing Service.

ROBERT E. PROBST is Assistant Professor of English Education at Georgia State University. He holds the Ph.D. in English education from Duke University, where his dissertation was entitled "Literature: A Mode of Knowing." Professor Probst has been a teacher at Milford Mill High School in Baltimore, an instructor in Education at Duke University, and Supervisor in English for the Norfolk, Virginia Public Schools. He has published widely and has most recently produced a definitive article, "The Influence of Francis Bacon's Concept of Knowledge on the Evolution of Seventeenth-Century Literary Criticism," which appeared in the *Revue des Langues Vivantes.*

R. W. REISING has taught at the University of South Carolina, Fort Hayes State College, Furman University, the University of South Florida, Virginia Commonwealth University, and presently is in the Department of Communication Arts at Pembroke State University. He holds the Ed.D. in English education from Duke University. Professor Reising has published some 25 articles and is presently collaborating on a book entitled *The Poetry of Baseball.* He is also writing a biography of Jim Thorpe.

BERTRAND F. RICHARDS is an Associate Professor of English at Indiana State University. He holds the Ph.D. in English education from Duke University, where he was elected to membership in Phi Beta Kappa. He directed the Effingham Experiment, which he reported on in the *Teacher College Journal* (March 1967). Professor Richards is on the Board of Directors of the National Council of Teachers of English and is a member of the National Committee on Semantics in the Secondary Schools. Prior to entering college teaching, he taught for several years in secondary schools.

R. BAIRD SHUMAN is Professor of Education at Duke University where he specializes in English education. He holds the Ph.D. in English from the University of Pennsylvania and has taught in the public schools of Philadelphia. He has also taught at the University of Pennsylvania, Drexel Institute of Technology, San José State College, the Moore Institute of Art, and the Philadelphia Conservatory of Music. He is the author of over 150 articles and three books of literary criticism. He has edited *Nine Black Poets, A Galaxy of Black Writing,* and Clarence Darrow's naturalistic novel, *An Eye for an Eye.*

ROBERT E. PROBST
Georgia State University

1 Literature

John Fisher, one of the National Council of Teachers of English's Distinguished Lecturers for 1972, remarks in the conclusion of his talk that

Language and literature must be *both* practical and imaginative. Society cannot exist without communication, and the more complex it becomes the more vital becomes the clarity and integrity of its communication. But without an ability imaginatively to conceptualize the world around us and our relations with one another, we would have nothing to communicate — indeed, we would not even recognize ourselves as human beings. Literature is the storehouse of these concepts, and it is the richness and variety of the concepts that justifies our studying literature, just as much as the accuracy and lucidity of its expression (16, pp. 15-16).

Two years earlier, also in a Distinguished Lecture, Louise Rosenblatt had stated that "surely, of all the arts, literature is most immediately implicated with life itself" (57, p. 4). Their comments suggest quite clearly that the teacher of literature is dealing with something of almost infinite scope. The mathematician and the physicist are bound to a consideration of certain phenomena by the principles of their disciplines, but the student of literature is limited to the confines ... of what? "Life itself," Rosenblatt has suggested, with all the variety and complexity that that implies.

"Life itself" is an imprecise term, and yet it is hard to imagine a more appropriate statement of the subject matter of literature, for there is probably little in human experience that has not at one time or another found itself confined within the pages of a book. And this is much as we should expect it to be, for language, in almost all its manifestations, is an effort to come to terms with experience, to grasp it or conceptualize it in such a way that it becomes manageable or comprehensible. The psychologist Joseph Church has identified this use of language by young children and has labeled the process "thematizing." "It is worth emphasizing," he says, "that the solution to the child's perplexities lies in thematizing them — reducing them to manageable symbolic forms — which is, after all, the goal of the philosopher, the artist, and the scientific theorist" (7, p. 97). It is also, and perhaps most obviously, the goal of the writer, who sits down at his typewriter with a head full of characters, events, motives, notions about the world, and the people in it, and from that morass attempts to create some literary form with meaning and significance for himself, at least, and possibly for others.

It is with those "others" that the teacher of literature is concerned. The reader, like the writer, is interested in meaning, in the manageable symbolic forms that impose order on the chaos of experience. Kenneth Burke's definition of man as "the symbol using (symbol-making, symbol-misusing) animal" (3, p. 16) applies equally well to both author and audience. Expounding upon that definition, Burke argues that the motives that lead to the production of works of literature and the motives that lead to the production of common, normal converse among men, are, in fact, the same. Men speak and write poetry for the same reason, and that reason is that man's natural reaction to experience is to put it in symbolic form. Poetry is the result of man's natural delight in exercising one of his powers. The reader is also naturally inclined toward symbolizing. Burke would probably find it more difficult to explain a lack of interest in things literary and linguistic than to account for the presence of that interest. Man is, by his definition, interested in the symbolizing processes that result in literary art.

That is to say, man may usually be expected to take an interest in understanding his world and his life and should therefore take a natural interest in the literature that contributes substantially to that understanding. Unfortunately, but obviously, not all students demonstrate that interest, despite Burke's definition. The English teacher in most public high schools will face enough students for whom the study of literature is an unpleasant obligation to realize that a natural interest in literature cannot be depended on. For whatever the reasons, many students enter the English class under protest. Nonetheless, a good number of these protesting students do seem to read. The National Study of High School English Programs, reported by James R. Squire and Roger K. Applebee in *High School English Instruction Today,* discovered that high school students were encountering, by choice, an unexpectedly high number of books. A survey of 16,089 students in both college-preparatory and noncollege-preparatory classes at all grade levels indicated that "An astounding 127,629 books had been obtained by students during the month before they were surveyed, an average of almost eight books per student" (62, p. 181).

So a great many students are reading, and, as Daniel Fader's experiments have proved, many of the students who are not reading can be enticed to read. His program, reported in *Hooked on Books,* has had such success that he can say of his list of recommended paperbacks that it

represents books so attractive to young people that the average boy at B.T.S., who arrives with a reading rate of no books per lifetime, is reading one library book every two days by the time he leaves. And that *average* includes all the boys—those who still never read anything as well as those who devour a book a day. However, it does not include the large number of paperbound books used as texts, or the immense number of newspapers and magazines devoured by newly awakened appetites (15, p. 58).

There is, in other words, some evidence that the interest in literature implicit in Burke's definition of man is, in fact, a characteristic, or potentially a characteristic, of many high school students. The English teacher should be able to turn that characteristic of his students into profit in the classroom, but in order to do so he must first understand, insofar as possible, what constitutes interest in literature for high school students.

WHY PEOPLE READ

It should not be at all surprising to discover that the literary interests of adolescents are not exactly the same as those of literary scholars. Not only are the two groups of readers frequently attracted to different works, but they also seem stimulated to read by different motives. Few adolescents, for example, show interest in the complications of literary history, in the problems raised by variant texts, in the theories of genre or of prosody, or in many of the other subtleties of scholarship in the field of literature. They are interested instead in an exciting story, intriguing characters, adventure, love—all those things, in other words, that seem to be part of life as it might be. They are interested, of course, in their immediate world, the problems of adolescence, of family relationships, of physical and emotional maturation, but they are also likely to be concerned about the problems of the future—their adult roles, their work, the beliefs and values that will influence their decisions.

G. Robert Carlsen, in *Books and the Teen-Age Reader: A Guide for Teachers, Librarians and Parents*, a reference text very useful to the English teacher, lists the following steps through which the adolescent will progress, as a guide to the adolescent's reading interests:

1. Discovering and accepting his sex's role in our culture.
2. Developing new relationships with members of his own sex.
3. Achieving an easy relationship with members of the opposite sex.
4. Accepting his physical body.
5. Changing his relationship with his parents.
6. Working for pay.
7. Finding a vocation.
8. Becoming aware of his value patterns (5, pp. 11-13).*

Carlsen remarks that "If books are to have any meaning, they must be related to the young person's personal and social needs" (5, p. 11) and suggests that a list such as the one he has offered might provide valuable clues to a teacher concerned about finding literature to which his classes will be responsive. Similar lists crop up, not unexpectedly, in other places. The tables of contents of such works as *High Interest—Easy Reading for Junior and Senior High School Students* and *Books for You*, although not tabulations of the characteristics of high school students, can serve well as checklists of possible interests. And the books themselves, of course, serve well as bibliographic aids. All of these lists of characteristics or interests indicate quite clearly that the adolescent's focus is not upon formal or stylistic elements, but upon the relationship of the work to life, either real or imagined.

---

*From *Books and the Teen-age Reader*, Rev. and Updated by G. Robert Carlsen. Copyright © 1967, 1971 by G. Robert Carlsen. Reprinted by permission of Harper and Row, Publishers, Inc.

LITERATURE

Louise Rosenblatt, commenting upon the reasons offered by a group of college students for reading novels, summarizes neatly the purposes for reading:

> The college students . . . placed greatest emphasis on literature as a means of broadening one's knowledge of people and society. This reflected their curiosity about life, a curiosity shared with younger adolescent and preadolescent students. For the average adult reader as well, literature contributes to the enlargement of experience. We participate in imaginary situations, we look on at characters living through crises, we explore ourselves and the world about us, through the medium of literature (58, p. 37).

As her phrase, "the enlargement of experience," implies, the reading interests of students will frequently extend beyond immediate concerns. Although a great deal of the reading of both children and adults is simple entertainment—escapist reading—there is also the possibility of encountering literature that expands the limited perspective of one man. Dwight Burton sees this as the principle value of literature:

> Literature is liberating in the sense that it helps to free us from the inherent shackles fastened upon us by our society. Crucial in the quest for identity, as opposed to a deadening relating to the crowd, is the ability to shake off, when necessary, the emotional censors of society. One can accomplish this in the literary experience and therein lies the great enduring value of literature (4, pp. 5-6).

He continues, arguing that "Experience with literature enables the reader to build a level of imaginative living which is real in itself, lying somewhere between dead-level literalness and hallucination. Even in so-called escape reading, for example, one comes to terms with experience while escaping from it at the same time" (4, p. 6).

Literature for the adolescent—and probably for the adult—provides an opportunity to find out about life. It provides vicarious experience of the most valuable sort, serving as a stimulus and focal point for reflection about one's self and one's world. The young girl engrossed in a romantic novel is likely to be experimenting with her own feelings, testing her own notions of love against those of the author or of the characters, and the young man deep in an adventure story may well be imagining himself in the situations portrayed, imaginatively testing his own reactions, attitudes, and skills. Literature provides, vicariously, a range of experience far beyond that which is possible for one man actually to achieve, and is thus a most valuable stimulus for intellectual and emotional growth.

That is not to say that people read imaginative literature for information. The intellectual growth and liberation referred to here result not from the acquisition of more factual knowledge, but from the imaginative encounter with experience. The reader of *Hamlet* may learn very little that a historian or a political scientist would consider significant about the governing of old Denmark, but he may instead acquire insight into the emotions and thoughts of a man torn by the desire to act and uncertain about the merits of the actions he contemplates. J. N. Hook argues that the important distinction is between facts and insights. He says that literature "gives information of a kind not available in encyclopedias. If we want facts, we go to reference books. But, if we want insights different from those afforded by facts, we go to literature" (26, p. 128).

Literature's most important offering to the reader is, then, a form of experience. It is obviously not real experience—reading *Moby Dick* is not the same thing as hunting the white whale—but neither is it simply the acquisition of factual information. If it were, then *Moby Dick* would have long since been replaced by a more contemporary work. The reading of *Moby Dick* provides instead vicarious entry into the mind of a man obsessed with one goal, and a vicarious Nantucket sleigh ride. It is not a substitute for the real experience, but rather an alternative experience, characterized by the opportunity for reflection and thought. Building upon Burke's definition of man as the symbol-using animal we might refer to the act of reading as "symbolic experience"—that is to say, a form of experience that is not in any sense unreal, but that is obtained through a symbol system rather than through physical encounter. Wallace Bacon and Robert Breen argue this point persuasively, contending that "A reader's experience with a book is no different in its nature than his experience with other objects in life. All experience is interactive; it is a traffic between the object and the subject. Actually, the sense of living through an event characterizes the experience of reading as it does the experience of living" (1, p. 5).

THE APPROACHES TO LITERATURE

We should expect the teaching of literature to take into consideration the nature of literature as a form of symbolic experience, but unfortunately there is some evidence that it has not always done so. Too frequently, courses in literature seem to have concentrated upon the dissemination of factual information about the literary works, the authors, the critics, and so on. Valuable as that information may be, to emphasize it in the high school classroom is to ignore the motives from which most students read. In their report on the National Study of High School English programs, Squire and Applebee note that

> More often than not, observers found the hours of literary study devoted to formal or informal talks by teacher or student on the age or period in which a work was written, on the writer himself, on the literary genre as an abstraction to be perceived in and for itself without reference to text, or on isolated facts extracted from the selection. Students were asked not to examine passages and incidents to determine how a specific image or episode contributes to the author's unified effect, but rather to accept blandly the theme or idea emerging from the work (or almost as frequently from the teacher's comments on the work) and to apply it to "everyday life," to "their own experience," or to other reading. Attempts to relate the reading to experiences which have meaning to the reader are commendable, of course, but not at the expense of understanding what the author has to say or how he says it. In too many classrooms, students discuss in vague and uncertain terms concepts which they would be sorely pressed to find for themselves in any work they had read (62, pp. 106-7).

The authors refer to these practices as "evasions of literary study" (62, p. 107), and speculate that they are the products of a misconception about the nature of literature: "Here indeed may be one of the difficulties in schools today: too many teachers seem to think that the ultimate end of instruction in literature is knowledge of and about *Macbeth* or *Silas Marner,* rather than refinement of the processes of learning to read *Macbeth* or *Silas Marner* with insight and discrimination" (62, p. 107). The literary scholar may well have developed an interest in the "knowledge about," but the high school student is still most likely to prefer literature as a source of experience. If that preference is ignored, it seems probable that the student's natural interest in literature will decline. If, on the other hand, that preference is respected, then it is quite possible that the interest will flourish, and perhaps expand to include the peripheral information.

Louise Rosenblatt cautions us about the corrupting influence of literary instruction that values data more highly than experience:

> The adolescent can be easily led into an artificial relationship with literature. Year after year as freshman come into college, one finds that even the most verbally proficient of them, often those most intimately drawn to literature, have already acquired a hard veneer, a pseudo-professional approach. They are anxious to have the correct labels—the right period, the biographical

background, the correct evaluation. They read literary histories and biographies, critical essays, and then, if they have time, they read the works (56, p. 71).

Instruction that cultivates the "pseudo-professional approach" can only be considered a perversion of the English classroom.

Unfortunately, other approaches to the teaching of literature seem to be difficult to define. Northrop Frye insists, in fact, that teaching literature is an impossibility:

> Art, like nature, has to be distinguished from the systematic study of it, which is criticism of literature. Similarly, the difficulty often felt in "teaching literature" arises from the fact that it cannot be done: the criticism of literature is all that can be directly taught. Literature is not a subject of study, but an object of study: the fact that it consists of words, as we have seen, makes us confuse it with the talking verbal disciplines (20, pp. 11-12).

He argues further that "The reading of literature should, like prayer in the Gospels, step out of the talking world of criticism into the private and secret presence of literature. Otherwise the reading will not be a genuine literary experience, but a mere reflection of critical conventions, memories, and prejudices" (20, p. 27). He implies here that the literary experience is beyond the reach of a third party, that it is a totally private and secret matter between reader and work, an area into which a teacher cannot intrude. In one sense, of course, this is undeniably true. There will inevitably be much in a student's reading of a work that is not exposed to and cannot be touched by a teacher. Nonetheless, if we exclude the teacher completely from this realm, then we cast the student entirely on his own resources. Frye's analysis may lead us to take a more hopeless view of the teaching of literature than is necessary.

Frye lies at one extreme of what James E. Miller, Jr., sees as "the slow swinging of a pendulum between two poles of emphasis which may be variously described as substance and psychology, subject matter and student, or intellectuality and society" (41, p. 26). At the time he was writing, in 1967, Miller saw the teaching of English moving away from the subject-matter pole, represented by Frye and his insistence that literature itself cannot be taught. Miller expected the following years to be characterized by greater attention to the student, and diminished reverence for such hallowed educational principles as "We must cover the material" and for some of the approaches, such as those described by Hook, that had determined organization and method in the preceding years.

J. N. Hook finds that the teaching of literature follows one of six different paths, each of which, he argues, has value in the high school classroom. The *historical approach,* perhaps the most common in college and the upper grades of the high schools, is well represented by a vast collection of textbooks. According to Bertrand Evans and James Lynch, chronological organization is the most frequent method of arranging literature anthologies intended for use in the 11th and 12th grades (37, p. 132). According to Hook, this approach, with its emphasis upon biography and period, can be of great value in developing the perspective upon matters both literary and personal, but it runs the risk of subordinating the literature to the history. Evans and Lynch are more outspoken, insisting that, "as the anthologies themselves indicate, chronological and geographical arrangements tend to pervert the study of literature, for the teacher is likely to find himself conducting a class in geography or literary history rather than literature" (37, p. 42).

The second approach, the *sociopsychological,* is distinguished by its concern with people. Rather than concentrate upon the life and times of the writer, as the historical approach presumably does, the sociopsychological approach would focus upon the life and times of the characters within the story, attempting to comprehend their actions, understand their motivations, and relate all to the lives of the student. Hook says the method is popular with students, a predictable reaction after reviewing Carlsen's list of the steps the adolescent takes toward adulthood.

The *emotive approach,* although it frequently degenerates into extolling the virtues of a writer or a work, has the distinction of emphasizing the pleasure to be derived from literature, as the *didactic approach,* although it may sink to the level of moralizing, emphasizes the insights, the truths to be abstracted from a work. The *paraphrastic approach,* as its name suggests, concentrates upon exact understanding of a work, as demonstrated by accurately paraphrasing the words of the author.

The sixth approach, the *analytical,* is a complex array of techniques borrowed from literary critics such as Northrop Frye, John Crowe Ransom, and Allan Tate. It emphasizes close reading of the text and detailed analysis of the techniques and the ideas of the writer. It can be a laborious process, but it can result in a sophisticated understanding of the way a literary work achieves its effects. Reservations about its value as a technique for high schools are common, however. Virginia Joki offers some precise recommendations: "I suggest that we teach analysis only as one of several approaches to literature, that we teach it only in our college divisions, only in grades eleven and twelve, and only four or five times a year" (31, p. 569). It is inappropriate, she feels, at lower grade levels or in greater quantity. Nonetheless, analysis remains a popular method, especially with teachers whose college training was influenced by the New Critics.

That there is some danger of some of these approaches transforming into what Rosenblatt has called "the *Pseudo-professional approach*" should be fairly obvious. Perhaps the one for which this is least likely to occur is the sociopsychological, and there, Hook points out, we find the other side of the coin—the danger of ignoring literary elements. Despite the dangers, Hook asserts that "the six categories provide an accurate taxonomy of instruction in literature." He adds, however, that "the techniques suggested for each approach have been modified in light of the present trend toward enhancing student responsiveness" (26, p. 143). Hook obviously felt the swing of the pendulum back toward the student, and though he desired to retain his six approaches, recognized the need to revise some of the methods within each approach.

One of the most powerful forces upon the pendulum within the past decade, turning it back in the direction of the student, has been the Dartmouth Conference. Its effect has been to stimulate the trend with which Hook has attempted to make his book conform. Because of its extensive influence on the approach to the teaching of English, we should perhaps explore some of the findings of the Conference before attempting to discuss in detail the techniques of instruction.

THE ANGLO-AMERICAN CONFERENCE ON THE TEACHING OF ENGLISH: THE DARTMOUTH CONFERENCE

The Dartmouth Conference was a meeting of approximately 50 educators representing the United States, England, and Canada. Their mutual concern was the state of the teaching of English, and they convened during the fall of 1966 to discuss what they saw to be the critical problems of the profession. Two major publications resulted from the Conference—John Dixon's *Growth through English* (8) and Herbert J. Muller's *The Uses of English* (44)—along with several pamphlets, one of which, *Response to Literature* (61), edited by James R. Squire, is particularly relevant here.

The Conference was enlivened by a wide range of opinion making it rash to ascribe one stance to the entire body. Several interesting points about the teaching of literature did, however, emerge from the discussions. One point, on which the British especially placed heavy emphasis, was that "the teacher must bring into a vivid relationship life as it is enacted and life as it is represented" (8, p. 54). Members of the Conference expressed widespread dissatisfaction with approaches to the teaching of literature that attempt to separate literature and life, and were more inclined to "look to literature to bring order and control to our world, and perhaps to offer an encounter with difficult areas of experience without exacting from us the full price" (8, p. 57). Literature, in other words, is to be taught as experience, not as a body of knowledge to be absorbed.

The position is not a new one. It was strongly argued in 1938 in Louise Rosenblatt's *Literature as Exploration* (58), still the most important book on the teaching of literature (a revised edition was published in 1968 by Noble and Noble); but if the National Study is correct, it is a position that has not had sufficient representation in the classroom. The Conference, too, expressed "dismay about prevailing approaches to the teaching of literature, not only at school level. So many seemed in the process to sap the central enjoyment and satisfaction of the act of reading and responding" (8, p. 58). One of the major complaints was about techniques in which the teacher seemed to play a more prominent role than the students. At several points Dixon comments about teaching of this sort:

There is a widespread and self-defeating refusal on both sides of the Atlantic to see that literature cannot be "taught" by a direct approach, and that the teacher who weighs in with talk or lecture is more likely to kill a personal response than to support and develop it (8, p. 58).*

The implication of many things said at the Conference, here made explicit, is that the teacher can intervene between the student and the literary work only in the most discreet and delicate manner. The heavy hand of authority—lecturing, demanding, assigning, cajoling, exhorting, and testing—can accomplish little of significance in an area of experience so deeply personal and private as literature. It is not a study to be pursued under duress:

There is no short cut then to each pupil learning to read for himself. Even a presented reading or a play has to be taken up by each individual in the audience out of his sense that the pattern and quality of the experience is a

---

*From *Growth through English*, 2nd edition, by John Dixon. Copyright © 1969 by Oxford University Press. Reprinted by permission of The Clarendon Press, Oxford.

matter of inner satisfaction and enjoyment. So whenever a group reads together we can reckon on a variety of satisfactions developing, according to the level of investment each pupil has made in his response (8, p. 56).

Although the Conference strongly recommends that the teacher not do the work for the student, it does not despair entirely of helping the student pursue his own course through the literature. The Study Group on Response to Literature identified three "Modes of Approach to Literature," all of which, the group thought, would be appropriate at one time or another. The first of these, "The Individual Child with the Individual Book" (61, p. 16), clearly demonstrates the willingness of the Conference to reduce the teacher's intervention between student and work. Basically, the teacher's task here is to help the student find the right book at the right time. That task, of course, is not a simple one, requiring "availability of a wide variety of appropriate titles, teacher acquaintance with the books, and teacher understanding of the individual child" (61, p. 16). Despite the difficulties of individualizing instruction in this way for the large number of students most teachers face, the study group insists upon viewing "guided individual reading as central to the literary education of the child, rather than as an appendage or adjunct to be relegated to book lists, 'outside' reading, or out-of-school activity" (61, p. 16).

The second mode, "Literature as Group Experience," emphasizes literature-related activities in which the entire class, or groups within the class, may participate. Storytelling, role-playing, and creative dramatics are representative of this treatment of literature. The purpose of such activities is twofold: to encourage a sense of community among the members of the class, and to stimulate more intense involvement with the literary work.

"Presentation of Literary Material Accompanied by Discussion" (61, p. 17), the third mode, is probably the most common. In some classrooms, it seems to be the one invariable method, and in those classrooms, unfortunately, discussion is frequently not discussion, but simply question and answer. The sort of discussion intended by the study group, however, is not the old-fashioned, formal recitation, but a more relaxed, open exchange of responses and ideas. Dixon says that "When talk does arise, at its best it springs from the pupils" (8, p. 59). If the materials read are suitable, talk that arises from the students is most likely to center on topics and questions which the students find to be truly significant. Dixon offers further criteria for talk in the classroom:

LITERATURE 13

The essential talk that springs from literature is talk about experience—as we know it, as *he* sees it (correcting our partiality and his; exploring the fullness of his vision, and ours). Conversely, only in a classroom where talk explores experience is literature drawn into the dialogue—otherwise it has no place. The demand for interpretation—was it this or that he meant?—arises in the course of such talk: otherwise it is a dead hand (8, p. 60).

We may note a few points of comparison between Hook's approaches and those of the study group. The six approaches outlined by Hook all seem to be distinguished from one another by the aspect of the literary work with which they concern themselves. The historical approach, for instance, emphasizes the biography of the author and the events contemporaneous with the writing of the work. The sociopsychological approach, concentrates upon the characters and the relationships that obtain between them. The modes identified by the study group, on the other hand, are characterized not by the aspects of the literary work under consideration, but by the relationships between the teacher and the students, and by the activity within the classroom. In the first mode, for example, the teacher does little more than assist the student to find appropriate books, and perhaps arrange for students with mutual interests to get together for discussion. In the second mode, a group may participate in role-playing, storytelling, or some other activity in which literature is performed or observed in performance. In neither mode do we find prescribed which aspect of the work is to be considered.

The study group thus seems less concerned with what the student knows about the work than with how intensely or completely he responds to it. It is concerned, in other words, more with the affective than with the cognitive. "We must constantly remind ourselves," Dixon says, "that 'the principle of organization of a critical statement is cognitive; that of a work of literature is, in the final analysis, affective'" (8, pp. 59-60).

The conception of literature and of literary instruction that emerges from the writings on the Conference is one in which the teacher's control is somewhat diminished. The approaches of Hook, in which emphasis falls more heavily upon cognitive elements, lend themselves more readily to organization and direction. One reason for this, of course, is that they are more predictable. A teacher who intends to have his class analyze a work can identify those elements he wishes to bring under discussion and, through carefully arranged questions, lead the class to them. On the other hand, a teacher who hopes to build his lesson on the responses of the students, on talk that springs from the pupils, builds his castle on shifting sands. The study group cautions that "overt response (verbal, etc.) may indicate very little of the inner response" (61, p. 11), and Dixon readily admits that talk may not always be the best way of dealing with a work: "Nor is it the case that talk is the appropriate and only testimony to the power of literature. Have we not all known the occasion when the best comment was silence—not a dead silence, but the shared silence of reflection and quiet brooding over what has moved us deeply" (8, p. 59). It is sometimes difficult, however, for the teacher to deal with silence—either silence of reflection or dead silence—but if he wishes to encourage honest responses he must be prepared for the possibility that the honest response will be silence, indifference, or rejection of a work; he must be willing to drop it, to initiate a line of questioning that may evoke response, or to follow some other alternative route. The teacher who would rely upon the responses of his students poses for himself a difficult, but necessary, job.

The relationship between student and teacher assumed by the Conference is clearly one characterized by mutual trust and respect. The response of an individual, whether teacher or student, is likely to be a very personal matter, touching private areas perhaps not easily revealed in a large group. For such matters to constitute the heart of literary instruction, members of the class must be on comfortable terms with one another, able to relax and speak openly without fear of ridicule or rejection, able to endure the silences without nervousness. The developing of this happy atmosphere in the classroom can be as difficult a task as any faced by the teacher, but it is a necessary prelude—or perhaps accompaniment—to teaching that attends to the responses of the students. Many educators are confident that once that pleasant tone is established in the classroom, the results will be dramatic. Charles Cooper, whose work has been primarily on the nature of student response to literature, concludes an article dealing largely with the Dartmouth Conference by declaring without reservation that "When the student in English class knows that his distinctness and humanness are wanted there, he will come to anticipate and enjoy his encounters with literature" (6, p. 1071).

CLASSROOM ATMOSPHERE

There are several obvious ways to encourage the climate in which free and open response is possible—unfortunately, not all of these are available to the teacher. One of the simplest would be to eliminate the absurdity of grading, surely the most ridiculous of the obligations that interfere with the teacher's job. Few teachers, however, even at the university level, have that option, or the option to modify the grading, even though several alternatives are readily available (see, for example, Merla Sparks' article, "An Alternative to the Traditional Grading System," *English Journal,* 56 [October 1967], pp. 1032-34).

A second possibility, almost as simple as the first and equally inaccessible to the English teacher, is to make school a voluntary activity. Arnold J. Rosenberg, an assistant principal in a Maryland junior high school, has spoken out eloquently for this idea:

> Compulsory education is the most self-defeating, paradox-ridden institution of our society. So long as young people are forced to attend school or be subject to penalties, there is little chance that schools will ever be more than barracks for an army of young automatons. Fulfillment of potential, self-actualization and individualization must remain empty terms for as long as the form and substance of education are determined by everyone but the recipients (55, p. 27).

The idea is unlikely to grow popular quickly, however, and so we must content ourselves with changes that can be made within the confines of one classroom. Happily, even these limited changes can have a significant effect. One such change, for example, might result from adopting, as an operating principle, that the model of cooperation shall prevail over the model of competition. The implementation of this principle can take a multitude of forms in the classroom.

The principle requires, for example, that the teacher not make a fetish of correct answers. To praise one child for supplying the "right" answer after criticizing another for offering a "wrong" answer is to give the first a small victory over the second. There should be no penalty for mistakes in the classroom—mistakes are, after all, a natural part of any learning process and they should be accepted as such, without embarrassment or condemnation. To do otherwise is to encourage a competitiveness that is not conducive to the discussion of personal responses upon which instruction in literature is based. In a classroom where primary attention is given to response and examination of that response, it is unlikely that a great many questions would require the sort of factual answers that could be labeled right or wrong. Still, they do inevitably arise, and they must not be treated as little battles to be won or lost by the student.

It is, of course, even more important to eliminate concern with correctness when the questions raised deal not with factual matters but with the thoughts and feelings of the reader. As Dixon has argued, the reading of a work of literature is an intensely personal event. A reader's response is determined not only by the text, but also by who he is and by what he brings to the text. For anyone other than the reader himself to pass judgment on that response would be presumptuous in the extreme. Abraham Bernstein warns that even in regard to questions of fact, "The wrongest answer you ever will get has a tincture of rightness about it; we have no measure of absolute zero in psychology, and we have not reached it in physics. Be careful with 'Wrong!' because you are untenably saying that you have hit on -273 degrees centigrade in human affairs" (2, p. 355). That is doubly true in matters of opinion. Even when the response seems to betray the grossest misreading of the text, it is more appropriate to arrange for clarification in some manner that does not suggest condemnation of the response.

The principle of cooperation is equally applicable to other areas. It has been unshakable tradition in most schools that each student shall do his own work entirely by himself. That demand implies, by the separation it specifies between students, a highly competitive atmosphere. Why should the students not cooperate? Presumably because they are to be judged by their products. The teacher needs to know who did what to ensure that the final rank-in-class is accurate. But a great deal of good is to be derived from arrangements in which work is shared by two or more students. Writing clinics, which can depend heavily upon students working together, have proved successful. Much of the writing that results from work with literature might be adapted to the group setting.

James Moffett recommends, for instance, the writing of Socratic dialogue as a means of increasing the student's ability to deal with alternative possibilities (42). As an example he offers a short dialogue on the question, "Should we aid the enemy?", a point of discussion that had arisen during a reading of Pearl Buck's "The Enemy." Although Moffett's purpose in such an assignment is to induce the student, operating on his own, to consider various sides to a question, the same effect might be achieved by having a small group prepare the dialogue, with the added benefit of encouraging the students to work with one another, evaluating ideas objectively, rather than to work competitively. The teacher might ask the group to adopt the nonjudgmental attitude of a brainstorming group while they attempt to conceive of the ideas their imaginary discussants might propose.

Thus the recurring question for the group might be, "What would character B say in reply to such-and-such a remark by character A?" The group, having discussed that point, would move on to formulate A's reply to B. The point is that the students would not be debating, but would be cooperating in the joint creation of an imaginary debate between two imaginary characters. They would be learning, in other words, to treat each other as partners in a verbal transaction, building upon one another's ideas rather than countering, rejecting, or debating those ideas. Such an attitude will be invaluable in other discussions that focus upon more personal matters. We should hope that students and teachers who felt this supportive relationship with one another will be better able to learn about both themselves and the literature.

Louise Rosenblatt, in suggesting the sort of questions that a reader might profitably ask himself, points up the importance of the willingness to learn from one another: "What meanings did others see in it—my classmates, my teacher, perhaps critics in published comments. Do they defend their interpretations by pointing to things in the story that I overlooked? Does this help me to see my blind spots" (56, p. 73)? The attitude she is recommending is not that of a debater, but of a partner in the learning process.

The establishment of a cooperative, relaxed atmosphere in the classroom is an obvious prerequisite for a literature program that intends to deal with such private matters as an individual's response to a literary work. There are ways to compel work, to demand some kind of quantifiable production, but there is no possible way to compel honesty, sensitivity, self-examination, or any of the other attitudes or activities necessary to the intelligent reading of literature. The teacher can hope only to build a mood in which those attitudes can take hold. Barrett John Mandel, in an excellent book primarily about college-level English teaching but equally applicable to high school, says,

The teacher's job—simple to state, difficult to perform—is to create the atmosphere in which natural fraternity and learning can develop. Our job is not to deliver information or even, really, to point out where it is. Teachers are not merely reference sources. As I understand my obligation to the students, I am a person prepared to work as imaginatively as I can to establish conditions in which students will *want* to learn. I create the conditions; they do the learning. . . . The teacher turns his class, whether it is meeting in a traditional setting or more naturally, into a community . . . (39, p. 42).

His position echoes that expressed by the Dartmouth Conference in both its conception of the job of the teacher and its demand for a sense of community in the classroom.

SELECTION OF LITERARY WORKS

The necessity of cooperation for many of the activities of the English classroom is self-apparent. It is somewhat less obvious insofar as the selection of materials is concerned, for the selection of materials is traditionally a part of the instructional process in which the individual teacher has almost nothing to say. The publishers of the textbooks have frequently been the ones to determine what shall be taught, though this situation may now be changing as paperbacks and the more flexible three- or four-volume paperback anthologies, such as McDougal, Littell and Company's *Man* series, become more and more popular. Still, unfortunately, there are school systems that refuse to put money designated for textbooks into anything other than hardbound texts. It can be a very dubious investment.

Perhaps the single most important criterion in selecting books for the high school classroom is, as we might expect, the interests of the student. To offer adolescent boys interested in adventure and excitement *Pride and Prejudice,* and to give adolescent girls seeking romance *Moby Dick,* is to increase their already disproportionate affinity for television. The teacher who establishes rapport with the class is much more likely to find himself learning about the interests of individuals and of the group, and thus better able to guide individual reading and to select works which the entire class will read.

Knowledge of student interests will come as a result of acquaintance with the students, but that will, of course, require time. The interest survey is one technique for quickly acquiring some information about reading preferences. Olson's Reading Interest Inventory (47, p. 165-67) is a good model for such a survey. It is a comprehensive list of reading interests, distinguished by both form and content, for which the students are asked to indicate one of six responses ranging from "Like very much" to "Dislike very much." Although the information it provides is fairly general, it is nonetheless better than following the table of contents of the anthology.

Arthur Olson and Wilbur Ames (47) suggest several other tactics well worth considering. An imaginative teacher may draw up a list of fictitious titles and annotations and request the students to indicate which ones they would be most, and least, interested in reading.

Perhaps even more informative would be a similar list written by the students themselves, perhaps in a session of brainstorming, an activity that most secondary school students seem to enjoy, and one, incidentally, at which they excel.

R. Baird Shuman proposes an intriguing variation of the survey technique, designed primarily to stimulate dialogue that may lead to a deeper insight into one's self, but also extremely valuable as a guide for the teacher to the concerns of the students. Some representative questions follow:

1. Why, aside from obeying the law, are you in school?
2. What, if anything, would you rather be doing?

* * * * *

4. What would you most like to be doing five years from now?

* * * * *

14. Do you think you have missed much in life? If so, what?

* * * * *

18. Did you tell the truth in answering questions one and two? If not, why not? (59, p. 1339).

Although the questions do not ask specifically for information about reading interests, they range over hobbies, dress, movies, books, early childhood memories, and the like, encouraging introspection and honesty, and revealing a great deal about the student that can be useful both in the selection of literature and in the planning of composition work. Again, the individual teacher may do well to try compiling his own questionnaire, and might at some point want to ask for the assistance of the class in doing so.

Shuman's technique is more personal and probing than are most surveys, and thus shares some of the characteristics of the interview, which may be the most useful method of all for eliciting information about reading interests. Its problem is the amount of time necessary to meet individually with the large number of students assigned most teachers. That is a problem for which there is no easy solution — some teachers have attacked it by combining interviews about reading interests with periods in the library — but if the interview proves useful to the teacher, he would do well to find time for it somehow.

In this section we have so far spoken primarily of ways of determining the interests of individuals. We must look also at the general pattern of adolescent reading interest, for that, too, can provide significant information for the teacher of literature. Carlsen says that "The patterns are amazingly similar for all of us. Our problem in guiding teen-age readers is one of knowing stages, being ready with the right suggestions when one stage is ending and another about to begin, and recognizing that each stage is but a rung on the ladder toward the truly cultivated human being" (5, p. 33).*

Carlsen distinguishes three major periods in the development of the adolescent's reading interests. The early period, about ages 11 to 14, is characterized by interest in stories dealing with animals, adventure, mystery, the supernatural, sports, adolescence in other cultures, family life, broad humor, and the past. Naturally, differences exist between the interests of boys and girls, with adventure stories more popular among the boys, and stories of the family more popular among the girls, but there is broad overlapping. In middle adolescence, ages 15 and 16, the interests of boys and girls divide most sharply, with boys showing preference for nonfiction adventure and war stories, girls for historical novels and mystical romance, and both sexes interested in stories about adolescence. Late adolescence, ages 16 to 18, is the period of transition to adult reading. Social problems, personal values, strange human experiences, and the assuming of adult roles are the central interests of this period.

Carlsen also points out that one feature of adolescent readers is that their reading interests often anticipate their own development by a few years. Thus a boy approaching the age of 16 may begin to show an interest in stories dealing with automobiles and young girls about to begin dating may become deeply interested in romantic stories. Dwight Burton's concept of literature as a liberating force may help to explain this phenomenon. He suggests that "One reason why imaginative literature is so important in the quest for the 'I', for identity, is that it serves as pre-experience on the imaginative level. Thus the thirteen-year-old girl may enjoy reading a novel about a seventeen-year-old girl's first serious love affair more than would an actual seventeen-year-old girl" (4, p. 7).

As Carlsen's analysis of the adolescent's reading interests suggests, many of the books that adults enjoy, many of the works that have come to be considered classics, are likely to be beyond the adolescent's range of interest, and conversely, many of the books that appeal to teen-agers would not be considered worth reading by adults.

---

*From *Books and the Teen-age Reader,* Rev. and Updated by G. Robert Carlsen. Copyright © 1967, 1971 by G. Robert Carlsen. Reprinted by permission of Harper and Row, Publishers, Inc.

The teacher must be careful to evaluate books by a set of standards that is a mixture of adult judgment and adolescent interest. Naturally, he does not want to waste time and energy on completely worthless materials; but on the other hand, he must guard against the inclination to require students to read material which they are not yet mature enough to comprehend and enjoy. Loban, Ryan, and Squire warn that "permanent damage to the reader's attitude may result if teachers disregard the level of maturity and experience of adolescents" (36, p. 439). Although the teacher naturally desires to extend the capabilities of his students, he must be willing to do so gradually.

At the upper levels of the high school, when the interests of many of the students are very nearly those of adults, the warning may seem unnecessary. Probably a more frequent error is made in attempting to "protect" mature students from works that some consider too sophisticated for them. At the junior high school level, however, caution is advisable. It is more important that students read than that they read what we want them to read. In a recent study, Alan C. Purves and Richard Beach report that "the amount of voluntary literature reading reaches a high point in junior high school . . . (53, p. 71). If this is the case, it should not be difficult to guide students gently toward works of higher literary quality. Frank Whitehead, writing about literature instruction in England, remarks encouragingly,

So long as this factor of "appeal" is given full weight, there is usually no need for the school librarian to pitch his standards unduly low, for experience shows that to stock a children's library with books of good quality tends to increase the number of books borrowed rather than to reduce it (69, p. 61).

Whitehead's remark points up the other side of the problem—not only must the teacher know about the students, but he must also know about the books. Again, at the upper levels the problem is less noticeable than at the lower levels. Teachers of juniors and seniors will quite likely find that many of the books they are themselves reading are suitable for recommendation to their students. Teachers of junior high school students are less likely to find themselves drawn to books that their classes will enjoy. Consequently they need to plan to devote some time to acquaint themselves with the available works. Of invaluable assistance in keeping up with adolescent literature are librarians, both in the school and in neighborhood libraries. Their records can also be useful in determining which titles are most popular, which areas of reading draw the most students. There are also a number of valuable reference books on the topic; the following are some of the most useful:

Burton, Dwight L. *Literature Study in the High Schools.* 3d ed.; New York: Holt, Rinehart & Winston, Inc., 1970.
Carlsen, G. Robert. *Books and the Teen-Age Reader: A Guide for Teachers, Librarians and Parents.* New York: Bantam Books, Inc., 1967.
Dodds, Barbara. *Negro Literature for High School Students.* Champaign, Ill.: National Council of Teachers of English, 1968.
Fader, Daniel N. and McNeil, Elton B. *Hooked on Books: Program and Proof.* New York: Berkley Publishing Corporation, 1968.
O'Neal, Robert. *Teacher's Guide to World Literature for the High School.* Champaign, Ill.: National Council of Teachers of English, 1966.
Perkins, Flossie L. *Book and Non-Book Media: Annotated Guide to Selection Aid for Educational Materials.* Urbana, Ill.: National Council of Teachers of English, 1972.
Weber, J. Sherwood (ed.). *Good Reading.* 35th ed.; New York: New American Library, 1969.
White, Marian E. *High Interest—Easy Reading for Junior and Senior High School Students.* 2d ed.; New York: Citation Press, 1972.
Willard, Charles B. (ed.). *Your Reading: Book List for Junior High Schools.* New York: New American Library, Inc., 1966.
Wilson, Jean (ed.). *Books for You.* Rev. ed.; New York: Washington Square Press, 1971.

The *English Journal's* "Book Marks" column offers a monthly review of several new books suitable for junior and senior high schools, and thus provides a convenient way for teachers to expand their personal book lists continually. Two other works, although they do not suggest readings for the classroom, deserve mention in this section. *Literature and the Reader: Research in Response to Literature, Reading Interests, and the Teaching of Literature* (53), by Alan C. Purves and Richard Beach, is an interesting and concise review of the research in this area, and merits inclusion in the English department's library. *Unrequired Reading: An Annotated Bibliography for Teachers and School Administrators* (66), by Iris M. and Sidney W. Tiedt, is a list of books that serve to "give us a new perspective of the student, the teacher, and the administrator" (66, p. 1). It is a bibliography that would be particularly useful to those preparing themselves for the teaching profession.

Ultimately, the selection of books is a matter of literary taste and judgment, which the teacher has presumably spent a lifetime developing, and for which there can be no substitute. Continued immersion in the best literature will prepare the teacher in the best possible way for the task of guiding the reading of his students.

INDIVIDUAL READING

We have dealt at such length with the problems of book selection primarily because the independent study of literature is so important in the secondary English program. If the teacher needed only to worry about choosing several novels, a larger number of short stories, and a collection of poems for his entire class to read, his problems would be slight. He would, of course, have to accept the impossibility of finding works that would satisfy everyone; but, that compromise being made, he would have only a small number of items to search out. An English program in which everyone reads the same works does not require an extensive collection. On the other hand, a program that hopes to take into account the individuality of the students must be prepared to offer a wide range of books, and to devote much time to the "guided individual reading" that the Dartmouth Conference Study Group on Literature insisted was "central to the literary education of the child" (61, p. 16).

That individual reading must be central to the English program should be fairly obvious when we consider how most reading is done. For adults, very little literary experience occurs in groups. In the past, this may not have been so. A large group may have sat at Homer's feet to listen to his recitations; but today, when one reads *The Iliad,* he reads it alone. Literature has become a solitary activity, not a communal one. Even when we expand the definition of literature to include the film and live drama, where large groups gather for performances, the experience, except in the rarest of cases, remains a private, solitary experience. If the student does not develop the ability to read and respond on his own, then we cannot hope that he will remain an active reader when he leaves school. As Michael Flanigan says, "The natural patterns of reading that students create for themselves, sometimes with our cooperation, are a better guarantee that they will continue to value reading than if patterns are created for them to follow" (17, p. 146).*

The literature program in which the concentration falls upon works to be read by the entire class seems to assume a uniformity among the students that does not, in fact, exist. Children read for a wide variety of reasons, to satisfy a great many different needs. A literature program that tries to ignore these differences stands little chance of affecting its students.

---

*From "Literature as an Individual's Thing" by Michael C. Flanigan in *The Creative Teacher,* edited by William Evans. Copyright © 1971 by Bantam Books, Inc.

A literature program that recognizes and attempts to take into consideration these differences, however, can be an unwieldy thing. A student load of 120 to 180 seems to forbid any efforts to individualize. In order to deal more comfortably with the large numbers of students, and to find out more about them, Flanigan recommends beginning an individualized literature program with a half step, breaking classes down into small groups: "This provides a flexible structure and gives more students a chance to talk and respond. The topics for discussion should be current or student-generated" (17, p. 147).

From these discussions will emerge a list of interests, concerns, and problems, one of which Flanigan would ask each group to select for further exploration. He would then suggest appropriate readings for the groups, perhaps guiding them into lines of inquiry that might otherwise be ignored. Flanigan would also allow students to break off from the group if they so choose, hoping that the initial discussions would have stimulated some interest for them to pursue either independently or with other dissidents. Although these strategies do not result immediately in complete individualization of the literature program, they do provide a start, a comfortable way of making the transition from whole class work to independent work.

Another convenient starting point is the work which the entire class has read. If the work is sufficiently rich in ideas, it should trigger some interest in the minds of most readers. The teacher's problem is then to find out what that interest is and suggest readings that will satisfy it. Asking the students to keep a journal during the reading of a work is one way to find out about individual responses and unique interest. The teacher may discover, for instance, that a week with *Death of a Salesman* has aroused in one student an interest in other works by Arthur Miller. For him the teacher might recommend *All My Sons* and *The Crucible*. Should the students become interested in the author himself, appropriate readings might be Sheila Huftel's *Arthur Miller: The Burning Glass,* or Denis Welland's *Arthur Miller.* If the student shows concern with the conflicts within the family he might wish to read William Saroyan's *The Human Comedy,* Carson McCuller's *The Member of the Wedding,* or perhaps *Family,* a collection of photographs and writings compiled by Margaret Mead and Ken Heyman. Other students may be attracted to other themes in the play—deception; infidelity; the coming of age; the value, or lack thereof, of the individual man; the problems of responsibility; success and failure—and they could be directed to other works that also deal with those themes.

A similar approach is recommended in "Individual Reading: Report of the Committee on Extensive Reading" (23, pp. 337-50). The Committee says that

Every essay or poem or novel or play poses a problem in human relationships. If it has been taught so that the culmination of the student's understanding about it is its relation to the enduring concerns of humanity — birth and death, love and hatred, fear, anger, greed, and pain — presented so that they impinge on the student's perception of life, then the ramifications of that essay, that play, are unlimited, both in variety and range. Each student can be shown an area of investigation and reading which appeals to him alone (23, p. 342).

The goal of the committee is, as for Flanigan, the eventual assumption by the student of full responsibility for the direction of his own reading. Other efforts to initiate individual study of literature may take other forms, but they generally share this goal. Andreas Lehner reports success with a course that began by listing the books the students had recently read and distributing that list to the class. Although the titles ranged from *Wuthering Heights* to *Street Rod* the results were that "the students are reading widely, discussing books with each other and with their teachers, and generally shattering our predictions about who's ready for what" (35, p. 808).

Other teachers have achieved some impact on the reading habits of their students simply by making a collection of books, usually paperbacks, available to the students. A classroom library of paperbacks, and time to use them, can be an invaluable asset for the English classroom. The success of the program reported in Daniel Fader's *Hooked on Books* seems to be attributable in large part to the easy access to a great many titles for the students. Similarly, Edward G. Winner reports the accomplishments of a massive program in the Washington, D.C., schools during which $50,000 worth of paperback books were given away to the students. No reports were required, no promises exacted — the books were offered free and clear — though informal seminars provided a place for the students to discuss the books they were reading if they so desired (71). The individual teacher cannot hope to equal the scope of a program like this, but he can adopt some of its strategies. He can, for instance, relieve some of the pressure on the students, making it clear that the books are to be a source of pleasure rather than a source of tests and book reports. And he can assist in arranging for the trading of books among the students, the establishing of a paperback store for the school, the allotting of time for free, unstructured discussion of reading, and any other strategems that might result in getting more books into the hands of the students.

LITERATURE WITH GROUPS

Although we have placed heavy emphasis on the student's individual reading, untrammelled by the customary demands of the English classroom, there are many activities applicable to the communal study of literature, and at times it may be appropriate to suggest several of these to the student. The most obvious activity is discussion, with other students, with the teacher, or both. Some teachers prefer that these discussions be organized in terms of study questions, that conferences with the individual student be scheduled and that the conference follow a prescribed sequence of questions. Others have found some virtue in informality. Flanigan reports a conversation with a student who appeared constrained and uneasy in discussions organized by the teacher, but free and relaxed in discussions that allowed him to follow his own inclinations: "I gathered from what he said that he felt my questions were not designed to help him or his fellow students nor were they designed to find out anything I really wanted to know, but instead were to show how little the students know and to show how much I already knew" (17, p. 140).

Discussion, directed or undirected, and many of the wide variety of other activities for groups, all run the risk pointed out in the incident Flanigan cites — the risk of once again subordinating the needs of the individual to those of the group or those of the teacher. Regardless of the importance placed upon individual reading in the literature program, the teacher must still find ways of dealing with the entire class, and those ways must not create the sort of feeling Flanigan discovered in that unhappy pupil.

On the importance of group activity, Purves says, "For most students in school, it takes two or more to read a piece of literature" (53, p. 71). Traditionally, the necessary second person was the teacher, who led discussions, made assignments, and evaluated work. Discussions in the classroom frequently resolved themselves into a series of dialogues between the teacher and individual students, or into question and answer sessions. The assumption underlying the carefully organized, sometimes rigidly structured, planning of the teacher was that he had knowledge to impart to the students. He comprehended the meaning and significance of a work, and his task was to bring the student as far along toward that comprehension as possible. The Dartmouth Conference pointed out vividly that the flaw in that conception of literary knowledge is that it ignores the individuality of the student, and denies the inevitable influence on the work's meaning of that individuality.

The inductive lesson, in which the teacher tries, through a planned sequence of questions, to lead the students to an understanding of some literary point, too often becomes what Alan Purves has referred to as "a script with the teacher's lines (usually questions) included and the students' lines (usually answers) omitted" (53, p. 77). Such a plan gives the teacher control. It gives the lesson a direction and purpose. But it also eliminates the possibility of other directions, other purposes emerging from the talk of the students. And, of course, it ignores the variations in meaning that result from the differences among people.

In order to accept and encourage individual response, the teacher must adopt a much more tentative, restrained approach to questioning than that of the highly structured inductive lesson plan. Rather than plan with conclusions in mind, the teacher might instead search for those points at which individuals might diverge or disagree. He might, in fact, encourage that divergence of ideas by asking at first for raw, unexamined reaction. Of a poem, he might ask simply, "How did the reading make you feel?" Of a short story, he might ask, "With which character did you feel most in sympathy" or "Were you pleased or upset with the outcome of the story?" Ideally, talk would arise from the students without the need for provocative questions; but when this does not happen, the best questions will be those that elicit the most natural talk. Quite obviously, the most natural talk at first is not a carefully considered critical estimate of the literary worth of the selection, but rather a simple statement of reaction. One's first response to a literary work is frequently a vague feeling—perhaps of uneasiness, perhaps of satisfaction and pleasure—that becomes clear and distinct only after some reflection.

Discussion beginning at this point will very likely lead to the consideration of the relevant literary concepts. A discussion of Thomas Hardy's "The Man He Killed," for example, could not very well neglect to consider the strange incongruity between the tone of voice of the speaker and the topic he is discussing. The slightly bemused expression, indicating that the speaker is troubled, aware of some problem, seems by understatement to emphasize the pointlessness of killing a man because he happens to be "my foe."

The teacher could lead the class to some such statement about the voice in the poem by asking pointed questions: What reason does the speaker give for killing the man? Is that a good reason? Why was the man his foe? Does he give any serious reasons—ideological differences, political differences, or the like, for being enemies? How adequate is "quaint and curious" as a description of circumstances that cause pointless killing? Such questions will make the class aware of the element of understatement in the voice of the speaker; but they may also, by virtue of the direction they impose upon the talk in the classroom, interfere with students' natural responses to the poem, responses that could lead to equally important revelations about the poem.

A student's response to the poem might, for instance, be one of anger toward the speaker. The student may feel that the voice betrays a callous, unfeeling attitude toward the victim, an inhuman casualness about killing. Another student may feel that the speaker is simply stupid, unaware of the important reasons that can send a nation to war and that make one life insignificant by comparison. Still another may feel that the speaker shows evidence of more intelligence than most, that his reflections on killing the man represent the first steps toward a realistic appraisal of the inhumanity of war. If responses like these are allowed to surface in the classroom, the discussion will touch both upon matters of literary technique and questions of more personal import.

Discussion that begins with these responses will also be more likely to lead to personal insight and, perhaps, changes in attitude, than will more rigidly structured talk. The student who argues that wars may be fought for good reasons, that a man should see what those reasons are, may come to realize that his political convictions occasionally obscure his view of the impact of such great events as wars upon the common man. The student who at first protests the callousness of the speaker may temper his condemnation when he sees that men sometimes find themselves in situations where survival is a more compelling consideration than an abstract moral code. The discussion that we may imagine ensuing between these students could yield insight into themselves and their classmates, and into the poem. A rigid sequence of questions, religiously followed, would be unlikely to range so widely.

We do not mean to imply that the teacher should avoid asking questions. Rather, he should keep his questions as open-ended as possible in order to invite diverse response. And he should be able to use questions to help students clarify and understand their responses. As Purves says, "While on the one hand it is counterproductive to place a value judgment on pupils' responses, it is important at the same time to realize that there are many kinds of responses, and that one of the goals of this program is to broaden the students' responses — in effect, to make them aware that there is more than one way of responding to a work of literature" (52, p. 87). Probing questions will be helpful in achieving this effect. Still, at first, the more tentative the question is, the better, since the teacher does not wish to suggest that there is a most correct, or most desirable, answer. If he feels the need to make the question more concrete, he might do so, not by proposing possible answers from which the students may choose, but by establishing a context for the poem. For example, he might ask them to imagine themselves seated at a bar in conversation with a stranger and to consider how they feel, under those circumstances, about the speaker in the poem. He might then read the poem aloud, have a student who reads well do it, or play a recording of the poem. The presentation of the poem in the context of the imagined situation introduces an element of role-playing into the lesson. The students are now doing more than looking at words on the page — they are instead involved in a recreation of a dramatic situation, and are consequently more likely to respond.

Discussions of this sort can also lead into individual or group projects of the kind referred to in the section on individual reading. The conversation in the class will reveal the concerns of the students, who can then be encouraged to pursue them. A well-prepared teacher might be able to predict some of the points of interest in the poem and compile a short list of readings to accommodate students who wish to explore them. Carlsen's analysis of reading interests indicates that 9th and 10th graders will be interested in war stories, so the teacher might gamble that several students, at least, will be curious about other poetic depictions of war after reading "The Man He Killed," and come to class armed with Henry Reed's "Naming of Parts," Robert Southey's "After Blenheim," Siegfried Sassoon's "Does It Matter?" and Wilfred Owen's "Dulce et Decorum Est." The wise teacher, however, will refrain from imposing his predictions on the class if they prove to be wrong. If the teacher considers "The Man He Killed" a good entry into *The Iliad* but his class develops an interest in comparing the literature of World War II with that produced during the Vietnamese War, he would be well advised to reshelve Homer until a more opportune moment.

The pursuit of valid questions raised by the class should take priority in the English classroom. Neil Postman and Charles Weingartner, in arguing that all modern curricula must be centered upon questions, rather than upon lists of required readings, topics to be covered, objectives to be achieved, or any of the other items customary in curriculum guides, insist that "question asking, if it is not to be a sterile and ritualized activity, has to deal with problems that are perceived as useful and realistic by the learners" (50, p. 81). If such questions arise, it would be folly to ignore them.

Regardless of where the students' interests lead, the teacher will still have in mind certain objectives that he wishes to accomplish. If he is concerned with teaching the process of reading literature rather than with convincing the students of the accuracy of his evaluations of literary works or with conveying certain facts of literary history, then he should have little trouble adapting to the demands of the class. Let us say, for instance, that he hopes to increase his students' awareness of the importance of characterization in short stories. No matter which stories he uses, his fundamental principle will be to begin with the students' responses. Thus he may begin, as with "The Man He Killed," by asking for initial reactions. Or he may instead try another tack. If he has the class translate the story into dramatic form, he will be requiring, subtly, that they attend closely to the characterization. Questions about how lines are to be spoken will arise, and they must be answered on the basis of clues contained in the text of the story. Is the man bitter or sad? His intonation will depend on their interpretation of his character. Are his intentions honest or deceitful? Again, the class must interpret character. Are his movements nervous and quick, or calm and deliberate? Dramatizing the story poses many questions that can be answered only by appeal to the text. By putting the students in a situation where the questions arise naturally, he makes the questions realistic and significant. If, instead, he presents the typical anthology question—"How does the author establish the hero's character?"—he risks turning the lesson into a pointless exercise.

Similar strategies will occur to the inventive teacher for the solution of other problems. To encourage his students to attend more carefully to elements of foreshadowing, he may teach a short unit on detective fiction in which he withholds the conclusion to several of the stories and asks the class to predict the endings on the basis of the information they acquire in the first parts of the works. A work like Lord Dunsany's "The Two Bottles of Relish" lends itself well to this activity. He may ask skillful students to transform stories they read outside class into problems for others in the class to solve, taking care to include enough information so that solution of the problem is possible. That is, however, an extremely difficult task, and seems to attract only the most intrepid readers of mysteries. Predicting the outcome of stories is an activity that need not be restricted to the mystery genre; nor need that genre be used only as a vehicle for teaching certain literary techniques. Verda Evans strongly recommends the "charms and fascination of the mystery as one way to catch the attention of the bored, the disenchanted, the alienated" (12, p. 501). To use the detective story or any story only as an example of literary devices would be to neglect many of its virtues.

The teacher should also be willing to draw upon the diversity of talents and interests within any group to broaden the possibilities of response for all the members. The artistically inclined student may be urged to draw or paint a picture representing the setting of a story in which that element is important. Musicians in the class may be asked to select, perform, or compose, depending on their capabilities, music that would be suitable background for the reading of passages. All students can learn to operate simple cameras well enough to provide slides for a visual interpretation of poems. The teacher's most valuable resources in the literature classroom are his students—he must not overlook them.

LITERATURE AND FILM

Perhaps because they strike at so many of the senses at one time, commercial film and television offer a form of the drama in which we may confidently expect many of our students to take an immediate interest. Although we may question the literary worth of many movies and of most television, the fact remains that most people manage to see more movies than plays, and more television than anything else. The teacher of literature can put this broad acquaintance with film and television to good use in the classroom. Robert Meadows recommends an activity that culminates in the preparation of a television show (40). He breaks his class into groups and has each group select a television show it will enjoy watching. The groups then watch the shows, taking careful notes on plot, structure, locale, costuming, and the like. Armed with these notes, each group undertakes the writing of a script for the show, which presents them with a multitude of problems—they must agree on plot sequences, the dialogue must be appropriate to the characters, the number of scene changes must be manageable, the timing must be relatively accurate, and movements on the set must be blocked. After some time for rehearsal the show is performed and evaluated.

The activity, as Meadows says, "encourages dynamic television viewing while it offers valuable experience with almost every communication tool we hope to sharpen in the English classroom" (40, p. 121). It involves the students in both the reception and production of a literary form, and in so doing motivates careful attention to elements of the show that would otherwise be ignored. The subsequent manipulation of these elements in the planning and production of a show is a creative exercise that should deepen the student's understanding of some of the aspects of drama. Meadows reports that another of the outcomes of the activity is that the students seem to become much more sophisticated as an audience for television.

Activities such as Meadows' are made even more realistic by the use of video tape equipment or movie cameras. Although video tape equipment remains prohibitively expensive, eight-millimeter and super-eight-millimeter cameras and projectors are within the reach of many school budgets. The very presence of the equipment seems to serve as powerful motivation for most students, so film-making is consequently an easy project to initiate. Part of its motivational value, perhaps, is that it offers opportunities for successful involvement to students who may have come to feel too verbally or socially inept for the classroom. Film-making is a multifaceted job requiring actors, directors, cameramen, editors, costumers, writers, artists—almost everyone can find a role in which he is comfortable.

The relationship of film-making to the study of literature is quite direct—film-making involves the student in the production of literature. Patrick A. O'Keefe, writing of his first uncertain venture into classroom movies, reports that "The creative thinking, the oral discussions, the class presentations, the acting, the literary interpretation and adaptation of plot, the writing—they all exceeded my expectations" (46, p. 959). The production of a movie is as much a literary activity as is the production of a play or the writing of a poem.

One of the added virtues of film-making derives from the fact that most teachers who attempt it know very little about it at the start. They are thus required to learn with the students a process that can do much to improve communication in the classroom. Film-making is also likely to motivate the study of professional films. Students involved in writing and producing their own movies are eager to discuss the techniques, both verbal and visual, of commercial films.

Several valuable references are now available for the teacher who desires to prepare himself before attempting either film-making or film study. *Behind the Camera* (34), by William Kuhns and Thomas F. Giardino deals with the problems of producing a film. *The Compleat Guide to Film Study* (51), edited by G. Howard Poteet is a more comprehensive work, dealing with both the production and study of film.

LITERATURE AND WRITING

In many English programs, work in composition is based largely upon the literature read. The compositions required are frequently analytical essays in which the student is asked to explain some aspect of the work, to paraphrase or interpret, to prove some point. The essay he writes usually must be argumentative in nature, building a strong logical case for the position he has elected to defend. Keith Fort objects to writing assignments of this sort because the "form of the essay tends to insist that the only possible relation of critic to work is that of thesis-hunter to source of thesis" (18, p. 638). In other words, the nature of the assignment severely limits the possible responses. Fort argues that there are other valid responses to a work of literature than the critical essay.

One of the most valuable, and most neglected, responses to reading is the effort to produce a literary work of one's own. Opportunities for the writing of poetry, short shories and plays, in addition to essays, must be provided if the students are to develop their literary sensitivities to the fullest. But the study of literature need not include a course in creative writing. Most important is that the teacher approach the students' writings—at least those writings that relate to the literature under study—with the same forebearance and discretion he demonstrates in dealing with the student himself. There is a place for the tightly reasoned essay, and it will serve the student well to be able to achieve the discipline of logic in his writing; but there is also a place for the personal essay, the subjective exploration of thoughts and feelings. If discussion of literature begins with individual response, writing about literature may well begin there, too.

Dixon says that "The writing that springs from literature takes us in two directions: outwards into our own shaping of experience, tapped and activated by our reading—and that is the usual direction—or in towards the writer's experience, sifting and savouring the thing for itself—and that is the rarer" (8, p. 65). The student must be free, in writing as well as in reading, to examine his own responses, to attempt to learn more about both himself and the literature.

REFERENCES

1. Bacon, Wallace A., and Breen, Robert S. *Literature as Interpretation.* New York: McGraw-Hill Book Company, 1959.
2. Bernstein, Abraham. *Teaching English in High School.* New York: Random House, Inc., 1961.
3. Burke, Kenneth. *Language as Symbolic Action.* Berkeley: University of California Press, 1966.
4. Burton, Dwight L. *Literature Study in the High Schools.* 3d ed.; New York: Holt, Rinehart & Winston, Inc., 1970.
5. Carlsen, G. Robert. *Books and the Teen-Age Reader: A Guide for Teachers, Librarians and Parents.* New York: Bantam Books, Inc., 1971.
6. Cooper, Charles R. "The New Climate for Personal Responses to Literature in the Classroom," *English Journal,* 60 (1971), 1063–71.
7. Church, Joseph. *Language and the Discovery of Reality.* New York: Vintage Books, 1961.
8. Dixon, John. *Growth through English.* 2nd edition. London: Oxford University Press, 1969.
9. Dodds, Barbara. *Negro Literature for High School Students.* Champaign, Ill.: National Council of Teachers of English, 1968.
10. Dunning, Stephen. *Teaching Literature to Adolescents: Poetry.* Glenview, Ill.: Scott, Foresman and Company, 1966.
11. _____.*Teaching Literature to Adolescents: Short Stories.* Glenview, Ill.: Scott, Foresman and Company, 1968.
12. Evans, Verda. "The Mystery as Mind-Stretcher," *English Journal,* 56 (1967), 121–24.
13. Evans, William. *The Creative Teacher.* New York: Bantam Books, Inc., 1971.
14. Evans, William H., and Walker, Jerry L. *New Trends in the Teaching of English in Secondary Schools.* Chicago: Rand McNally & Company, 1966.
15. Fader, Daniel N., and McNeil, Elton B. *Hooked on Books:*

Program and Proof. New York: Berkley Publishing Corporation, 1968.
16. Fisher, John H. "Truth vs. Beauty: An Inquiry into the Function of Language and Literature in an Articulate Society," *The Humanity of English: NCTE 1972 Distinguished Lectures.* Urbana, Ill.: National Council of Teachers of English, 1972, 1-16.
17. Flanigan, Michael C. "Literature as an Individual's Thing," in William Evans (ed.), *The Creative Teacher.* New York: Bantam Books, Inc., 1971, 138-50.
18. Fort, Keith. "Form, Authority, and the Critical Essay," *College English,* 32 (1971), 629-39.
19. Fowler, Mary Elizabeth. *Teaching Language, Composition, and Literature.* New York: McGraw-Hill Book Company, 1965.
20. Frye, Northrop. *Anatomy of Criticism: Four Essays.* New York: Atheneum, Publishers, 1968.
21. Goodman, Paul. *Speaking and Language: Defense of Poetry.* New York: Vintage Books, 1971.
22. Gordon, Edward J. (ed.). *Writing and Literature in the Secondary School.* New York: Holt, Rinehart & Winston, Inc., 1965.
23. Gordon, Edward J., and Noyes, Edward S. (eds.). *Essays on the Teaching of English.* New York: Appleton-Century-Crofts, 1960.
24. Guth, Hans. *English Today and Tomorrow.* Englewood Cliffs, N.J.: Prentice-Hall, Inc., 1964.
25. Hillocks, George, et al. *The Dynamics of English Instruction.* New York: Random House, Inc., 1971.
26. Hook, J. N. *The Teaching of High School English.* 4th ed.; New York: The Ronald Press Company, 1972.
27. Howes, Alan B. *Teaching Literature to Adolescents: Plays.* Glenview, Ill.: Scott, Foresman and Company, 1968.
28. Jenkinson, Edward B., and Daghlian, Philip B. (eds.). *Teaching Literature in Grades Ten through Twelve.* Bloomington, Ind.: Indiana University Press, 1968.
29. Jenkinson, Edward B., and Hawley, Jane (eds.). *On Teaching Literature: Essays for Secondary School Teachers.* Bloomington, Ind.: Indiana University Press, 1967.
30. _____*Teaching Literature in Grades Seven through Nine.* Bloomington, Ind.: Indiana University Press, 1968.
31. Joki, Virginia. "So Who Needs Analysis?" *English Journal,* 57 (1968), 568-71.
32. Josephs, Lois S., and Steinberg, Erwin R. (eds.). *English Educa-*

tion Today. New York: Noble and Noble, Publishers, Inc., 1970.
33. Knapton, James, and Evans, Bertrand. *Teaching a Literature-Centered English Program.* New York: Random House, Inc., 1967.
34. Kuhns, William, and Giardino, Thomas F. *Behind the Camera.* Dayton, Ohio: Geo. A. Pflaum, Publishers, 1970.
35. Lehner, Andreas P. "The Laissez-Faire Curriculum in the Democratic School," *English Journal,* 59 (1970), 803–10.
36. Loban, Walter; Ryan, Margaret; and Squire, James R. *Teaching Language and Literature: Grades Seven-Twelve.* 2d ed.; New York: Harcourt, Brace & World, Inc., 1969.
37. Lynch, James J., and Evans, Bertrand. *High School English Textbooks: A Critical Examination.* Boston: Little, Brown and Company, 1963.
38. Malmstrom, Jean, and Lee, Janice. *Teaching English Linguistically.* New York: Appleton-Century-Crofts, 1971.
39. Mandel, Barrett John. *Literature and the English Department.* Champaign, Ill.: National Council of Teachers of English, 1970.
40. Meadows, Robert. "Get Smart: Let TV Work for You," *English Journal,* 56 (1967), 121–24.
41. Miller, James E., Jr. "Literature in the Revitalized Curriculum," *NASSP Bulletin,* 38 (1967), 25–38.
42. Moffett, James. *A Student-Centered Language Arts Curriculum Grades K-13: A Handbook.* Boston: Houghton Mifflin Company, 1968.
43. ———. *Teaching the Universe of Discourse.* Boston: Houghton Mifflin Company, 1968.
44. Muller, Herbert J. *The Uses of English.* New York: Holt, Rinehart & Winston, Inc., 1967.
45. Murphy, Geraldine. *The Study of Literature in High School.* Waltham, Mass.: Ginn/Blaisdell, 1968.
46. O'Keefe, Patrick A. "The Movie's the Message," *English Journal,* 60 (1971), 957–59.
47. Olson, Arthur V., and Ames, Wilbur S. *Teaching Reading Skills in Secondary Schools.* Scranton: Intext Educational Publishers, 1972.
48. O'Neal, Robert. *Teacher's Guide to World Literature for the High School.* Champaign, Ill.: National Council of Teachers of English, 1966.
49. Perkins, Flossie L. *Book and Non-Book Media: Annotated*

Guide to Selection Aid for Educational Materials. Urbana, Ill.: National Council of Teachers of English, 1969.
50. Postman, Neil, and Weingartner, Charles. *Teaching as a Subversive Activity.* New York: The Delacorte Press, 1969.
51. Poteet, G. Howard (ed.). *The Compleat Guide to Film Study.* Urbana, Ill.: National Council of Teachers of English, 1972.
52. Purves, Alan C. *How Porcupines Make Love; Notes on a Response-Centered Curriculum.* Lexington, Mass.: Xerox College Publishing, 1972.
53. Purves, Alan C., and Beach, Richard. *Literature and the Reader: Research in Response to Literature, Reading Interests, and the Teaching of Literature.* Urbana, Ill.: National Council of Teachers of English, 1972.
54. Purves, Alan C., and Rippere, Victoria. *Elements of Writing about a Literary Work: A Study of Response to Literature.* Champaign, Ill.: National Council of Teachers of English, 1968.
55. Rosenberg, Arnold J. "An Angry Principal Speaks Out," *Learning,* I (1973), 26-28.
56. Rosenblatt, Louise. "The Acid Test in Teaching Literature," *English Journal,* 45 (1956), 66-74.
57. _____ "Literature and the Invisible Reader," *The Promise of English: NCTE 1970 Distinguished Lectures.* Champaign, Ill.: National Council of Teachers of English, 1970.
58. _____ *Literature as Exploration.* Rev. ed.; New York: Noble and Noble, Publishers, 1968.
59. Shuman, R. Baird. "Establishing a Basis for Classroom Dialog," *English Journal,* 61 (1972), 1338-40.
60. Sparks, Merla. "An Alternative to the Traditional Grading System," *English Journal,* 56 (1967), 1032-34.
61. Squire, James R. (ed.). *Response to Literature.* Champaign, Ill.: National Council of Teachers of English, 1968.
62. Squire, James R., and Applebee, Roger K. *High School English Instruction Today.* New York: Appleton-Century-Crofts, 1968.
63. _____ *Teaching English in the United Kingdom.* Champaign, Ill.: National Council of Teachers of English, 1969.
64. Stone, George Winchester (ed.). *Issues, Problems, and Approaches in the Teaching of English.* New York: Holt, Rinehart & Winston, Inc., 1964.
65. Thompson, Denys. *Directions in the Teaching of English.* London: Cambridge University Press, 1969.

66. Tiedt, Iris M., and Tiedt, Sidney W. *Unrequired Reading: An Annotated Bibliography for Teachers and School Administrators.* Corvallis,Or.: Oregon State University Press, 1963.
67. Weber, J. Sherwood (ed.). *Good Reading.* 35th ed.; New York: New American Library, 1969.
68. White, Marian E. *High Interest—Easy Reading for Junior and Senior High School Students.* 2d ed.; New York: Citation Press, 1972.
69. Whitehead, Frank. *The Disappearing Dais: A Study of the Principles and Practice of English Teaching.* London: Chatto and Windus, 1966.
70. Wilson, Jean (ed.). *Books for You.* Rev. ed.; New York: Washington Square Press, 1971.
71. Winner, Edward G. "The Paperback Goes Home," *English Journal,* 56 (1967), 453-89.

CHARLES R. DUKE
Plymouth State College

2 Drama

The state of knowledge about teaching drama in the secondary school seems to be a confused one. A quick scanning of current educational journals reveals that little, if anything, is being said on a consistent basis about drama and its place in the curriculum. Undoubtedly much of this present state can be traced to the conceptions that many English teachers have about drama. For too many teachers, as Dwight Burton points out (10, p. 131), "drama has been looked upon as a pleasant interlude between the more serious concerns of the novel, the poem, the short story and the essay."

No one denies the acceptance of drama as entertainment; but too often students come away from their experiences with drama in the classroom with only two impressions. First, drama is Shakespeare in the minds of many students; frequently the only exposure to drama which students receive is centered on the reading of a Shakespearean play each of the four years a student is in high school. His other impression of drama usually is associated with the yearly senior play, often produced strictly as a money-raising venture; whatever dramatic appreciation occurs is a secondary and very minor consideration.

Little wonder, then, that the secondary school student has little awareness and appreciation of the rich dramatic tradition within his own country as well as throughout the world. One might speculate that if Shakespeare had not produced the works he did, drama as a subject might never have appeared in the secondary classroom.

The very strong emphasis upon Shakespeare as the carrier of dramatic tradition has probably set the teaching of drama back at least 50 years. The reason for this is pointed out by Barry Robinson who suggests that "for far too many years, teachers, both academic and thespic, have been insisting that Shakespeare and other playwrights of similar stature are so great that their very words should be worshipped without virtually any regard for the overall relevance of what their dramas are saying" (43, p. 38). This attitude closely parallels that which governs the traditional approach to the teaching of poetry and fiction; the result is a kind of closet drama, with the student groping his way through a foreign-looking text and concluding his study little wiser or more appreciative than when he began.

George Bernard Shaw was familiar with the manner in which plays were treated by educators. Once asked if he would be willing to have his plays studied in schools, Shaw replied, "No! I lay my eternal curse on whomsoever shall now or at any time hereafter make schoolbooks of my works and make me as hated as Shakespeare is hated. My plays were not designed as instruments of torture. All the schools that lust after them get this answer, and will never get any other from G. Bernard Shaw" (38, p. 12). Despite his wishes, Shaw and his plays have made it into the classroom, but one assumes that Shaw's reaction would be the same today.

Remarkably little progress has occurred in expanding the study of drama in the classroom. Joseph Mersand (30) traced the development of instruction in drama in the secondary schools and found that not until 1910 were some plays other than Shakespeare's added to the curriculum and then these consisted of such plays as Oliver Goldsmith's *She Stoops to Conquer* and some of the early English plays like *Ralph Roister Doister*. Play selection has improved somewhat over the last 60 years, for we can now find instances where modern playwrights such as Edward Albee, Arthur Miller, and Eugene O'Neill are being studied in the classroom, but still not on any consistent basis.

WHY DRAMA IN THE CLASSROOM?

Many justifications are available for making the study and appreciation of drama a more integral part of the English curriculum. One of the most fundamental reasons lies in the fact that man constitutes the central subject matter of all drama and, therefore, through the study of drama, an individual can come to discover more about what it means to be a human being. Then, too, as Gabriel Barnfield suggests, drama is "that form of creative expression which deals with the person directly and entails only himself as the instrument of expression—his outward appearance and vocal impressions under the guidance of mind and imagination" (8, p. 4). James Moffett, one of the foremost proponents for increased emphasis upon drama in the classroom states:

Drama is the most accessible form of literature for young and uneducated people. It is made up of action; and the verbal action is of a sort we all practice all the time. A kindergarten child or an older illiterate can soliloquize and converse, verbalize to himself and vocalize to others (32, p. 3).

Moffet also stresses that one of the principal values of drama in the classroom is that drama is "oral and behavioral and functional, evolving directly out of real-life activities..." (32, p. 3). Still another reason for the inclusion of drama in the curriculum is offered by Walter Loban. He suggests that since students give so much time to the spoken word as it comes to them through the mass media rather than through reading, drama offers an excellent means for training discriminating readers; students have to become involved with the text while reading or seeing a play because no guiding voice is there to show them the way, or to summarize or to explain (25, p. 480).

In the past, English teachers have thought of dramatic awareness, dramatic appreciation, and content retention as synonymous. Yet it does not necessarily follow that simply because a student does not exhibit a high level of content knowledge that he is unaware of drama. Perhaps it will be helpful to draw some distinctions here which will clarify the reasons that drama has often been misused and misunderstood in the classroom.

Drama as literature allows one the opportunity to explore the relationship between the play's message and the spectator or reader. Drama as theater, on the other hand, involves an interaction among the play's message, the actor, and the spectator. Drama as literature offers an internalized production; drama as theater offers a backdrop against which the spectator tests his "internal production," reshapes his attitudes and reforms his values. Hence drama calls for a different understanding than that found in other forms of literature. Peter J.

Sheehan summarizes the difference in this way: "Drama is a study of human nature directed at the common denominator, everyman. Serious novels require adult experience for complete empathy while poetry usually grabs only those sensitive to it.... Drama makes the most intensive and creative demands on the imagination, drawing from the individual a more or less total commitment of the self, whereas poetry hits a limited part of the mind, and novels often leave the mind untouched" (45, p. 562-63).

Not only does drama require a different kind of consideration from other forms of literature, but it also meets some of the primary objectives that most English teachers feel are important for the student. Dwight Burton sees the primary objectives for the teaching of drama in the secondary school as the following:

1. To develop pleasure and skill in reading and interpreting drama, and to acquaint students with some dramatic works and lists of plays for future reading.
2. To acquaint students with the dramatic tradition, the role of drama in the history of man.
3. To develop critical standards and taste in drama, film, and television.
4. To encourage interest in playgoing and the support of community ventures in drama.
5. To increase students' understanding of the importance of drama as a source of insight into personal and social problems (10, p. 136-40).

The teacher who wishes to make drama an important part of the English classroom experience faces a tremendous challenge. On the one hand, he knows that a common impulse toward dramatic expression exists in his students; nor is it unnatural to assume in a society where the primary emphasis is placed on the materialistic and the physical, that an impulse toward dramatic expression should be contrastingly deep and intense. On the other hand, never has there been a generation which has burst forth with such a flood of expression as the mechanisms of this age have made possible. Motion pictures, television, radio, all within immediate access of today's young people, make it difficult for the English teacher to convince students that what may be found on the printed page and on the stage will be of some lasting value.

Simply putting more plays into the curriculum is not the answer. What must happen, first of all, is a drastic change in the present attitude that many English teachers exhibit toward drama. Part of the problem can be traced to the preparation of teachers of English; according to a recent study by Joseph L. Peluso, most have little background in drama (39). The usual preparation consists of a course or two in Shakespeare, possibly a course in theater history and nothing more. Knowledge of contemporary theater is negligible and awareness of what plays might be suitable for secondary school students is weak. Missing, too, is a clear understanding of the particular problems students will encounter when reading drama in the classroom. Hence we must not be surprised when we encounter resistance against increasing the emphasis upon drama in the curriculum.

The Anglo-American Conference on the Teaching of English, held at Dartmouth College in 1966, made it quite clear, however, that some of the primary considerations to which English teachers should be addressing themselves lie in the field of drama. Both British and American educators agreed quite closely on the need for such increased emphasis. From this Conference came the following guidelines for the use of drama—in its largest context—and oral communication:

1. Drama and oral communication should become the centrality of pupil's exploring, extending, and shaping of experience in the classroom.
2. There is a definite urgency for developing classroom approaches stressing the vital, creative dramatic involvement of young people in language experiences.
3. The importance of directing more attention to speaking and listening for pupils at all levels, particularly in those experiences which involve vigorous interaction among children, should be apparent.
4. The wisdom of providing young people at all levels with significant opportunities for the creative use of language—creative dramatics, imaginative writing, improvisation, role playing and similar activities—has become increasingly evident (13, p. 33).

The participants of the Anglo-American Conference viewed drama in a much wider perspective than has traditionally been the case in American schools. To these educators, drama embraced not just the printed page, the stage performance, and the Broadway show; more important in their eyes was the total involvement of the student in dramatic activities which allowed him to explore and test his own identity. This constitutes a new approach to the teaching of drama which many teachers will have to consider closely in the coming years.

One should see, then, that the solution is more complex than simply having teachers take more courses in drama and theater, although this should not be discarded. More important, however, is that the English teacher himself genuinely value the reading of plays, the attending of theatrical productions, the reading of periodicals dealing with the dramatic arts, the viewing of effective television and film productions and of following closely the development of drama in all its forms—street, avant garde, academic, creative—within American culture and throughout the world.

RESOURCES FOR THE TEACHING OF DRAMA

The English teacher who recognizes the need for increased emphasis upon drama in the classroom will have to undertake some preparation before he can be thoroughly comfortable with the dramatic mode. One of his first tasks will be to acquaint himself as much as possible with the state of theater today and to be certain that he has a thorough knowledge of its development.

Every secondary school library should have some basic references on drama and approaches to its teaching, as well as collections of plays and types of drama. Of equal importance to the teacher will be information about the contemporary theater, most easily gained, perhaps, through careful reading in selected journals and reviews. A further aid is available in the numerous organizations which a teacher may join or call upon to provide him with assistance and materials.

A basic reference library in drama should include as many of the following titles as possible; some of these should be a permanent part of any library's collection; others the English teacher undoubtedly will wish to have for his personal use as he becomes more familiar with the directions in which he wishes to move as he uses drama in the classroom.

General

Anderson, Michael, et al. *Crowell's Handbook of Contemporary Drama.* New York: Thomas Y. Crowell Company, 1971.

Baker, George Pierce. *Dramatic Technique.* Boston: Houghton Mifflin Company, 1919.

Barnfield, Gabriel. *Creative Drama in the Schools.* New York: Hart Publishing Company, Inc., 1968.

Barton, Lucy. *Historic Costume for the Stage.* Rev. ed.: Boston: Walter H. Baker Co., 1961.

Beckerman, Bernard. *Dynamics of Drama.* New York: Alfred A. Knopf Inc., 1970.

Bentley, Eric. *The Life of the Drama.* New York: Atheneum Publishers, 1964.
Blau, Herbert. *The Impossible Theater, a Manifesto.* New York: The Macmillan Company, 1964.
Bowman, Walter P., and Ball, Robert H. *Theatre Language.* New York: Theatre Arts Books, 1961.
Breed, Paul Francis. *Dramatic Criticism Index,* Detroit: Gale Research Company, 1972.
Brockett, Oscar F. *History of the Theatre.* Boston: Allyn & Bacon, Inc., 1968.
Brustein, Robert S. *The Theatre of Revolt: An Approach to the Modern Drama.* Boston: Little Brown and Company, 1964.
Burton, Dwight L. *Literature Study in the High Schools.* 3d ed., New York: Holt, Rinehart & Winston, Inc., 1970.
Campbell, Oscar J. and Quinn, Edward C. *The Reader's Encyclopedia of Shakespeare.* New York: Thomas Y. Crowell Company, 1966.
Conner, J. M. and Conner, B. M. *Ottemiller's Index to Plays in Collections.* 5th ed., Metuchen, N.J. Scarecrow Press, Inc., 1971.
Downer, Alan S. (ed.). *The American Theater Today,* New York: Basic Books, Inc., Publishers, 1967.
Drew, Elizabeth. *Discovering Drama.* Port Washington, N.Y. Kennikat Press Inc., 1937.
Esslin, Martin. *Theatre of the Absurd.* Rev. ed.: Garden City, N.Y. Anchor Books, 1969.
———. *Reflections, Essays on Modern Theatre.* Garden City, N.Y. Doubleday & Company, Inc., 1969.
Gassner, John. *The Theatre in Our Times.* New York: Crown Publishers, Inc., 1954.
———. *Theatre at the Crossroads: Plays and Playwrights of the Mid-Century American Stage.* New York: Holt, Rinehart & Winston, Inc., 1960.
———. *Dramatic Soundings.* New York: Crown Publishers, Inc., 1968.
Hansen, Henry H. *Costumes and Styles, the Evolution of Fashion from Early Egypt to the Present.* New York: E. P. Dutton, Co., Inc., 1956.
Kernan, Alvin B. (ed.). *The Modern American Theater: A Collection of Critical Essays.* Englewood Cliffs, N.J. Prentice-Hall, Inc., 1967.
Kernodle, George R. *Invitation to the Theatre.* New York: Harcourt, Brace & World, Inc., 1967.
Lass, Abraham H. (ed.). *A Student's Guide to 50 American Plays.* New York: Washington Square Press, 1969.
Lewis, Allan. *American Plays and Playwrights of the Contemporary Theatre.* New York: Crown Publishers, Inc., 1965.
Lumley, Frederick. *New Trends in 20th Century Drama.* New York: Oxford University Press, 1967.
Matlaw, Myron. *Modern World Drama, an Encyclopedia.* New York: E. P. Dutton & Co., Inc., 1972.
Mersand, Joseph. *Index to Plays with Suggestions for Teaching.* Metuchen, N.J.: Scarecrow Press, Inc., 1966.
Meserve, Walter J. (ed.). *Discussions of Modern American Drama.* Boston, D. C. Heath & Company, 1965.

Nagler, A. M. *A Source Book in Theatrical History.* New York: Dover Publications, Inc., 1952.
Nicoll, Allardyce. *The Development of the Theatre.* New York: Harcourt, Brace & World, Inc., 1966.
Roose-Evans, James. *Experimental Theatre: From Stanislavsky to Today.* New York: Universe Books, 1970.
Rowe, Kenneth Thorp. *Theater in Your Head.* New York: Funk and Wagnalls, Inc., 1966.
Shank, Theodore J. (ed.). *A Digest of 500 Plays.* New York: Crowell-Collier Publishing Company, 1963.
Sprinchorn, Evert. (ed.). *20th Century Plays in Synopsis.* New York: Thomas Y. Crowell Company, 1966.
Taubman, Howard. *The Making of the American Theatre.* New York: Coward McCann, Inc., 1965.
Taylor, William E. (ed.). *Modern American Drama: Essays in Criticism.* Deland, Fla.: Everett/Edwards Inc., 1968.
Wilde, Percival. *The Craftsmanship of the One-Act Play.* New York: Crown Publishers, Inc., 1951.
Williams, Clifford J. *Theatre and Audiences.* London: Longman Group Ltd., 1970.
Williams, Raymond. *Drama from Ibsen to Brecht.* New York: Oxford University Press, 1969.

Teaching of Drama

Barnes, Douglas (ed.). *Drama in the English Classroom.* Champaign, Ill. National Council of Teachers of English, 1968.
Beck, Roy A. *Group Reading: Reader's Theatre.* Skokie, Ill. National Textbook Company, 1969.
Creber, Patrick. "The Dramatic Experience," *Sense and Sensitivity,* London: University of London Press, 1965, pp. 85–108.
Dunning, Stephen and Sams, Henry W. (eds.). *Scholarly Appraisals of Literary Works Taught in High Schools.* Champaign, Ill. National Council of Teachers of English, 1965.
Harris, Peter (ed.). *Drama in Education.* London: Bodley Head, 1967. (Available from NCTE.)
Hodgson, John and Banham, Martin (eds.). *Drama in Education I, The Annual Survey.* New York: Pitman Publishing Corporation, 1972.
Hoetker, James. *Dramatics and the Teaching of Literature.* Champaign, Ill. National Council of Teachers of English, 1969.
———. *Students as Audiences: An Experimental Study of the Relationship between Classroom Study of Drama and Attendance at the Theatre.* Champaign, Ill.: National Council of Teachers of English, 1971.
Howes, Alan B. *Teaching Literature to Adolescents: Plays.* Glenview, Ill.: Scott Foresman and Company, 1968.
Loban, Walter; Ryan, Margaret; and Squire, James R. "Literature: Drama and Poetry," Chapter 11 in *Teaching Language and Literature,* 2d ed.; New York: Harcourt, Brace & World, Inc., 1969.

Moffett, James. *Drama: What Is Happening?* Champaign, Ill.: National Council of Teachers of English 1967.

―――. *Student-Centered Language Arts Curriculum, Grades K-13.* Boston: Houghton Mifflin Company, 1968.

Motter, Charlotte. *Theatre in High School, Planning, Teaching, Directing.* Englewood Cliffs, N.J.: Prentice-Hall, Inc., 1970.

Mersand, Joseph. *Drama in the Secondary Schools.* Metuchen, N.J.: Scarecrow Press, Inc., 1969.

Muller, Herbert J. "Creativity and Drama," Chapter 7 in *The Uses of English,* New York: Holt, Rinehart & Winston, Inc., 1967.

Ontario Institute for Studies in Education. *Courses of Study in the Theatre Arts Grades 7-12.* Toronto, Canada: Ontario Institute for Studies in Education, 1969.

Play List Revision Committee of the Secondary School Theatre Conference. *Plays Recommended for High Schools.* Rev. ed.: Washington, D.C.: American Educational Theatre Association, 1967.

Rabkin, Gerald. "On Teaching Drama," in Edward B. Jenkinson and Jane S. Hawley, (eds.), *On Teaching Literature.* Bloomington, Ind. Indiana University Press, 1967, pp. 106-34.

Secondary School Theatre Conference. *A Course Guide in the Theatre Arts at the Secondary School Level,* Rev. ed.; Washington, D.C.: American Educational Theatre Association, Inc., 1968.

Way, Brian. *Development through Drama.* London: Longman Group Ltd., 1967.

Wolf, Mary H., and Miller, Victor B. *Theatre's Different Demands.* Study Developed by Title III Program and administered by Connecticut State Department of Education and the American Shakespearean Festival, 1970.

PERIODICALS

Most of the periodicals currently publishing articles about theater arts tend to emphasize either academic theater or production; few journals address themselves specifically to the teaching of drama in the secondary school. The exceptions are the *English Journal* and *College English,* both publications of the National Council of Teachers of English. Other periodicals which will prove helpful from time to time include the following: (asterisked titles will be most likely to carry topics of immediate interest to secondary teachers).

Children's Theater Review (4 issues; $8: articles on production and texts of children's theater; American Theatre Association, John F. Kennedy Center for the Performing Arts, Suite 500, 1701 Pennsylvania Ave., N.W., Washington, D.C. 20006).

*Drama Review (4 issues; $7.50; scholarly appraisals of dramatic literature; considered one of the best of its kind. The Drama Review, 32 Washington Place, Room 73, New York, New York 10003).

Drama Survey (3 issues; $2.50; scholarly appraisals of dramatic literature. *Drama Survey,* Box 4098, University Station, Minneapolis, Minnesota 35414).

*Dramatics (8 issues; directed toward secondary school teaching and production of drama; content is suitable for students as well as teachers. *Dramatics,* Dept. D/Box E, College Hill Station, Cincinnati, Ohio 45224).

*Educational Theatre Journal (4 issues; $12.50; scholarly articles pertaining to drama as well as articles dealing with educational theater. American Theatre Association, John F. Kennedy Center for the Performing Arts, Suite 500, 1701 Pennsylvania Ave., N.W., Washington, D.C. 20006).

Modern Drama (4 issues; $4; scholarly articles pertaining to modern playwrights. Virginia B. Edwards, Dept. of English, University of Kansas, Lawrence, Kansas 66044).

Modern International Drama (2 issues; $4.50; translations of plays from various foreign countries. *Modern International Drama,* Max Reinhardt Archives, State University of New York, Binghamton, New York 13901).

*Plays (monthly; $8; scripts of plays suitable for junior and senior high students. Plays Inc., 8 Arlington Street, Boston, Mass. 02116).

Quarterly Journal of Speech (4 issues; $15; occasionally contains articles directed toward drama and theater. Speech Communication Association, Statler Hilton Hotel, New York, New York 10001).

*Secondary School Theatre (3 issues; $6; articles pertaining both to production and teaching of drama on secondary level. American Theatre Association, John F. Kennedy Center for Performing Arts, Suite 500, 1701 Pennsylvania Ave., N.W., Washington, D.C. 20006).

The following magazines are of less immediate value but the teacher of drama should look at them occasionally.

Black Theatre Bulletin (biannual newsletter; $3; reports on significant black theater activities in Africa, Latin America, and the United States. American Theatre Association, John F. Kennedy Center for Performing Arts, Suite 500, 1701 Pennsylvania Ave., N.W., Washington, D.C. 20006).

Scripts ($7.50; publishes scripts of plays not found usually in regular anthologies; tends toward avant garde. 425 Lafayette St., New York, New York 10003).

Theatre Crafts (6 issues; $5; emphasizes technical aspects of theater production; often has interesting articles and pictures dealing with set designs which are helpful in class discussions about the physical aspects of theater. *Theatre Crafts,* Emmaus, Pennsylvania 18049).

Theatre Notebook (4 issues; $6; concentrates on history and techniques of British theater; available from 14 Woronzow Road, London, NW 8, England).

THEATER ORGANIZATIONS

Still another consideration for the English teacher is his association with professional organizations whose primary concern is drama. In addition to regional and state theater and speech associations, which vary from area to area, the following organizations will provide valuable assistance and materials to their members. The parent organization for most of these groups is the American Theatre Association (ATA) which has the following branches:

American Community Theatre Association (ACTA)
Children's Theatre Conference (CTC)
Secondary School Theatre Conference (SSTC)
National Contemporary Theatre Conference (NCTC)

All of these organizations have their main headquarters at the John F. Kennedy Center for the Performing Arts, Suite 500, 1701 Pennsylvania Avenue, N.W., Washington, D.C. 20006. Other organizations which will be of help include the following:

National Association of Dramatic and Speech Arts (NADSA) (headquarters: Fort Valley State College, Fort Valley, Georgia)
National Thespian Society (NTS) (headquarters: College Hill Station, Cincinnati, Ohio 45224)
Speech Association of America (headquarters: Statler Hilton Hotel, New York, New York 10001)

ACADEMIC AND COMMUNITY THEATER AND THE SCHOOLS

Potential sources of information, advice, and live theater exist with two resources often overlooked by secondary school teachers. Academic theater departments which may exist in neighboring colleges and universities frequently are eager to work with secondary schools in developing curriculum and providing materials and productions to augment the regular program of the school. Often students majoring in theater at nearby institutions can, as part of their course work, spend time in the high schools introducing students to drama and improvisational activities. Another source exists with the professional repertory companies that often locate in cities throughout the country. These companies are interested in building an audience and one of the ways to do this is by cultivating students' taste for theater. Consequently, members of such companies often are willing to spend time with students explaining drama, offering short programs for school assemblies and eventually working out programs with school authorities so that live theater experiences become a regular part of student education. Some of these joint efforts have produced marked improvement in both teacher and student attitudes toward drama.

Educational Laboratory Theatre Project, centered in three areas—Rhode Island, New Orleans, and Los Angeles—was conducted to determine the relationship between students' appreciation of drama and their attendance at theatrical productions. The project, funded by a federal grant, was based on the assumptions that classroom study of plays would maximize the benefits of theater experience and that the availability of a professional performance would enliven and enrich the classroom study of the play. Past proposals for using creative and performing artists in a variety of humanities programs have not always been realistic in determining the difficulties which arise when educators and working artists are asked to cooperate in a joint venture.

The communication problems arising in such joint efforts usually stem from preconceptions that each group brings to the task. For example, it was found in the Educational Laboratory Theatre Project, evaluated quite fully by James Hoetker in *Students as Audiences* (22), that the opinions about literature teaching to which the English teachers in all three project sites subscribed, seemed to be learned and professional specifics. Teachers gave priority to the literary text of a play and looked upon production as merely an illustration of the text. The professional theater people, however, saw the performance of the play as the primary consideration and classroom instruction as simply a preparation for viewing. Neither point of view was surprising, considering the lack of understanding of each person's role in developing appreciation of drama. Such differences had to be resolved before the project could get under way. Eventually theater people and English teachers combined to produce a workable plan for the project with each group contributing to the preparation, performing and evaluating which took place for each theater experience.

Some of the conclusions of this study offer valuable information for the classroom teacher of drama. It was found, for example, that little significant difference existed between the effects of one or two periods of study of a play prior to viewing it and four to seven periods of study; in most schools, teachers discussing the play tended to spend about three periods before the performance and one after. The Educational Laboratory Theatre project also showed that dramatic enrichment of this type—discussing and viewing of professional performances—is appropriate and beneficial for all ability levels, with the average student benefiting slightly more than those of above average or below average ability. Students also seemed to have an increased sensitivity to stimuli, paid more attention to reflecting on what was said, heard, and done around them and placed more importance upon values as a result of their exposure to this type of dramatic program.

The kinds of plays presented to the students varied from site to site, but some of the titles included *Macbeth, Ah! Wilderness, Tartuffe, A Raisin in the Sun, Enemy of the People, The Crucible, The Chairs,* and *The Bald Soprano.* Teachers received curriculum packets, compiled by educators and professional theater people, that included illustrated materials on stage and scenery designs, transcripts of interviews with directors, artists and technicians, critical essays, a teacher's study guide, and historical information. Of all the materials produced, the most frequently used by teachers were the study guides and the critical essays. In the case of Eugene Ionesco's *The Chairs* and *The Bald Soprano,* the professional company put together a short assembly program dealing with theater of the absurd and toured participating schools before the performance date of the two plays. Student reaction to this procedure indicated they found such a practice helpful.

Other information gained from the project that should help the classroom teacher centers on student attitudes. It was found that the timing of the preparation for viewing a play seems to affect a student's expressed liking for the play, but it does not affect students' reported involvement with the production. Often, because of scheduling difficulties, the preliminary introduction to a play slated for viewing is done some time before the production; although such a practice is not desirable, it apparently does not have quite the negative effect that some teachers would anticipate. Ideally, of course, preparation and viewing should come as close as possible. Another development of interest to those teachers working with contemporary drama occurred during the study. It was discovered that preparing students for a conventional production may facilitate their enjoyment of it, but similar preparation may inhibit student enjoyment of a total theater production which relies heavily on scenic and acoustical effects.

It will not always be possible to discover community or academic theaters willing to go to the amount of preparation found in the Educational Laboratory Theatre project. But, if we feel that the theater-going habit is of any value to a person, then it must be developed while the student is still in high school and just mere acquaintance with dramatic texts is unlikely to accomplish this. Once the habit is developed in the secondary school, it is fairly certain that it will continue into the college and adult years. The Tyrone Guthrie Theater of Minneapolis has found that their most faithful and enthusiastic audiences are drawn from the secondary school population in the area rather than from the colleges and universities. These secondary school students come to realize what Gerald Rabkin points out in his essay "On Teaching Drama": "Drama is literature, but it is something more. With certain exceptions, the history of drama as a literary form is very largely the history of those works which have survived on stage" (42, p. 106).

The communal experience of theater, as suggested by such studies as the Educational Laboratory Theatre project, provides what otherwise might be a purely "literary" experience with an extra dimension of pleasure that is as real as it is difficult to define. It appears that the realities of transferring the play into theatrical actuality force the student to compare his imaginative reconstruction of the script with that of theatrical artists, and out of this comes a deeper and lasting understanding of the dimensions of drama.

PLAY SELECTION

Once the teacher accepts the need for dramatic experiences, however, he is faced with a qualitative judgment as well as a quantitative one. Just how does he know which plays he should select and how does he determine whether students should see a production? One of the first sources of information lies with the various compilations of criticism such as Paul F. Breed's *Dramatic Criticism Index;* here the teacher will find extensive listings of sources that will provide him with a large spectrum of critical judgment.

Other helpful sources include Joseph Mersand's *Index to Plays with Suggestions for Teaching,* Abraham Lass's *A Student's Guide to 50 American Plays,* and a publication of the American Theatre Association entitled *Plays Recommended for High Schools.* For extremely modern plays, reviews from major newspapers and magazines will provide some clue to the English teacher as to whether a production might be suitable for his students.

Joseph Mersand offers the following characteristics as a guide for determining great drama:

1. Universality of appeal in time as well as space
2. Creation of living characters in convincing situations

3. Action which stirs, moves, enriches or transforms the spectator or reader
4. Information about life, how people think and act
5. Help in strengthening a student to face his own problems (30, p. 124-28).

The number of plays students view will depend largely upon their availability. It has been found, however, that students who are aware of the text and its problems, and the production and its problems can profit from a "bad production" of a "bad play" just as much as from a "good production" of a "great play." For this reason, the teacher should not summarily dismiss plays which seem on first glance to be less than excellent. He may find that he can accomplish much by careful previewing and then careful preparation of students for such experiences.

PLAYS SUITABLE FOR CLASSROOM STUDY

A number of play lists are available and a quick perusal of the catalogs of the play publishing houses will give teachers an idea of the offerings available to them. As a help in this direction, however, the following list is offered. No attempt is made to indicate at what grade level the plays should be taught since reading abilities and interest levels vary so widely that the teacher will undoubtedly wish to make his own selections; neither have sources for the plays been indicated since most are readily available either in anthologies or acting scripts.

One Act Plays

The Browning Version by Terence Rattigan
Fumed Oak by Noel Coward
The Valiant by Holworthy Hall and Robert Middlemas
The Ghost Story by Booth Tarkington
Hands Across the Sea by Noel Coward
Happy Journey to Camden and Trenton by Thornton Wilder
The Informer by Bertolt Brecht
The Monkey's Paw by W. W. Jacobs and Louis N. Parker
The Old Lady Shows Her Medals by J. M. Barrie
Once around the Block by William Saroyan
Hello out There by William Saroyan
The Private Ear by Peter Shaffer
The Public Eye by Peter Shaffer
Riders to the Sea by J. M. Synge
Trifles by Susan Glaspell
The Apollo of Bellac by Jean Giraudoux

The Tiger by Murray Schisgal
The Typists by Murray Schisgal
Mrs. Dally Has A Lover by William Hanley
Whisper into My Good Ear by William Hanley
The Mother by Paddy Chayefsky

Three Act Plays

The Shrike by Joseph Kramm
A View from the Bridge by Arthur Miller
All My Sons by Arthur Miller
The Crucible by Arthur Miller
Death of a Salesman by Arthur Miller
Cry Havoc by Allan R. Kenward
The House of Bernada Alba by Frederico Gracia Lorca
The Iceman Cometh by Eugene O'Neill
Desire under the Elms by Eugene O'Neill
A Streetcar Named Desire by Tennessee Williams
A Glass Menagerie by Tennessee Williams
Come Back Little Sheba by William Inge
Look Back in Anger by John Osborne
Luv by Murray Schisgal
The Doctor and the Devils by Dylan Thomas
I Remember Mama by John Van Druten
The Winslow Boy by Terence Rattigan
The Admirable Crichton by J. M. Barrie
Arms and the Man by George Bernard Shaw
Man and Superman by George Bernard Shaw
Pygmalion by George Bernard Shaw
Androcles and the Lion by George Bernard Shaw
Our Town by Thornton Wilder
The Skin of Our Teeth by Thornton Wilder
The Matchmaker by Thornton Wilder
The Time of Your Life by William Saroyan
Idiot's Delight by Robert Sherwood
Of Mice and Men by John Steinbeck
Awake and Sing! by Clifford Odets
Golden Boy by Clifford Odets
End of Summer by S. N. Behrman
The Investigation by Peter Weiss
The Miracle Worker by William Gibson
A Cry of Players by William Gibson
The Odd Couple by Neil Simon
Last of the Red Hot Lovers by Neil Simon
Barefoot in the Park by Neil Simon
The Star Spangled Girl by Neil Simon
Jimmy Shine by Murray Schisgal
The Little Foxes by Lillian Hellman
The Rainmaker by Richard Nash

Requiem for a Heavyweight by Rod Serling
Harvey by Mary Chase
A Member of the Wedding by Carson McCullers
West Side Story by Arthur Laurents, Leonard Bernstein, and Stephen Sondheim
The Desperate Hours by Joseph Hayes
Sunrise at Campobello by Dore Schary
Twelve Angry Men by Reginald Rose
The Andersonville Trial by Saul Levitt
The Caine Mutiny by Herman Wouk
The Night Thoreau Spent in Jail by Jerome Lawrence and Robert Lee
The Cherry Orchard by Anton Chekhov

GENERAL APPROACHES TO TEACHING DRAMA

The teacher using drama in the classroom may utilize a number of general approaches to organize his instruction. He should not expect that one approach will necessarily be better than another; instead, he should be looking for those activities and approaches which will fit the immediate and long-range needs of his students. Each class is different; each play is different. The general approaches suggested below indicate some of the possibilities for organizing instruction in drama.

Historical. Many teachers feel that a student needs a sense of the dramatic tradition to appreciate the trends in contemporary theater. An introduction to the origins of drama, perhaps beginning with the early Greek theater and tracing the development of drama through the medieval morality and miracle plays and then through Shakespeare to the modern day will set the history of dramatic literature in perspective.

Such an approach might follow the general outline adopted from Helen Louise Cohen's *Milestones of the Drama* (14, pp. 552-56).

I. *The Greek Drama*
   A. Origins
   B. The Theater
   C. Playwrights and their work
   D. Conventions of Greek drama
II. *Medieval Drama*
   A. Historical background including the transitions from classical times
   B. Liturgical drama
   C. Miracle plays

      D. Morality plays
      E. Interludes
III. *Elizabethan Drama*
      A. Renaissance
      B. Christopher Marlowe
      C. Elizabethan theater
      D. Study of Elizabethan drama
IV. *Drama of the Eighteenth and Nineteenth Centuries*
      A. Eighteenth Century — Richard Brinsley Sheridan
      B. Nineteenth Century — Henrik Ibsen
V. *Contemporary Drama*
      A. Edmond Rostand
      B. Eugene O'Neill
      C. Arthur Miller

Difficulties in the historical approach arise with selecting materials and devising time schedules to assure equal coverage of each period. If the teacher uses drama as only a part of the overall course in English, then the historical approach will need considerable modification. The straight historical/chronological approach is better suited to the elective system now being used in many secondary schools. For the regular English class, the teacher will have to select short samplings from various periods and perhaps spread them over a period of four years; this method follows the traditional pattern in which primary emphasis upon historical developments in drama appear in the 11th and 12th grades where American literature and British literature customarily have been emphasized.

Sequential Development. Another approach which the classroom teacher may wish to consider is that of the sequential teaching of drama. Such an approach allows the student to become immersed gradually in dramatic literature and establishes a basis of skills and experiences upon which later learning may be built. Dwight Burton recommends a sequential program for the regular classroom (10, pp. 140–50). He suggests that in the 9th grade, the principal emphasis should be placed on one-act plays, with three-acts reserved for the very able student. At this level, the student becomes familiar with basic stage conventions and reading skills such as visualizing setting, interpreting characters, following stage directions, and identifying themes. At the 10th grade, the student begins working with three-act plays and receives his introduction to Shakespeare; a review of concepts taught in the 9th grade prepares the way for learning how to deal with Shakespeare's blank verse and the Elizabethan stage conventions.

The 11th and 12th grades continue the development of reading skills in dramatic literature and students work with both American and English drama. Emphasis falls on relating drama to larger themes such as individualism, Romanticism, and the world at large. In addition, 12th-grade students explore Greek and modern drama and develop a thorough acquaintance with present theatrical developments as well as an ability to recognize the different specific dramatic genres such as melodrama, the comedy of manners, and the tragedy. Extra emphasis on the contributions of media also appear at this level.

Thematic. The thematic approach appears frequently in the study of literature at the secondary level. Teachers find that the flexibility which can be built into such an approach makes it easier to meet the varied interests and reading needs of students. Drama, however, often is left out of thematic treatments; usually the reason for the omission can be traced to a teacher's unawareness of what plays might fit a particular theme. An extensive knowledge of plays suitable for young people needs to be cultivated if the teacher is going to use the thematic approach.

Lois Josephs recommends one plan that should suggest additional possibilities to teachers (24). Although her approach is geared to meet the needs of an elective program, the general format is easily introduced into the regular English class. For instance, Josephs centers her study on groupings of plays; one group stresses the problems of the individual in society; plays suggested for this theme include Kenneth Cameron's *The Hundred and First,* and Lee Kalehiem's *The Match Play.* Another grouping centers on the inability of man to communicate with man. Here such plays as Eugene Ionesco's *The Bald Soprano* appear.

Another possibility for thematic grouping stems from a study of the Bible and its impact on dramatic literature. Archibald MacLeish's *J.B.* is a natural selection because of its interesting parallels with the Book of Job (12, 20). Still further possibilities lie in historical tradition and experiences. Eugene O'Neill's *The Emperor Jones,* and Arthur Miller's *A View from the Bridge* or *All My Sons* are appropriate for treatment in this general area.

Some dangers exist with the thematic approach, however, and the teacher must be alert to avoid them. Sometimes the desire for establishing a thematic focus leads to relating pieces of literature on very flimsy rationalizations. The results do not further a student's knowledge of a work and usually tend to confuse his understanding of how basic themes may recur in various pieces of literature. A careful analysis of a piece's thematic merits before a complete study is developed will help the teacher be certain the material he is using fits his teaching objectives. Far better not to use a particular play in a thematic study than to risk confusing the student and obscuring major goals.

Social Development. Much of the recent emphasis on drama has focused upon the close relationship among drama and social experience and expression. British educators at the Anglo-American Conference on the Teaching of English offered a number of examples of situations where students had developed greater social poise and relationships as a result of work with classroom drama. Douglas Barnes claims that our society offers a wide range of roles for young people and that this same society tolerates differences of opinions, attitudes, and conclusions. As he points out, "our society partakes of the nature of drama: it speaks not with one voice but with many, and these often contradict one another in ways that not even the wisest of us can resolve. But this society with its contradictory voices is not only outside but inside each one of us. Each must learn to tolerate the many voices within himself, to recognize and express his own variousness, to learn how to live among uncertainties and divided loyalties" (7, p. 2). Hence, as Benjamin DeMott declares, "The drama class becomes the place where the talk aims at naming a feeling or sets of feelings, at understanding the complications and contradictions of human response" (7, p. 5).

Several authorities have suggested programs which offer a subject-matter sequence in drama that parallels the developing social patterns of young people and thus offers support for them as they reach out to develop new attitudes and values. James Moffett in his *A Student-Centered Language Arts Curriculum: Grades K-13* (33) offers a well reasoned and comprehensive program with drama at its center. Moffett explores the various applications of drama to all phases of the language arts and indicates that he feels the key to unlocking a student's potential lies in getting the student to express himself orally and dramatically.

David Adland outlines a sequence for the secondary school which follows a somewhat more conventional approach but still offers sufficient latitude for a student to explore and develop on his own (2). Adland recommends that during the first year in the secondary school, students deal with plays that emphasize fantasy and nonrealistic events because many of the young people at this stage are just beginning to cross the bridge into adolescence. In the second year, the content of plays begins moving toward realism and Adland would introduce more emphasis on types of drama. During the third year, a large part of the dramatic work is related to emotional growth. This means that students are free to explore a wide variety of dramatic approaches. These might include original open-ended incidents which spur student discussion and involvement; improvisational sketches which help students recognize their own potential for relating to other people; or experiences with symbolic drama. Students also are encouraged to develop experimental modes of theater using tape recordings, video tapes, chants and choruses, masks, paintings, movement and dance as well as becoming familiar with technical aspects of theater such as lighting and scenic design. The final year of the secondary school focuses on current events and contemporary problems and their relationship with the dramatic mode. Original work at this level is supported by material from all the genres of literature, with particular attention given to extracts from modern plays.

To use the social developmental approach calls for a wealth of knowledge on the part of the teacher. Not only must he know his drama well, but he must also know his students well—their needs, their degrees of social development, and their interests. Resources are important; experiences and materials which will help students find themselves often must be devised quickly and yet with thoroughness. The teacher's knowledge of what resources and materials are available must be extensive and he must be willing to improvise and experiment.

Genre

Some teachers may prefer a genre approach in the teaching of drama. Important to such an approach is a close consideration of the distinctions among drama and other genres. A composite of some of those differences will include the following:

1. A story tells; drama shows.
2. Narrative is not governed by length in the same way that a drama is influenced by the attention span of an audience.
3. A story may utilize great amounts of detail; drama must be economical.
4. The writer of narrative governs more directly a reader's response

to characters and actions; in drama, interpretation is influenced by actors, producers or directors, and the audience.
5. Narrative can go into the minds of characters; drama must rely heavily on the external, although conventions such as asides and soliloquies are available.
6. Narrative can develop characters slowly and let events occur at a slower pace than drama where stress is placed upon getting to the key situations quickly.
7. Narrators may interrupt a story to explain and comment: playwrights are forced to communicate indirectly.
8. Scenic change and mobility are of little concern in fiction; spatial movement is not as easily accomplished in the drama.

Although the genre approach often prompts the deadly line-by-line analysis of a text, which students deplore, the careful use of the approach can lead to increased reading skill on the part of a student and a more comprehensive appreciation of the art which lies inherent in drama. The genre approach also has the advantage of providing the teacher with a definite set of characteristics and reading skills upon which to focus his instruction. This enables him to plan his instruction more carefully in terms of the grade level at which he is teaching. As a guide for making appropriate selections of skills, Dorothy Matthews suggests the following outline (28, p. 9-12):[1]

THE PLAY IN TERMS OF PROBLEMS CONFRONTING THE DRAMATIST

I. Selection of Material
  A. Source of story:
   legend? history? work of another author? work in another genre? original?
  B. Choice of central action: (the single action the entire play demonstrates)
  C. Choice of central conflict or tension:
   man against God(s)? man against nature? man against society? man against man? man against himself?
  D. Selection of scenes:
   point of attack?
   parts of story to omit entirely? parts merely to report on? parts to summarize?
   parts of story with greatest dramatic potential?

---

[1]Courtesy of Professor Matthews.

DRAMA

choice of climax — emotional high point?
determination of other climactic moments?

II. Structuring of Play
   A. Plot decisions:
      simple? (clear plot line which first raises then settles issue of conflict)
      complex? (intricately planned interrelationship of story threads)
      single or double? (a sub-plot or not?)
      degree of contrivance in construction of plot?
         (examples of stock plotting devices: letters that miscarry, mistaken identity, misunderstandings, deceptions, trickery, secrets, surprises, reversals, coincidences)
   B. Arrangement of scenes:
      conventional structure:
         pyramidal: exposition, rising action, climax, falling action, denouement
         tri-partite: exposition, complication, resolution
         Shavian: exposition, situation, discussion
      less conventional structural patterns:
         cause-effect? thesis-proofs? state of affairs-typical aspects of it?
         situation-elaboration? loosely episodic? circular?

III. Handling of Time
   A. Arrangement of time sequence:
      tight chronology (strict unity of time with no significant breaks)
      loose chronology (general straight-forward movement within acts but with time gaps between the acts)
      broken chronology (occasional deviation from straight-forward movement)
      temporal flexibility (frequent backward and forward movement in time — as in memory sequences)
   B. Expository methods: (audience enlightenment to action not presented visually)
      artificial direct means: prologue? commentary by chorus or choral character?
      artificial means within action of play:
         minor characters discussing the background of a situation?
         reading of letters, newspaper accounts, etc.?
         introduction of stranger on scene to whom everything has to be explained?
      clearly expository speeches concentrated at beginning of play?
      gradual exposition worked in naturally through dialogue?
      more subtle means such as suggestions, hints, innuendoes throughout play?
   C. Means of showing passage of time:
      choral commentary? program notes and curtain? dialogue?
      lighting changes? musical cues? changes in costume, make-up?

IV. Handling of Space
   A. Methods of presenting locale:
      verbal descriptions?

physical set: realistic? suggestive only? symbolic?
  B. conventions of staging: foreshortening of space? use of plates?
V. Handling of Scenes
  A. Identification of "beats" (small segments of action demonstrating unity)
    function of each "beat":
      important to plot: as exposition? part of chain of events? transition?
      important to play: provide mood? comic relief? contrast?
      important to characterization?
    tempo of each "beat":
      determination of tempo by:
        amount of stage movement? physical action?
        number of pauses in delivery of dialogue?
        length of speeches? (long speeches, slow pace)
        emotion portrayed? (excitement increases pace)
    recognition of "beats" providing *agons* (an *agon* is a segment of dialogue which incorporates its own building and release of tension)
  B. Artistry of scenic arrangement or rhythm:
    arrangement of "beats" or scenes for special effect: contrast?
    gradual building of emotion? alternation of tempo?
VI. Characterization
  A. Choice of characters:
    protagonist:
      class: aristocratic? royal? middle class? lower class?
      kind of depiction: realistic or theatrical? heroic or nonheroic?
      basic skeletal type?
    antagonist? foil? confidente? raisonneur?
  B. Treatment of characters:
    flat or rounded?
    static or dynamic?
    stock characters? (braggart, sly servant, gossip, sweet young woman, lovesick young man, etc.)
  C. Function of each character:
    important to plot? — needed for causal chain of events?
    important to play? — as comic relief? contrast? representation of viewpoint?
VII. Choice of Diction
  A. General description of dialogue:
    representational: colloquial? naturalistic?
      somewhat formalized but simulating actual speech?
    presentational: frankly theatrical? stylized? witty? poetic? rhetorical?
  B. Dramatic possibilities offered by dialogue:
    opportunities for: movement? stage action? business? vocal variety? effective use of pause? audience inferences? character differentiation? creation of mood?
  C. Opportunities for tempo variation:

DRAMA

        variation in length of speeches?
        variation in density?
    D. Qualities of dialogue: economy? appropriateness? beauty? wit? power to evoke emotion? verisimilitude?
VIII. Means of Providing Emphasis
    A. Verbal means of giving emphasis:
        through dialogue: repeated phrases or words? verbal imagery?
        through character: raisonneur? (character who comments on action) choral character? (character who may address audience directly)
    B. Non-verbal means:
        sound effects: off-stage noises? silences, pauses? dramatic use of music?
        setting: scenic symbols? lighting? use of stage space? (pictorial composition of actors)
        stage movement: small gestures? stage business? movements required by dialogue or stage directions?
    C. Other possibilities for communicating meaning:
        repetition of any kind
        proportion (elements which receive the greatest expansion usually are considered most important)
        position (most emphatic positions are at beginnings and ends of scenes and of play)
        focus (unusual emphasis upon any element [mood, character, idea, etc.)
        choice of title

SPECIAL TYPES OF DRAMA

Although the English teacher may feel equipped to handle a rather general approach to the teaching of drama, he very likely will not always feel comfortable when dealing with certain special types of drama. Areas such as Shakespearean drama, black theater, theater of the absurd and television drama have particular qualities which separate them from the normal classroom drama study and call for different kinds of knowledge.

Shakespearean Drama

The traditional choice of drama in the secondary school has been the plays of Shakespeare. Looked upon with reverence by teachers, frequently despised by students, William Shakespeare and his work have occupied a central place in the English curriculum. Too often, however, the teaching of Shakespearean drama has degenerated into a rehash of notes and lectures taken from teachers' undergraduate and graduate courses. Frequently the novice teacher will approach Shakespeare with an enthusiasm not shared by students, but often not until it is too late does the teacher recognize the major difficulties which students have with Elizabethan drama.

Very few high school students are equipped to handle the conventions of Shakespearean drama on their own; the soliloquy, the lack of stage directions, the absence of description and the apparently strange language are just the beginnings of what a student views as a tortuous path through a maze of what to him is a completely foreign literature. Some authorities have suggested that Shakespeare be eliminated from the curriculum entirely; but this is not necessary. One does not have to prepare extensive mimeographed sheets of characters, history, and plot synopses to make the drama of Shakespeare come alive for high school students. What is needed are a clear understanding of some of the initial problems students have with a Shakespearean play and then an effort to overcome those problems with sympathy and careful attention.

Language. Probably the greatest difficulty for students when they encounter a Shakespearean play for the first time is the Elizabethan English which Shakespeare uses with such skill. The archaic terms, the inverted syntax, and the figurative language are baffling to the average student. The teacher, however, has a number of ways to overcome the language barrier.

One of the best ways to introduce students to the role of language in Shakespeare's plays is through the teacher's own voice and enthusiasm. A careful oral reading interspersed with discussion can do much to bring down the barriers of language. Reading the play aloud, which usually can be done in the matter of six or seven class meetings, may assure that the students have a basic grasp of the drama. This, then, can be followed by intensive discussion of specific segments of the drama, its characters, motivation and other pertinent details, all of which are revealed through the language of the play.

Occasionally students may read the text aloud in class. Contrary to popular belief, this practice does not ruin the beauty of the play nor of the language. Quite often it helps the student begin to sense the power of Shakespeare's word choice and the need for the inverted structure in many of the speeches. Coupled with this awareness comes a clearer realization of the importance of pacing and intonation of the speeches. After a scene has been read, for example, it is helpful to return to and focus on a certain passage as an illustration of the importance of dialogue and its delivery. A valuable exercise is to select key lines from a scene and place them on the chalkboard. From the teacher's request for different readings of the lines, students soon realize the importance of the voice in drama. A nuance, an innuendo, a revelation of emotion—all depend upon the interpretation of the voice; without a stage production to use as a guide, the student will frequently miss much of the underlying meaning in a scene unless he realizes what the voice can do for meaning. Because, however, we are not interested in teaching a course in oral interpretation, all discussion centers on the contribution of speech to the meaning of a character's actions and personality.

Students do not know that much of Shakespeare is still with us today in our modern language. An exercise which demonstrates just how much Shakespeare has influenced our language can be done by having students explain the following phrases and expressions, all of which are drawn from the plays of Shakespeare.

a) "winter of our discontent" (*King Richard III*, Act I, Sc. 1)
b) "plain as the nose on one's face" (*Two Gentlemen of Verona*, Act II, Sc. 1)
c) "a dish fit for the gods" (*Julius Caesar*, Act II, Sc. 1)
d) "every inch a king" (*King Lear*, Act IV, Sc. 6)
e) "the green-eyed monster" (*Othello*, Act III, Sc. 3)
f) "it was Greek to me" (*Julius Caesar*, Act I, Sc. 2)
g) "dead as a door nail" (*Henry IV*, Pt. II, Act V, Sc. 3)
h) "brave new world" (*Tempest*, Act V, Sc. 1)
i) "he has eaten me out of house and home" (*Henry IV*, Pt. II, Act II, Sc.1)
j) "neither rhyme nor reason" (*Comedy of Errors*, Act II, Sc. 1)
k) "the short and long of it" (*Merry Wives of Windsor*, Act I, Sc. 1)

Another aspect of Shakespeare's language which interests students is his use of various levels of language within his plays; one finds a mixture of Cockney and court language adding color to scenes. Of particular interest is the use of the lower class dialect, for this tends to give students the most difficulty when they are reading. Not only the pronunciation of the words but also the shift in their meaning confuse the modern reader. For instance, the word "gossip" in Elizabethan times referred to a friend or a neighbor while today the same word is used in a pejorative sense. Other examples of this problem include the word "go" which was used in place of "come." Colloquial expressions are in abundance. For example, the expression "I'll tickle your catastrophe" literally translated in modern English would mean "I'll prick your bottom." No wonder students are confused!

Punctuation and other stylistic devices should be explained to students. We cannot, of course, develop any set rules about the punctuation because in most cases we are dealing with the results of many editings; however, one or two examples will suggest some of the changes which have occurred. For instance, the comma often is used in place of the semicolon when the connection of thought is emphasized through parallel clauses or echoed wordings. The noun of direct address is seldom punctuated as in "How comes this Sir John?" but the comma is used for emphasis as in "Now, the Lord lighten thee, thou art a great fool." Many a frustrated English-teacher-grammarian might be tempted to sneak a semicolon into such a construction—but not Shakespeare.

Other devices are scattered throughout the plays and though most students will not notice them immediately, occasionally a passage may cause trouble because of an unusual device that students have not met before. For instance, malapropisms abound in the speech of many of his lower class characters and these can be shown to students with good effect. Shakespeare also uses transposition frequently such as in "Good my Lord" for "my good Lord." Ellipsis is another trait that students often have some difficulty comprehending as in the following: "Now Master Gower, what news?" "At Basingstoke my lord." If students have read carefully, they will have little problem supplying the missing information; but if they have never seen this type of device before, they may have difficulty following the direction of a conversation that may be central to a specific scene. One must examine the syntactical structures cautiously for clues, however, before using examples since sometimes these do not withstand careful scrutiny.

From these few examples, one should see why Shakespearean language often baffles students and teachers alike. If a teacher questions just how much has changed in the language of Shakespeare's plays, he should take the time to compare a modern version with the Variorum edition of the same play. Modern editing has done a great deal to ease the task of introducing students to Elizabethan language, but students should be made aware that they are reading an edited version, not an original.

Background. Whenever the teacher must deal with literature from another time or another country, he is faced with the problem of how much background to provide students. Modern texts range from heavily annotated ones to those with no reference material whatsoever. As a general rule, it is best to keep footnoting to the minimum needed to understand the general purpose of a larger context. Students can be presented with a short glossary of terms before the reading of a play; they also can be made responsible for looking up certain references if the key understanding of a passage depends upon such information. It is also helpful, particularly with Shakespearean drama, to spend a few minutes before a scene or the initial reading of the play to sketch a brief genealogy of characters on the chalkboard. One of the most frequent complaints of students is that they cannot keep characters straight. One teacher, to offset this problem, assigns parts in an introductory scene or two to students scattered throughout the room. As the parts are read aloud, the voices coming from different sections of the room seem to help students begin to sort out the characters and become aware of differences in personalities.

Another aid in this respect is to direct students' attention to key figures; students tend to think all characters are equally important when a play is first presented; hence they spend too much time trying to determine the relationships of the tribunes in *Julius Caesar,* for example, when really their attention should be directed elsewhere.

How much attention to pay to the era in which Shakespeare lived is another consideration. Certainly students should be somewhat familiar with the kinds of people who would come to view a Shakespeare play. Richard Mueller approaches the study of Shakespeare with his students by first introducing them to the groundlings of Shakespeare's time (34). He divides his approach into three sections: the spectacle of the groundlings, the reactions of the groundlings to Shakespeare's plays, and the actual study of the play. Mueller familiarizes his students with the appearance and atmosphere of the Globe Theater by showing them diagrams and describing where members of the audience might come from, what the physical conditions on a typical theater day might be, and what the general sensory experience might be. He then takes certain scenes from the play and speculates with students about how the groundlings might react to the action; he also tries to draw comparisons with how modern groundlings might react, using for examples the responses of audiences at circuses and puppet shows.

Approaches such as these allow the teacher to introduce background information but in such a way that students can see a clear relationship between its importance and the comprehension of the drama. Great care should be taken to assure that this relationship remains at the center of any extra material which is brought to the student's attention. The teacher's first concern is to assure himself that students have a good grasp of the play itself; the amount of supplementary material and the timing of its presentation will, in large measure, depend upon just how far the students are capable of going with their interpretations of the play.

Bibliography. References abound on Shakespeare, his plays, and his century. The teacher of secondary school English already will be familiar with a number of them, but the following titles may suggest some additional materials which he will wish to have in his personal library or in the school library.

Adams, J. C. *The Globe Playhouse: Its Design and Equipment.* Cambridge, Mass. Harvard University Press, 1942.
Bradley, A. C. *Shakespearean Tragedy.* New York: The Macmillan Company, 1904.
Browning, D. C. *Dictionary of Shakespeare Quotations.* New York: E. P. Dutton and Co. Inc., 1963.
Chute, Marchette. *Shakespeare of London.* New York: E. P. Dutton & Co., Inc., 1949.
Granville, Barker Harley, *Prefaces to Shakespeare.* Princeton, N. J: Princeton University Press, 1946 (2 vols.).
Harbage, Alfred. *Shakespeare's Audience.* New York: Columbia University Press, 1941.
――――. *William Shakespeare: A Reader's Guide.* New York: The Noonday Press, 1963.
――――, ed. *Shakespeare, The Tragedies, a Collection of Critical Essays.* Englewood Cliffs, N. J. Prentice-Hall, Inc., 1964.
Holzknecht, K. J. *The Backgrounds of Shakespeare's Plays.* New York: American Book Company, 1950.
Muir, Kenneth (ed.). *Shakespeare, the Comedies.* Englewood Cliffs, N. J.: Prentice-Hall, Inc., 1965.
Spurgeon, Carolyn F. *Shakespeare's Imagery and What It Tells Us.* New York: The Macmillan Company, 1935.
Van Doren, Mark. *Shakespeare.* New York: Holt, 1939.
Waith, Eugene M. (ed.). *Shakespeare, The Histories.* Englewood Cliffs, N. J.: Prentice-Hall, Inc., 1965.
Webster, Margaret. *Shakespeare without Tears.* New York: McGraw Hill Book Co., Inc., 1942. Rev. ed., Cleveland, Ohio: World Publishing Co., 1955.

Teaching Approaches for Shakespearean Drama

Cohen, Lauren W. "Romeo and Juliet: Living Is Being Relevant," *English Journal,* 59 (1970), 1263-65.
Eaves, Morris. "The Real Thing: A Plan for Producing Shakespeare in the Classroom," *College English,* 31 (1970), 463-72.

Eidenier, Elizabeth. "Bottom's Song: Shakespeare in Junior High," *English Journal*, LX (1971), 208-11.
Evans, Bertrand. *Teaching Shakespeare in the High School.* New York: Crowell-Collier-Macmillan, 1966.
Greene, J. Gordon. "Motivating Students to Study Shakespeare: A Creative Notebook Approach," *English Journal*, 61 (1972), 504-7.
Hook, Frank S. "So You're Going to Teach Shakespeare?" *English Journal*, 56 (1967), 1120-26.
Lewis, Anthony J. "Response to Prejudice in *Romeo and Juliet, The Merchant of Venice,* and *King Lear,*" *English Journal*, 61 (1972), 488-93.
Mack, Maynard. "Teaching Drama: *Julius Caesar,*" (Chap. 17) Edward J. Gordon and Edward S. Noyes, (eds.), in *Essays on the Teaching of English,* New York: Appleton-Century-Crofts, 1960.
Sargent, Seymour H. "Julius Caesar and the Historical Film," *English Journal*, 41 (1972), 230-35, 245.
Simmons, John S. "Shakespeare in the Boondocks," *English Journal*, 57 (1968), 972-76.
Trowbridge, Clinton W. "Hamlet and Holden," *English Journal*, 57 (1968), 30-33.

Audio-visual Resources for Shakespearean drama. Films and recordings of Shakespearean drama are plentiful. Most of the major film rental companies offer a number of different cinematic treatments of the major plays and many of these films can be rented reasonably. Some teachers, of course, may feel that turning to film destroys the integrity of the text. Such need not be the case if careful use of the two media—print and film—is planned. Gerald Camp argues that in comparing a Shakespearean play with a film of the same play, students not only learn about the play, but they also see more clearly the contributions which acting, direction, costuming and setting make to the interpretation of a play (11). In addition, students come to see the distinctive characteristics of the two media and what changes are prompted by adapting one medium to the requirements of the other. This need for change and its resulting effects on interpretation of the play can be seen clearly in Roman Polanski's production of *Macbeth.* Here we see a production that has freely interpreted some of the key scenes in the play; Polanski's ending is particularly striking and affords a fine opportunity for discussion of what dimensions film may bring to drama.

Still another example of the relationship between film and Shakespearean drama is seen in the different adaptations of *Romeo and Juliet. West Side Story,* first a musical and then a film, has been used with great success by teachers who wish to show the relevance of the Capulet and Montague feud and its effects upon the lovers. Franco

Zeffirelli's *Romeo and Juliet* brought an excitement to classes studying the play at the time. During one of its previews in New York City in 1968, a number of Negro youth leaders were present from Brooklyn's Bedford-Stuyvesant section. One of the comments overheard: "Man, we the Capulets and you the Montagues." Tom Andrews and Jan Austell had their students view the Zeffirelli film first and then turn to the text of the play (5). They found students able to "see" the words of the play more clearly and the ability to become involved with the action of the play was more marked.

Film Associates of California (11559 Santa Monica Boulevard, Los Angleles, California 90025) offers a film entitled "Four Views of Caesar." This consists of four staged playlets; the first profiles Julius Caesar as he was seen by himself, drawing upon his *Commentaries;* the second offers Plutarch's interpretation of Caesar's actions; the third playlet is derived from William Shakespeare's play and the fourth view is taken from George Bernard Shaw's dramatic interpretation of Caesar. Such an approach shows students how different generations offer their own interpretations of figures of the past and reminds students that the same material can be used for many different literary works.

Teachers should also consult the holdings of audiovisual departments in nearby colleges and universities; often these institutions lend films at very low cost. Large companies such as Encyclopaedia Britannica Films have prepared several series of films on Shakespeare's plays; one series deals with *Hamlet* and consists of four films tracing the themes and characters of the play and their possible meanings; another series does the same with *Macbeth*. The following companies offer audiovisual aids in Shakespearean drama:

Warren Schloat Productions, Inc., Pleasantville, New York 10570 (filmstrips and recordings).
International Film Bureau, Inc., 332 South Michigan Avenue Chicago, Illinois 60604 (films).
Audio Brandon Films, 34 MacQuesten Parkway South, Mt. Vernon, New York 10550 (films).
Encyclopaedia Britannica Films, 1150 Wilmette Avenue, Wilmette, Illinois 60091 (films).
Spoken Arts, Inc., 310 North Avenue, New Rochelle, New York 10801 (recordings).
Caedmon Records, 505 Eighth Avenue, New York, New York 10018 (recordings).
Visual Products 3M, Box 3100, St. Paul, Minnesota 55101 (transparencies and tapes).

Other sources include an extensive bibliography by Richard N. Albert entitled "An Annotated Guide to Audiovisual Materials for Teaching Shakespeare"(4). The National Council of Teachers of English, 1111 Kenyon Road, Urbana, Illinois, offers a number of aids which the teacher will find helpful in presenting Shakespeare to students. A comprehensive listing of recordings is available in Morris Schreiber's *An Annotated List of Recordings in the Language Arts with Supplement* (order from National Council of Teachers of English, stock no. 47906R; cost is $2). *Shakespeare in the Classroom* by Robert Ornstein offers glossy photos of different plays and a text describing approaches to the teaching of Shakespeare (37). Yorke Studio, 62 Kramer Street, Hicksville, New York, offers literary art prints of some Shakespearean plays; these are artists' sketches of specific scenes from the plays.

These aids, by suggesting many approaches, should equip the teacher, involve his students, and add to their appreciation of Shakespeare and his contribution to the development of drama. Teachers who accept the challenge of teaching Shakespeare as one which means helping their students read with greater clarity and comprehension, should find their students asking for more Shakespeare, rather than less.

Black Drama

Although the first play written by a black to reach Broadway was produced in 1925, little if anything has been done to bring black drama into the secondary school classroom. In fact, only recently has emphasis been placed upon the black culture's contribution to the American theater. Part of the reason for this is that the theater provides a special confrontation when the play is written by a black. Typically, theater audiences have been predominantly white; and when they are confronted with a world created by a black playwright out of his own experience, they find little immediate identification. As Douglas Turner Ward, a contemporary black playwright, points out: "Plays stand to be witnessed and assessed by a majority least equipped to understand his [the black playwright's] intentions, woefully apathetic or anesthetized to his experience, often prone to distort his purpose" (51, p. 1).

Because of these conditions, the black playwright has largely been ignored by textbook companies. Another problem lies with the language found in many of the contemporary black dramas. Strong, sometimes violent, the language depicts the frustration and rage of the black culture; the bluntness with which black playwrights face their problems and expose their experience makes many textbook publishers hesitant about anthologizing their material. What black drama has been anthologized has been written for the professional theater and little effort is made to locate plays which might meet the approval of textbook commissions in school districts throughout the country.

The English teacher who wishes to give his students an opportunity to explore and understand the black experience through drama must be certain that he himself enjoys and respects black literature or he should not attempt to teach black drama. Darwin Turner suggests that the teacher who desires to use black literature in the classroom should follow certain guidelines (50, pp. 12-20).

1. The teacher should prepare himself as meticulously as if he were teaching the drama of Shakespeare or Arthur Miller. This means that one must have a thorough knowledge of the history of Afro-Americans; just why this is important can be seen in the case of James Baldwin's *Blues for Mister Charlie*. A superficial reading of this play could lead to confusion about the motivations of the characters, but if the teacher is aware that the play is based upon an actual incident in which a 14-year-old black youth was tortured and murdered for whistling at a white woman, he can help students to see the true significance of the work. In his prefatory remarks to the play, James Baldwin explains why this understanding is so important. Talking of the murderer, Baldwin says the following:

In life, obviously, such people baffle and terrify me and, with one part of my mind at least, I hate them and would be willing to kill them. Yet, with another part of my mind, I am aware that now man is a villain in his own eyes. Something in the man knows—*must* know—that what he is doing is evil; but in order to accept the knowledge, the man would have to change.... The human being, then, in order to protect himself, closes his eyes, compulsively repeats his crimes, and enters a spiritual darkness which no one can describe (6, p. 6). [2]

2. The teacher of black drama must be familiar with attitudes which were characteristic of black people during various periods of history. Background reading in the history of the black people of the United States and of the development of the American theater will help to place in proper perspective important changes in values and attitudes.

---

[2]Courtesy of The Dial Press.

3. Comprehension of the jargon spoken in the black community is essential if one is to appreciate the black man's wit and his method of expressing his thoughts. Clarence Major's *Dictionary of Afro-American Slang* (26) will provide valuable information for the teacher unfamiliar with the language of the black culture.

4. A final consideration in teaching black drama is to remember that an integrated class *is* integrated and a balanced approach must be used. Just as in the selection of other literature, the teacher of drama should select his plays to provide students with a representation of drama as a whole; for those students who may not wish to explore the black experience in drama, alternative readings should be available; the same should be true when the class turns to other drama.

To aid the teacher in selecting black drama suitable for the classroom, the following list of plays and playwrights may be useful. Many of the plays exist only in acting editions and must be obtained from companies which specialize in publishing these; three such companies are Samuel French, Inc., 25 West 45th Street, New York, New York 10036; Walter H. Baker Plays, Boston, Massachusetts; and Dramatists' Play Service, New York, New York. All three companies will supply a catalog upon request.

Individual Black Playwrights and Plays Suitable for Secondary School

Baldwin, James. *The Amen Corner; Blues for Mister Charlie*
Bontemps, Arna, and Cullen, Countee. *St. Louis Woman*
Branch, William. *In Splendid Error*
Bullins, Ed. *In the Win Time; Goin' a Buffalo*
Childress, Alice. *Trouble in Mind*
Davis, Ossie. *Purlie Victorious*
Elder, Lonnie. *Ceremonies in Dark Old Men*
Gordone, Charles. *No Place to Be Somebody*
Hansberry, Lorraine. *Raisin in the Sun; The Sign in Sidney Brustein's Window*
Hughes, Langston. *Simply Heavenly*
Jones, LeRoi. *Dutchman*
Kennedy, Adrienne. *A Rat's Mass*
Mackey, William Wellington. *Family Meeting*
Milner, Ronald. *Who's Got His Own*
Mitchell, Loften. *A Look Beyond the River*
Peterson, Louis. *Take A Giant Step*
Ward, Douglas Turner. *Happy Ending; Day of Absence*

Anthologies of Black Drama

Bullins, Ed. *New Plays from the Black Theatre.* New York: Bantam Books, Inc., 1969.
Couch, William Jr. (ed.). *New Black Playwrights.* Baton Rouge, La.: Louisiana State University Press, 1968.
Edmonds, Randolph. *Six Plays for a Negro Theatre.* Boston: Walter H. Baker Company, 1934.
Litto, Frederic M. (ed.). *Plays from Black Africa.* New York: Hill and Wang, 1968.
Patterson, Lindsay (ed.). *Black Theatre.* New York: Dodd, Mead & Company, 1971.
Richardson, Willis. *The King's Dilemma and Other Plays for Children.* New York: Exposition Press, Inc., 1956.
Smalley, Webster (ed.). *Five Plays by Langston Hughes.* Bloomington, Ind.: Indiana University Press, 1963.
Turner, Darwin T. (ed.). *Black Drama in America: An Anthology.* Greenwich, Conn.: Fawcett World Library, 1971.

Reference Material and Background for Black Drama

Abramson, Doris E. *Negro Playwrights in the American Theatre 1925-1959.* New York: Columbia University Press, 1969.
Bond, Frederick W. *The Negro and the Drama: The Direct and Indirect Contributions Which the American Negro Has Made to Drama and the Legitimate Stage, with the Underlying Conditions Responsible.* Washington, D.C.: The Associated Publishers, 1941.
Brown, Sterling A. *Negro Poetry and Drama.* Washington, D.C.: The Associates in Negro Folk Education, 1937.
Dodds, Barbara. *Negro Literature for High School Students.* Champaign, Ill.: National Council of Teachers of English, 1968.
Hughes, Langston, and Meltzer, Milton. *Black Magic: A Pictorial History of the Negro in American Entertainment.* Englewood Cliffs, N. J.: Prentice-Hall, Inc., 1967.
Isaacs, Edith J. R. *The Negro in the American Theatre.* New York: Theatre Arts Books, 1947.
Johnson, James Weldon. *Black Manhattan.* New York: Alfred A. Knopf, Inc., 1930.
Mitchell, Loften. *Black Drama: The Story of the American Negro in the Theatre.* New York: Hawthorn Books, Inc., 1967.
Turner, Darwin T., and Stanford, Barbara Dodds. *Theory and Practice in the Teaching of Literature by Afro-Americans.* Urbana, Ill.: National Council of Teachers of English, 1971.

Theater of the Absurd

A *Time* magazine essay on the status of modern theater posed an interesting problem for the teacher of secondary school drama.

According to the essay, "... at the center of the contemporary stage remains the European drama represented by Beckett, Genet, Pinter and Osborne. None are alike; yet all raise a hemlock toast to the 20th century. Theirs is a drama of metaphysical anguish, rigorous negation, asocial stance, skin-prickling guilt and anxiety, and abidingly absurd humor" (31, p. 34).

Whether students should become involved with theater of the absurd is debatable. For many students, the absurdists offer a fascinating look at life in the 20th century. Peter J. Sheehan feels that using some of the plays of Harold Pinter, Edward Albee, and others helps to stimulate interest in drama and its present direction while allowing teacher and student to achieve a common ground where both can communicate through collective learning experiences (45). Theater of the absurd offers a fertile ground for the cultivation of new ideas and relationships that students may not have considered before. Another benefit is that students may examine their own natures through an introspective reaction to the drama as well as through open discussion.

But just what is theater of the absurd? The term, originally coined by Martin Esslin (16), tends to confuse people and often has been misinterpreted. What Esslin had intended to become a generic concept has, instead, become a fixed label in the minds of many teachers. Attempting to explain what he originally meant, Esslin writes in *Reflections, Essays on Modern Theatre* (17, p. 184): "what these writers express is not an ideological position but rather their bewilderment at the absence of a coherent and general integrating principle, ideology, ethical system, call it what you will, in our world." The term "theater of the absurd," then, is an attempt to describe certain characteristics in a number of works which in many other ways can be completely dissimilar.

Primarily through form, many contemporary playwrights express their confusion and sense of alienation. As Esslin points out, the form for much of contemporary drama consists of all the things normally thought to be contrary to dramatic principles. Language, plot, characterization, and resolution, have been de-emphasized while concrete stage imagery, repetition, and intensification, as well as a whole new stage language, are now down stage center.

Since the sudden turnabout in stage conventions often confuses students and teachers who approach theater of the absurd for the first time, the following list of general characteristics may help to clarify absurdist drama (25, pp. 487–88):

protagonist: Extreme neurotic, what psychiatrists call a "border-line personality."

his situation: When one resembling this type (Hamlet) appears in the classical or traditional play, he is placed within an established relationship; in the Absurd he is outside.

conflict: Between his intense desire to form a satisfying relationship and his intense fear that if he does he will destroy his own identity.

theme: Statement about such problems as isolation, loneliness, confusion between reality and illusion, despair, difficulty of communicating.

dialogue: For the most part, repetitious and monotonous; humor, inserted for relief, is likely to make a sensitive audience uncomfortable since it comes from the situation, which is not funny.

form: Although the playwright structures his material, his structure is not discernible; thus the content may seem amorphous to one knowing plays only in traditional form.

resolution: None.

Students frequently have great difficulty adjusting to the change in form and conventions. They have to learn that in theater of the absurd, what *happens* on the stage goes beyond, and often contradicts, the spoken words of the characters. Hence a student must get beyond the apparent aimlessness of conversation in *Waiting for Godot* if he is to begin to perceive the vision of the playwright. Still another problem for the student is the apparent lack of resolution in the absurdist drama; pondering existential questions which have no immediate answer, the absurdist playwright often turns the drama back to the viewer and leaves him with a feeling of frustration and bewilderment. As Herbert Adams indicates, this lack of answer or solution may have a negative effect upon students, particularly those who are very reliant upon a strong authoritarian atmosphere found in many classrooms. Adams says, "I fear that too few of us realize the impact that can be made by an Ionesco on a vulnerable adolescent who thinks he finds life meaningless already. I fear that many of us, who steer our students into philosophical speculation, have no way of steering them out when they ask for guidance" (1, p. 1047).

Robert Geller, on the other hand, feels that exposure to absurdist drama is profitable for students:

> ... I do not believe even for one minute that having my students read Beckett or Pinter will drive them to endless paralysis. They finish their reading restive as hell. They intuit what's happening and know that ironies and double talk are being strategically exploited, but they don't intend to lie down and quit because of the heavy futility of it all (19, p. 705).

Edward Albee, one of the foremost practitioners in the theater of the absurd, sees no reason why students should avoid such literature.

He claims that, "the young, of course, are always questioning values, knocking the status quo about, considering shibboleths to see if they are pronounceable. In time, it is to be regretted, most of them — the kids — will settle down to their own version of the easy, the standard; but in the meanwhile . . . they are a wonderful, alert, alive, accepting audience" (3, p. 173).

Handled in a controlled manner, short units on the theater of the absurd may offer excellent opportunities for able students. George Smith and Gay Sauer worked with their classes in a study of Samuel Beckett's *Waiting for Godot* and found that students responded well (46). The class study utilized small discussion groups and presentations dealing with the fusion of science and religion and the contributions of such individuals as Camus and Kierkegaard. Attendance at a performance of the play and then follow-up discussion proved fruitful. The class also studied Ionesco's one-act *The Leader*, which was dramatized and discussed by class members. Evaluation of the unit by students indicated a definite increase in their level of consciousness and a realization that many people share the same doubts and fears about the nature of man's existence.

Now that theater of the absurd has been performed on the legitimate stage for some time, the initial shock has worn off and a more careful evaluation has taken place. Actually the absurdists have not destroyed the theater, as some critics have suggested, but instead they have brought to us a clearer perspective of the dramatic tradition. Again, it is Martin Esslin who makes the case for the absurdists; he claims that the absurdists have brought back the full richness of the dramatic vocabulary, that the restrictions caused by the missing fourth wall have been eliminated and in their place has come a deeper dimension of drama, one that allows for actors to communicate directly with their audiences, to reveal their innermost thoughts via monologue and they create once again the "world of the dreamlike, the supernatural, and its stage machinery . . . " (17, p. 191).

Careful selection of plays and knowledge of students' abilities will allow the teacher to give at least some of his students an opportunity with the absurdists. The contrast between the traditional and the theater of the absurd should spark considerable interest in the direction of the theater today and this is a goal worth striving toward.

The following plays and playwrights have been used with some success in the secondary school program:

Albee, Edward: *The American Dream; The Sandbox; The Death of Bessie Smith: Zoo Story; Who's Afraid of Virginia Woolf?*

Beckett, Samuel: *Endgame; Waiting for Godot; Play.*
Ionesco, Eugene: *The Bald Soprano; The Chairs; Jack, or the Submission; The Lesson; Rhinoceros.*
Pirandello, Luigi: *Six Characters in Search of an Author.*
Pinter, Harold: *A Slight Ache; The Collection; The Dwarfs; The Dumb Waiter; The Caretakers; The Birthday Party.*
Sartre, Jean Paul: *No Exit.*
Stoppard, Tom: *Rosencrantz and Guildenstern Are Dead.*

Reference material discussing methods of teaching theater of the absurd is not abundant; however, the following books and articles may help a teacher begin to plan how he might use the works in his classes.

Adams, Herbert. "Albee, the Absurdists, and High School English?" *English Journal,* 55 (1966), 1045-48.
Blau, Herbert, *The Impossible Theater, a Manifesto.* New York: Macmillan, 1964.
Brown, John Russell, (ed.). *Modern British Dramatists.* Englewood Cliffs, N. J.: Prentice-Hall, Inc., 1968.
Brustein, Robert. *The Theatre of Revolt: An Approach to the Modern Drama.* Boston: Little, Brown and Company 1964.
Chevigny, Bell Gale (ed.). *Twentieth Century Interpretations of Endgame.* Englewood Cliffs, N. J.: Prentice-Hall, Inc., 1969.
Clare, Sister Jeanette. "Understanding the Theatre of the Absurd: Analyzing Ionesco's *The Chairs,*" *Catholic School Journal,* 68 (1968), 62-64.
Cronkhite, Gary. "Samuel Beckett: En Attendant Fin de L'Univers," *Quarterly Journal of Speech,* 55 (1969), 45-53.
Demetz, Peter (ed.). *Brecht.* Englewood Cliffs, N. J.: Prentice-Hall, Inc., 1962.
Dukore, Bernard F., and Gerould, Daniel C. "Explosion and Implosion: Avant Garde Drama between the Wars," *Educational Theatre Journal,* 21 (1969), 1-21.
Esslin, Martin (ed.). *Samuel Beckett.* Englewood Cliffs, N. J.: Prentice-Hall, Inc., 1965.
Grossman, Manuel L. "*Him* and the Modern Theatre," *Quarterly Journal of Speech,* 54 (1968), 212-19.
Hassan, Ihab. *The Literature of Silence: Henry Miller and Samuel Beckett.* New York: Alfred A. Knopf, Inc., 1967.
Hinchliffe, Arnold. *The Absurd.* London: Methuen Co., Ltd., 1969.
Ionesco, Eugene. *Notes and Counternotes.* New York: Grove Press, Inc., 1964.
Johnson, Carolyn. "In Defense of Albee," *English Journal,* 57 (1968), 21-23, 29.
Mussof, Leonore. "The Medium Is the Absurd," *English Journal,* 58 (1969), 566-70, 576.
Schroll, Herman T. *Harold Pinter: A Study of His Reputation (1958-1969) and a Checklist.* Metuchen, N. J.: The Scarecrow Press, Inc., 1971.

Television Drama

Quite a few English teachers operate on the assumption that the programs which appear on television are, for the most part, inane and unworthy of consideration. Such a view limits the English teacher severely in his attempts to discover materials and ideas which relate closely to the experience and interests of adolescents. For all its wasteland qualities, television has produced and continues to produce creative and worthwhile drama. In fact, the television script is far more adaptable to classroom study than the movie script.

Little has been said, however, in the professional journals about ways in which television may contribute to the classroom experience in drama. Yet the English teacher must make the effort to become familiar with television drama because it is affecting his students and their ability to become involved in the printed text. The adolescent, through his extensive exposure to television and movie, has become conditioned to respond to visual and auditory clues; somehow the student also must come to recognize similar clues in the printed text.

One of the best ways to help the student make the adjustment to the regular dramatic text is simply to begin where the student is — with television drama. Such an adjustment is not so farfetched as it may sound, for television as well as the limitations of time and space all contribute to making the teleplay more appropriate classroom material in the study of drama than movie scripts.

The mistake is often made by teachers that the stage play, the teleplay, and the movie have few important differences to consider. Actually, all three have significant distinctions in the methods by which they attempt to handle time and space, in their use of language and in the ways response is evoked from the audience. Probably the major distinction is in the method of handling time and space. The stage play is quite literally locked to the physical space of the stage itself. Changes of scene can be accomplished, of course, and much information about shifts of action is conveyed by characters and offstage action. Improvement in scenery design, the use of the revolving stage and the lack of formal scenery have made the regular stage a far more flexible instrument than was ever before possible.

If the television play is a live performance, it operates under similar restrictions. The teleplay put on film, however, allows greater latitude in scenery and time. It should be remembered that a live stage play must be presented in full view of an audience; hence, the viewer is able to see all parts of the stage while the action goes on; if he decides that a certain character is more interesting than the lead, the viewer may focus his attention in that direction; if a piece of scenery is not quite accurate or if a prop is out of place, the spectator may have his attention diverted. Viewing the teleplay, the spectator is far more limited in what he sees and what his interpretation will be, for the eye of the camera becomes the eye of the viewer; this shift of perspective is unconsciously accepted by the spectator and he does not have to rely so heavily on the printed or spoken word for clues as to what is taking place, while in the conventional stage play, the speech of the characters directs attention to them and to those nearby.

Changes in time are conveyed through dialogue or stage directions in the regular drama text. On television we may see devices such as printed captions that denote the passage of time, but we also are treated to obvious changes in scenery. At one moment we may be within an elevator on the 31st floor and the next scene we see is one played at ground level in front of the same building.

Another factor which is influenced by television lies in the use of gesture, facial reaction, and intonation. The student who finds it difficult to discern how a printed line in a play may be delivered has no such difficulty with the television performance since the camera leaves little to question; a close-up on a character's face quickly reveals the meaning of a line and the audio portion that accompanies such a shot quickly reinforces the student's understanding. As Rod Serling has said, "The key to TV drama was intimacy, and the facial study on a small screen carried with it a meaning and power far beyond its usage in the motion pictures" (41, p. 47).

We might assume, then, that with the impact which television has on the viewer that students would come to the classroom with problems of relating to the printed text. In a sense this is true, but they also come to us with more training in language than we sometimes expect. Television drama is more verbal than we give it credit for and because of this, students have learned to respond to the spoken word more quickly. To transfer this awareness to the plays of Arthur Miller, William Shakespeare and others is not easy, but the potential is there and can be capitalized on with careful balancing of television scripts and regular plays.

One successful way of helping students make the transition between stage and teleplay is through videotape. Many schools own equipment which makes it possible for a teleplay to be taped directly during its performance on television.* Several such tapes, used in

*Editor's Note: Be sure to clear permissions before taping.

conjunction with the teleplay scripts, will help focus students' attention on the adjustments to be made between printed page and the screen. An appreciation of the difficulties of the dramatist as he attempts to adjust to the restrictions of the various media becomes more likely as a result of such comparisons.

Alan Howe makes the following recommendations to the teacher who wishes to draw upon students' experience with television drama to make the classroom study of stage drama more pertinent (23). The teacher should make and invite comparisons of movies and television when they are relevant, and he should avoid giving the impression that what appears on the television screen is without merit. To help students visualize the staging of a scene or an entire play, reference to television techniques and comparisons to stage problems will help the student begin to see the characteristics peculiar to each medium. When discussing the language of a play, students should draw comparisons with examples of language appearing on television. Finally, the teacher should introduce television plays into the classroom as a legitimate artistic development of our times and as a suitable companion for the study of conventional stage drama.

Neil Postman in *Television and the Teaching of English* (41) urges that a section of a bulletin board in the classroom be reserved for reviews, notices and listings of recommended programs. Students may take turns as critics for the week, scanning program listings in newspapers, *TV Guide,* and weekly news magazines such as *Time* and *Newsweek* that frequently carry reviews of programs. Students might compile lists of programs they feel are worth viewing and offer brief critical reviews of each program's content; time can be allowed in class for some discussion after a performance to enable students to compare their reactions with the previewing comments made by the critics. An especially good source for listings of television drama appears in the telelog that is an integral part of *Media and Methods,* a monthly publication devoted to an examination of media and its uses in education. Subscriptions to this magazine are $7 a year and may be obtained by writing *Media and Methods,* 134 N. 13th Street, Philadelphia, Pennsylvania 19107.

Although straight television drama is somewhat scarce, adaptations of works of literature frequently appear and offer good sources for classroom study. For example, in 1971-72 the following programs were aired: *The Overcoat; Last of the Mohicans; Androcles and the Lion; The Andersonville Trial; Hamlet; The Possessed; Pere Goriot; Julius Caesar; To Be Young, Gifted and Black; The Ransom of Red*

Chief; Much Ado About Nothing; The First Churchills; Jane Eyre; Gideon; Jude the Obscure; The Snow Goose; Six Wives of Henry VIII.

Neil Postman suggests that such adaptations can promote cross media analysis. The purpose of such analysis is not to determine which form is better but more importantly to learn something about the literary forms under investigation. This analysis can look at character, setting, language, theme, structure, and ethical and moral standards to discover what changes have been made, both in form and interpretation.

The teacher's main difficulty with such programs is that few appear with any regularity on the three major commercial networks; the one notable exception is NBC's "Hallmark Hall of Fame." The Public Broadcasting System (PBS), however, offers several opportunities, namely "Hollywood Television Theatre," and "Masterpiece Theatre." The National Educational Television Network (NET) offers excellent television drama on "NET Playhouse." Teachers who find it difficult to view some of the special programs should consider contacting the Indiana University Audiovisual Center which makes 16 mm. prints of NET productions available shortly after they are aired. The Center also has a large catalog of past broadcasts. For information on rental or purchase write the Center at Bloomington, Indiana 47401. NBC Educational Enterprises offers some of its network telecasts in 16 mm. For information contact them at 30 Rockefeller Plaza, New York, New York.

Sources of television plays in print are not numerous; with increased emphasis on media study appearing in the schools, however, publishers should soon make available collections of teleplays which the secondary school teacher will find useful. Until such time, the English teacher should spend some time himself watching various dramatic productions on television to familiarize himself with the differences in technique and interpretation. Charles S. Steinberg, a vice-president of Public Information for CBS, makes the growing relationship between education and television quite clear. "Its [television's] contributions are too significant to be brushed aside. The teacher who does . . . effects no change in the student's viewing habits or attitudes. The teacher who seeks out television's infinite possibilities can make a positive contribution, not only to the education of the student but also to the medium itself. It is a matter of choice, but the possibilities for good are infinite" (48, p. 1368).

As has been indicated, anthologies of teleplays are scarce, but the following titles may be available in some libraries.

DRAMA

Chayefsky, Paddy. *Television Plays.* New York: Simon and Schuster, Inc., 1955.
Decker, Richard. *Plays for Our Times: Motion Pictures, TV, Radio.* New York: Oxford Book Co., Inc., 1959.
Foote, Horton. *Harrison, Texas: Eight Television Plays.* New York: Harcourt, Brace & World, Inc., 1956.
Kaufman, William (ed.). *The Best Television Plays. 1950-51.* New York: Merline Press, 1952.
_____. *Best Television Plays. 1957.* New York: Harcourt, Brace & World, Inc., 1958.
Mosel, Tad. *Other People's Houses—Six Television Plays.* New York: Simon and Schuster, Inc., 1956.
Rose, Reginald. *Six Television Plays.* New York: Simon and Schuster, Inc., 1956.
Vidal, Gore (ed.). *Best Television Plays.* New York: Ballantine Books, Inc., 1956.
Writers' Guild of America (eds.). *The Prize Plays of Television and Radio.* New York: Random House, Inc., 1956.

Teaching References

Good, Charles H. "Commercial Television—A Teaching Tool for English," in M. Jerry Weiss (ed.), *An English Teacher's Reader.* New York: Odyssey Press, 1962, pp. 84-90.
Howe, Alan. *Teaching Literature to Adolescents: Plays.* Glenview, Ill.: Scott Foresman and Company, 1968.
O'Sullivan, Eugene J. "What the English Teacher Should Know about Film and Television Drama," in M. Jerry Weiss (ed.), *An English Teacher's Reader.* New York: Odyssey Press, 1962, pp. 73-84.
Postman, Neil. *Television and the Teaching of English.* New York: Appleton Century-Crofts, 1961.
Trapnell, Coles. *Teleplay, An Introduction to Television Writing.* San Francisco: Chandler Publishing Company, 1966.

CLASSROOM ACTIVITIES FOR THE TEACHING OF DRAMA

As in any aspect of the field of English, each teacher will have certain activities he will use successfully with his students. Drama offers the student and the teacher a rich field for exploration and a wide range of experience should be made available to enhance this exploration.

The central classroom activity, of course, will be the reading of the play itself. Every attempt should be made to have the play read aloud or at least to give students through recordings, acted versions, or tape, a familiarity with the tone and pace of the drama. Teachers often become discouraged with the oral activities because students frequently do not give good readings; but much of the reason for the poor reading is attributable to the student's lack of knowledge about the play, and asking a student to read an unfamiliar text at short notice is putting him in a very awkward and potentially embarrassing position. Some ways for encouraging the better reading of plays include the possible assignment for home reading of some parts which can then be presented later in class. Other times groups can be given scenes or be asked to select scenes they would like to work on together and then present orally. Giving the opportunity to a group to work out its own production of a scene or a short play which can then be recorded on tape or produced live, encourages creativity in students and involves them more closely with the text and the meaning of the play.

For younger students, who often find it difficult to establish plot sequence and the significance of conflicts in a play, the teacher may ask them to watch and record some of the plots found in television serials; the nature of the medium tends to make the plots and conflicts more apparent and with some discussion with other class members, students will begin to understand such things as repetition of incidents, stereotyping of characters, building of suspense, and the resolution of conflicts. Questions arise about believability, and the concept of "suspension of disbelief" is easily illustrated.

Various elements of drama may be isolated and awareness of their function developed through other activities. James Hoetker in "Reading a Play: An Essay for Students" (21) suggests that students look closely at titles of plays such as *Oh Dad, Poor Dad, Mama's Hung You in the Closet and I'm Feeling So Sad";* what do they suggest about the tone of the play and its subject. The cast of characters, often overlooked by students, normally contains essential information about relationships, occupation and age. The scene and act divisions offer hints of time and place. This information may provide details that may not fit smoothly into dialogue or it may suggest mood, scenery and lighting. For instance, "just before morning"; "the tower clock has just struck twelve." Stage directions must be brought to the student's attention, for characters on stage often will react to a variety of things and the reader, unless he pays careful attention, may not perceive how a line is to be delivered, what facial expressions an actor may use, or what movements are occurring. Since often students ignore stage directions and setting clues, extra attention needs to be focused on such matters. A good way to alert students to the importance of setting is to take several examples of descriptions and demonstrate with students how these settings reveal tone and facts which are important to an understanding of the play. Have students attempt to visualize the settings as the facts of the description are read aloud and ask the students to determine what these facts suggest about the play. Settings can also be paired for comparative purposes as in the following:

The Ship of Dreams. The stage is divided into two sections. One half represents the living room. It is bright and comfortable, though not luxurious; there may even be an impression of rather meager resources made the most of by careful husbandry. There is a doorway to the kitchen, another to the upstairs, and a third to the other half of the stage, which is a small, overcrowded general store filled with everything that housewives need. It is a feeble one-man answer to Woolworths.

Raisin in the Sun. The Younger living room would be a comfortable and well-ordered room if it were not for a number of indestructible contradictions to this state of being . . .

. . . the once loved pattern of the couch upholstery has to fight to show itself from under acres of crocheted doilies and couch covers which have themselves finally come to be more important than the upholstery. And here a table or a chair has been moved to disguise the worn places in the carpet; but the carpet has fought back by showing its weariness, with depressing uniformity, elsewhere on its surface.

Once students become accustomed to the idea of gleaning information from setting and stage description, they can move to drawing implications from specific lines in a play. Walter Loban suggests that students can be asked to find lines in plays which combine two or more of the following purposes:

a) referring to a significant event of the past
b) foreshadowing of the future
c) revealing a character trait of the speaker
d) showing the speaker's opinion of another's character
e) helping create mood
f) showing an attempt of the speaker to evade an issue
g) showing an attempt of the speaker to conceal his thoughts or feelings
h) showing the speaker's attempt to persuade by appeal to another's needs or weaknesses (25, p. 502).

Comparative studies work well in drama; many novels and short stories have been dramatized and the changes for the adaptation help students become aware of the different demands in each form. Two of Broadway's longest running plays were originally novels. Howard Lindsay and Russell Crouse's *Life with Father* had 3,224 performances while Erskine Caldwell and Jack Kirkland's *Tobacco Road* tallied 3,182 performances (40).

Elizabeth Mapes works with her junior high school students during the reading of the dramatization *The Diary of Anne Frank* to help them see the special conventions of the stage as opposed to those of the book (27). She usually assigns the diary for reading prior to class study of the play. Then, as the reading of the play continues, students begin to think more closely about character and event. If the dramatists change an event or a character, the change usually points out something about the conventions of telling a story on stage rather than in a book. Often students are asked to read specific passages from the diary in relation to scenes in the play and are asked to explain the differences as well as describe them.

Older students can explore the parallels between plays such as Arthur Miller's *The Crucible* and Nathaniel Hawthorne's novel *The Scarlet Letter*. Strong parallels exist in these two works in terms of language, character and theme. David Bergeron suggests that such a comparative study helps to enlarge the vision of students about the nature of Miller's drama and also helps to suggest to students that modern American writers frequently are attuned to some of the traditional themes found in earlier works of American literature (9).

Still another possibility for comparing and contrasting genres occurs with the relationship between short stories and drama. Ellen Nold uses such a relationship to foster student awareness of choice of subject matter and technique. Taking two or three short stories, she selects the climactic scene in each story and gives the beginning lines of each scene; characters are limited to four. Students are then given the following instructions:

Pick a partner and choose one of the three scenes... Read the introductory material and decide what kind of people your main characters are. As you finish writing the scene, try to visualize and hear it. You may want to improvise a few times and write down the most pleasing solution. Make your scene long enough so each character's personality is evident and that the tension is raised high before it is resolved (36, p. 378).

After students complete their scripts, interest groups are formed, depending upon which scene the students selected; scripts are read in the groups and the best scripts are selected and presented to the entire class. Students then read the actual short stories and discuss the differences in their interpretations and those of the authors. Similar activities can be accomplished by selecting from plays to be studied and asking students to follow the same pattern of activity.

A number of teachers have broadened their approach in teaching drama to involve students in the process of playwriting. The development and analysis of scripts seem to help students as they read and discuss plays. Robert Meadows has his students begin with television, since he feels that students need to be more discriminating in their evaluation of what is seen on that medium (29). Using a six step procedure, consisting of organizing committees, observing television, writing of scripts, rehearsing, producing, and finally evaluating, Meadows' students learn from this how to make more accurate aesthetic judgments of the fine art not only in television but in all media. Briefly, the process works in the following manner: students work in groups, selecting certain television shows to view; each committee member selects a character to watch and takes notes on how his character communicates, how he moves, and how he relates to the plot of the story. Following the viewing time, committee members compare notes and begin to construct an actual drama. Much interaction occurs since each person must fit his character into the overall script, thus learning a great deal about casting, dialogue, and the whole problem of adaptation. Once the script is prepared, rehearsals begin and are followed by class productions. In the end, students evaluate each other's productions and offer comments about the dramatic qualities of each.

Bruce Sweet takes another approach with the script and discusses it in terms of the director and the final interpretation of a play (49). Although Sweet's approach may be most applicable with electives in theater arts, some of his comments about the manner in which a director interprets scripts will prove helpful to both students and teachers. The shift in focus from reader to director makes the student aware of a new set of problems in interpretation and can help him see drama as a rich literary medium open to varieties of interpretation.

Far too often the study of drama becomes anchored to the classroom and students come to think of dramatics as simply another subject. Some teachers and schools, however, have made radical changes in that view and helped to make drama a central activity of their curriculum. Don Evans, director of drama at Princeton High School in Princeton, New Jersey, was one of those individuals who felt drama should involve more than mere class reading (18). The Princeton High School Repertory Program, involving three companies, four teachers acting as directors, and over 200 students, has done much to make drama a living activity in Princeton High School. Companies formed around grade levels supply theatrical activity for different segments of the school's population.

The Provincetown Players, a 9th grade company, offers the student the opportunity to explore the various aspects of theater; in his first year of activity, the student experiences the roles of actor, designer, director, producer, stage manager, writer, and others. The 10th grade group, called The Mercury Players, tours junior high schools in the area and performs works from the 10th-grade curriculum. Students are given the opportunity to specialize in some facet of theater, emphasis being placed on the mastery of dramatic skills so the group becomes a true functioning ensemble. The third group, comprised of 11th and 12th graders, is known as The Repertory Company and tours with plays throughout the state of New Jersey. Students in this company are encouraged to express their abilities in particular areas; thus, productions often are staged and directed by members, scenery and lighting are designed by students, and costumes are created and sewn by members of the company. Although the company idea still does not involve all students, it suggests a way to complement the classroom experience with drama; the Princeton program especially takes note of this aspect by selecting plays normally studied in the regular English curriculum; they follow this with preperformance talks by faculty and students and after a production, small discussion groups are chaired by members of the performing company so that all members of the audience can participate in sharing reactions and questions.

Another approach to involving students in theater activity to complement classroom experiences was developed by Jack Nelson (35). To increase the number of students who can actively participate in drama and to develop intelligent audiences, his school established a special unit on theater which is presented on a two-three week basis each year with different material being offered on each class level. A rotating schedule of performances is worked out and plays are presented as 45 minute cuttings so that students can see them within a class period. Not only does the student see many plays but by the time he is graduated, he will have had the opportunity to participate in over 20 productions, as well as to attend lectures and discussions on costuming, lighting, dramatic forms, and scenery design. As a result of this program, the student should take his place as a knowledgeable and educated member of audiences for the future.

Teachers interested in complementing their classroom study with programs of this nature might find the project undertaken at Barrington High School, Barrington, Illinois, worthwhile. The school was enlarging its physical plant and with the changes came an architectural arrangement which is the envy of many English teachers.

DRAMA

What the English teachers at Barrington wanted was a suite of rooms that would cope with both traditional instruction and large group sessions as well as converting to an area for arena theater. The result was an extremely flexible room arrangement that not only provided for conventional teaching duties but also provided a theater with a seating capacity of 250. This central facility makes it easy for teachers to encourage student production and improvisation coupled with classroom study of drama. Students and faculty are enthusiastic about having live drama as an immediate adjunct to the classroom. Student interest in acting and participation in dramatic activities has risen. As Charles White, one of the faculty members at Barrington High School says:

To be able to see quality drama at the drop of a hat ... as a natural part of their classroom experience; to be able to take a role in a play and do justice to it despite one's amateur standing, because of the simplicity and directness of the arena staging which pares away everything but the essential, the play itself; and to generate an appreciation of quality dramatic literature through formal classroom study followed by the direct involvement of being either an actor or a member of the audience—these are the ultimate rewards and justification for incorporating into the English Department program and facilities an arena theatre (52, p. 133).

To introduce a play or the idea of theater to students, teachers use a variety of activities. One method is to recreate a situation similar to that which students will find in the opening scene of a particular play; through discussion with students about such a situation, additional details are established until most of the basic elements essential for an understanding of the opening scene are present. Then the actual text of the play is introduced; students are assigned roles and they take their places in front of the class or in small groups. Play scripts are taken away at this point and given to other students who serve as voiceover readers. As these readers render the text aloud, the actors pantomime the actions and relationships suggested; the remainder of the class watches the interpretations. At the end of the scene, discussion is encouraged to determine what was clear in the scene and what was not. Sometimes a replaying of the scene can show where certain elements were missed the first time.

AIRPORT GAME

Mary Wolf and Victor Miller use what they call the airport game to make students aware of some of the elements at work in theater

(53). A landing strip is constructed from two rows of chairs put back-to-back about 4 feet apart; a good length for the runway is 12 feet. The space between the chairs is strewn with obstacles: books, shoes, pocketbooks, boots. A student is blindfolded and he becomes a pilot who is attempting to land his plane on a foggy night on a runway covered with wrecks and potholes. The radio transmitter in his plane is dead; he can hear the control tower, but he cannot speak. Another student becomes the control tower and chooses one location from which to give directions. The pilot is placed at one end of the runway; his task is to get through the 12 feet without touching any of the objects, including the chairs. Any touch constitutes a crash and another student and control tower operator take over. The parallels with theater are numerous. We have a set, lighting of a sort, actors, and a dramatic situation which must be played out. An audience is present with sufficient empathy to suggest how audience and play become involved; the pilot becomes the main character and must overcome obstacles to reach a certain resolution of the action.

Such activities work well with a wide range of students and the improvisational nature of the experiences helps students begin to see the importance of visualization when reading a play. This aspect of visualization and improvisation can be stressed in still another way. Select a scene which is particularly forceful. Type several copies of a script, making certain that each character in the scene receives the same number of lines; these lines may or may not fit the character from the original scene. Using only the lines which they have been given, and in whatever order they wish, students immediately improvise a scene; they may use parts of each speech or whole speeches; they may repeat lines; as they speak they are to infer what action might go with the lines. Upon completion of the scene, students should discuss the difficulty of creating some type of order and some semblance of reality out of the jumbled lines. After discussing the results of the improvisation, students take the regular script and replay the scene. This activity makes students become closely involved with the text and helps them understand the sense of order which a playwright imposes upon his characters and the world of the drama.

No matter what device a teacher uses, however, he should keep the text of the play in a central position. Analysis of scenes, improvisation of related situations, oral reading — all should come from and return to the discussion of the play as an entity; each of the activities used becomes only a supplement and a means for shedding more light upon the drama and its characters, its world and its meaning.

CREATIVE DRAMA AND THE CLASSROOM

The tremors sent out in 1966 by the Anglo-American Conference on the Teaching of English held at Dartmouth College are still being felt in many areas of the teaching of English, especially in drama. People such as James Moffett and Douglas Barnes urge that English teachers consider drama from another viewpoint besides the one of drama as merely another genre. They suggest that drama may provide a focusing element for all we normally teach in the English classroom.

James Moffett argues that drama and speech are central to the language curriculum (32). What Moffett envisions is a program drawing upon all facets of drama as a medium for instruction. One of the keystones to such an approach is the use of creative dramatics. We must realize, though, that when we speak of creative dramatics we are not talking of the usual school productions for the public nor the intensive reading and analysis that go on in the classroom. We are, instead, referring to a form of drama which is completely student-centered. It includes all forms of improvised drama created and played by students with spontaneous dialogue and action. It is an art for students and a group experience that allows every person to express himself as he works and plays with others (15).

The values of such drama are numerous. First, work in creative drama can develop those characteristics which are essential for the processes of discussion, evaluation, and group interacting. Second, the promotion of creative expression of all kinds is another goal which can be realized through active use of creative dramatic techniques. There is also the opportunity to exercise and channel emotions which might otherwise spill out and cause disruption to the school and damage to the student.

But what really makes creative dramatics attractive to the English teacher is that little formal preparation or equipment is required. It is an approach that draws on all segments of the school population — the more mixed the better — and it is a natural adjunct for the regular study of drama in the classroom.

Various approaches exist for the teaching of creative drama. The order of developing the many aspects of it is not too important, but teachers just beginning will find it helpful to spend time on a sequence of activities to ensure some kind of continuity. The first of these activities will involve work with movement and the senses. High school students tend to be quite inhibited and need to feel that there is no threat to free expression of emotion and action. To develop such an atmosphere, the teacher should work with the class as a whole or in groups. There should be no emphasis upon audience; everyone should be a participant. Attempts to show emotional reactions, to develop different ways of moving through space—all are designed to give the student a heightened awareness of himself and of his ability to express what he feels.

A number of ways exist for introducing the student to the concept of expressing himself through movement. For instance, the teacher might discuss with students the following questions: How does the basketball player feel at the moment in the championship game when, with 8,000 fans watching him, he must make the foul shot that can mean victory for his team? From the discussion of one's feeling in such a situation, a person is only a short distance from discussing what an individual does to express that feeling. Another method is to use Edward Steichen's *The Family of Man* (47); select carefully some of the photographs which seem to convey emotion clearly. Show these to the class and ask them to consider what emotions are being portrayed; have the students give specific details which helped determine what emotion is pictured; have them pay particular attention to body stance and facial expression. If this book is not available, carefully chosen pictures from magazines—minus captions—can be used.

Still another approach to the relationship between space, movement, and feeling can be made. Divide the class into two groups; form two lines, facing each other; one line stands and the other is seated; each group is to look at the other without talking or laughing. The teacher should observe the standing group carefully; when they seem quite uncomfortable, usually evidenced through shifting feet, tightness of neck muscles and posture, introduce a task for them such as counting the number of chairs in the room, the number of squares in the ceiling etc.—but have the seated group continue to look at the standing one. When the standing group appears to have relaxed somewhat, the teacher should then switch the groups and repeat the process. Once this has been accomplished, the entire class should discuss their feelings, the effects of the sudden isolation, and the change, if any, when a task is introduced. Such an activity makes students aware of themselves as individuals as well as introducing them to the acting situation and the idea of focus.

The senses are also important to a development of a student's awareness of his surroundings and his place in them. Students may be asked to close their eyes and listen to sounds around them; they are to identify not only the sound but also its cause—if the sound is made by a person, they are to fill in details: What does the person look like? What is he doing? Why is he associated with the sound? A variation on this activity is to ask students to associate several sounds as if they were part of a television or film sound track—Where are you in the story: beginning, middle or end—What is happening?

Work with sight suggests many possibilities for helping students become more imaginative. For instance, arrange a series of objects on a table where students can see them easily; let the students look for 30 seconds and then have them close their eyes. Rearrange the objects slightly and then have the students look again and tell what has been changed. This activity can be done a number of times with the changes becoming progressively more subtle as students' powers of observation and concentration increase.

In terms of movement, if possible students should be working all at the same time in the beginning, lessening the chance for inhibition. One exercise helpful in this respect is called mirroring. Pair students and designate one of each pair as the initiator of action, the other to be the reflector. The initiator of each pair begins some movement which is reflected simultaneously by the reflector; concentration should be placed on the movement and speech is not encouraged. Roles should be changed frequently; eventually students should be able to signal the exchange without using verbal means. This type of exercise develops students' concentration and attention to movement, factors helpful in later pantomime and improvisation work.

Students also can be asked to demonstrate how they would do certain things such as: eat an ice cream cone, walk through deep snow, walk in army boots, walk with a cast on one leg, handle a clod of dirt, eat a hot, toasted marshmallow. From actions such as these, students can next work with facial expression. For instance, ask students how they would perform the following with particular emphasis on facial expression: a girl receives a phone call from her date telling her that he cannot take her to the dance. Teachers can help students with progressive or side coaching. The teacher tells students details of a situation; and as each detail is offered, students attempt to portray the different reactions required. As an example: a student insulted by another is resentful—his resentment grows to anger and the change of feeling becomes evident in his face; then, as the anger becomes uncontrollable, he is moved to strike at something.

Once students seem comfortable with movement, they are ready to move to pantomime. It is a common misconception that pantomime is simply a way of doing without words. Actually, pantomime is more like thinking overheard; it begins and ends before words have been formed. Feeling is extremely important to effective pantomime. There is a striking difference between the pantomine of a boy woodenly doing the supper dishes and that of the boy who is washing dishes while the ball team waits impatiently under the kitchen window, his mother having threatened to withdraw his allowance if the dishes are not washed. Here are the tension and conflict which make successful drama. Pantomime also illustrates that drama develops from within; the pantomimist who does a good job is the one who, through the powers of movement, is able to communicate his ideas and inner emotions to others.

Students may begin with simple pantomime such as the act of brushing one's teeth, washing one's face, putting on heavy shoes or boots, or fixing a flat tire. From these, the student can go to object involvement; students are given such objects as chairs, books, coat hangers, pieces of paper, articles of clothing; individually or in groups the students are to form a meaningful pantomime using as many of the objects as possible. The emphasis here is not so much on what is being done but rather on the imaginative uses to which each article may be put. Students may wish to work with character mime once they become accustomed to transmitting meaning through body movement and facial expression. For this a simple setting such as that of a bus stop, railroad station, or airport lobby may be established. Volunteers are asked to show people of different ages and types. The student before he begins his pantomime writes the age of the person to be portrayed on a slip of paper and hands it to the teacher; then the student demonstrates how a character of that age might act in the provided environment; evaluation by group members determines his success; the exercise may be done many times with emphasis placed on different character traits.

Eventually students will wish to develop more involved pantomime which shows a sequence of events or the development of a plot. Here are some suggestions for starters in such activity:

1. Three teammates arguing with an umpire over a bad call in a close baseball game.
2. You have a painful blister on your heel; you know that you are late for school and you are only halfway there; show what you would do.
3. You are a burglar picking the lock on a safe; you hear something and turn to face (a policeman, the owner of the house, a little baby, a dog); what do you do?

DRAMA

Success with pantomime leads to the next aspect of creative dramatics—improvisation. This part of the dramatic art goes back to the very source of drama, for it was through improvisation that the Dionysian ritual took the first step which led to Greek tragedy.

Improvisation is often confused with pantomime; the two are closely related, but some important differences exist. First, improvisation is unplanned and unpredictable. Often the only structure offered is that of an opening situation. Ideally, of course, there should be no structure but simply raw ideas which are developed into dramatic form as the players work with them. Improvisation also leads to dialogue. Usually as pantomime becomes more efficient, students find themselves spontaneously developing dialogue which then moves them into improvisation suggesting a number of activities which can be developed in this respect. One of these is obviously the scripted play; students can improvise, evaluate, play, and play again until they have a product which they like. One way to foster this type of activity is to have students construct short duologues—these are two character scenes with fixed setting, obvious conflict, and playable in 5 minutes or less; later these may become triadic or even more complex. The following script developed in a span of 10 minutes by a high school student offers an example.

ME: Hey, Mom, I got two tickets to the important Red Sox playoff's for tomorrow so can I have the car for me and Darrell?
MOM: Michael, didn't you promise to take your brother John one of these days?
ME: Yeah, but I only have two tickets and after all it's one of the biggest games of the year. I'll take him another time.
MOM: Well, let me ask John if he wants to go now or wait till next time.
ME: I'll go ask him for you. Hey, John, come here. Listen, Mom is going to ask you if you want to go to a Red Sox game and you're going to say no, okay?
JOHN: But, I want to go.
ME: I'll take you another time.
JOHN: I'm going.
ME: But, I promised Darrell, so wait till next time.
JOHN: Only if you give me your glove.
ME: I'll give it to you if you agree.
JOHN: Okay.
MOM: John, do you want to go to the ball game?
JOHN: Yes, and look, mother, Mike gave me his glove to go to the game with.

At this point in developing the relationship between creative drama and students' lives, opportunities should exist for students to explore drama that exists outside the classroom. Introduce the newspaper, for example, as a potential source of drama. Let students select events which they feel contain the necessary elements for convincing drama; then have students work out their own interpretation of the news. Dramatic situations can be created which call not only for acting but for serious consideration of the values involved. Leo Schools offers one such activity which he calls Lifeboat. Students are given the following situation:

There are ten (more or less) people on a lifeboat; only room, food and provisions for four people are available. The group must decide who stays and who is to be sacrificed. Initially it may be helpful to assign character roles such as an elderly man, a young child, an expectant mother, a sailor, a millionaire. Students must come up with reasons for their choices and present them to the class for decision (44).

As improvisation progresses, the teacher will find that students move in and out of it easily; there will be periods of discussion and evaluation which will slide smoothly into improvisation and then out again. The student is learning constantly about group process and inter-action; he is exposed to group criticism and development. Other aspects of creative drama can be introduced as the need or time allow; for instance, role-playing, socio-drama, and reality theater are all possibilities; but the teacher will probably find that students will move into these areas naturally.

The following sources will help the teacher familiarize himself with the concept of creative drama and its application to the English classroom.

Creative Drama References

Aubert, Charles. *The Art of Pantomime.* New York: Henry Holt and Company, 1927.
Barnes, Douglas (ed.). *Drama in the English Classroom.* Champaign, Ill.: National Council of Teachers of English, 1968.
Cullum, Albert. *Push back the Desks.* New York: Citation Press, 1967.
Moffet, James. *Drama: What Is Happening?* Champaign, Ill.: National Council of Teachers of English, 1967.
———. *A Student-Centered Language Arts Curriculum, Grades K-13: A Handbook for Teachers.* Boston: Houghton Mifflin Company, 1968.
Sayre, Gwenda. *Creative Miming.* London: Herbert Jenkins, 1959.
Siks, Geraldine Brain. *Creative Dramatics.* New York: Harper and Brothers, 1958.
Slade, Peter. *Child Drama.* New York: Philosophical Library, 1955.

Spolin, Viola. *Improvisation for the Theatre.* Evanston, Ill.: Northwestern University Press, 1963.
Way, Brian. *Development through Drama.* London: Longman Group, Limited, 1967.

Articles

Atkinson, Claudene D. "A New Approach: Drama in the Classroom," *English Journal,* 60 (1971), 947–56.
Christensen, J. A. "School Drama," *Media and Methods,* 8 (1972), 33, 52–56.
Denby, Robert. "NCTE/ERIC Report: Oral/Dramatics Approach to Teaching English," *English Journal,* 58 (1969), 614–21.
Dixon, John. "Creative Expression in Great Britain," *English Journal,* 57 (1968), 795–802.
Duke, Charles R. "Creative Dramatics: A Natural for the Multiple Elective Program," *Virginia English Bulletin,* 21 (Winter, 1971), 9–12, 22.
_____. "Space and Body English: Keys to Speech Evaluation," *Classroom Practices in Teaching English, 1972-1973:* in Allen Berger and Blanche Hope Smith (eds.), *Measure for Measure.* Urbana, Ill.: National Council of Teachers of English, 1972.
Heathcote, Dorothy. "How Does Drama Serve Thinking, Talking and Writing?" *Elementary English,* 47 (1970), 1077–81.
_____. "Drama," in Arthur Daigon and Ronald LaConte (eds.). *Challenge and Change in the Teaching of English.* Boston: Allyn and Bacon, Inc., 1971, 138–46.
Lewis, George L. and Burkart, Kammerling. "Creative Dramatics: A Selective Bibliography," *Elementary English,* 39 (1962), 91–100.
Magers, Joan. "Role Playing Technique in Teaching a Novel," *English Journal,* 57 (1968), 990–91.
McCaffrey, Marilyn, and Sandberg, Nancy. "Improvised Drama: A Recipe," *Arizona English Bulletin,* 14 (1971), 65–67.
Schwartz, Sheila. "New Methods in Creative Dramatics," *Elementary English,* 36 (1959), 484–87.
Shuman, R. Baird. "Drama in the Schools: A Well-Spring of Creativity," *Journal of English Teaching Techniques,* V (Winter, 1972–73), 16–22.
Simon, Marianne P., and Simon, Sidney B. "Dramatic Improvisation: Path to Discovery," *English Journal,* 54 (1965), 323–27.
Trad, Lyovonne M. "Acting as Awareness," *English Journal,* 61 (1972), 76–77.

REFERENCES

1. Adams, Herbert R. "Albee, the Absurdists, and High School English?" *English Journal,* 55 (1966), 1045–48.
2. Adland, David. "Drama as a Social Activity," *Opinion,* 12 (1968), 7–18.

3. Albee, Edward. "Which Theater Is the Absurd One?" in Horst Frenz (ed.), *American Playwrights on Drama,* New York: Hill and Wang, 1965, 168-74.
4. Albert, Richard N. "An Annotated Guide to Audio-Visual Materials for Teaching Shakespeare," *English Journal,* 54 (1965), 704-15.
5. Andrews, Tom, and Austell, Jan. "Who Are These People?" *Media and Methods,* 5 (1968), 27-29, 35.
6. Baldwin, James. *Blues for Mister Charlie.* New York: Dial Publications, 1964.
7. Barnes, Douglas (ed.). *Drama in the English Classroom.* Champaign, Ill.: National Council of Teachers of English, 1968.
8. Barnfield, Gabriel. *Creative Drama in the Schools.* New York: Hart Publishing Company, Inc., 1968.
9. Bergeron, David M. "Arthur Miller's *The Crucible* and Nathaniel Hawthorne: Some Parallels," *English Journal,* 58 (1969), 47-55.
10. Burton, Dwight L. "Drama in the Literature Program," in *Literature Study in the High Schools,* 3d ed.; New York: Holt, Rinehart & Winston, Inc., 1970.
11. Camp, Gerald. "Shakespeare Lives," *Media and Methods,* 5 (1968), 42-45.
12. Campbell, Shannon O. "The Book of Job and MacLeish's *J.B.:* A Cultural Comparison," *English Journal,* 61 (1972), 653-57.
13. Christensen, J.A. "School Drama," *Media and Methods,* 8 (1972), 33, 52-56.
14. Cohen, Helen Louise. *Milestones of The Drama.* New York: Harcourt Brace and Co., 1940.
15. Duke, Charles R. "Creative Dramatics: A Natural for the Multiple Elective Program," *Virginia English Bulletin,* 21 (1971), 9-12, 22. (Much of the material in this section has been adapted from this article.)
16. Esslin, Martin. *Theatre of the Absurd.* Rev. ed.; Garden City, N.Y.: Anchor Books, 1969.
17. _____. *Reflections, Essays on Modern Theatre.* Garden City, N.Y.: Doubleday and Company, Inc., 1969.
18. Evans, Don. "Educational Theatre in the High School," *English Journal,* 57 (1968), 387-90.
19. Geller, Robert. "The Absurd Theater: No Taste of Honey. But—," *English Journal,* 56 (1967), 702-7.
20. Hallman, Ruth D. "Teaching Job and *J.B.,*" *English Journal,* 61 (1972), 658-62.

21. Hoetker, James. "Reading a Play: An Essay for Students," *English Journal*, 57 (1968), 1193-96.
22. ———. *Students as Audiences, an Experimental Study of the Relationship between Classroom Study of Drama and Attendance at the Theatre.* Champaign, Ill.: National Council of Teachers of English, 1971.
23. Howe, Alan. *Teaching Literature to Adolescents: Plays.* Glenview, Ill.: Scott, Foresman and Company, 1968.
24. Josephs, Lois. "Electives in the English High School Program: Drama and Flexibility," *English Journal*, 60 (1971), 246-50.
25. Loban, Walter; Ryan, Margaret; and Squire, James R. "Literature: Drama and Poetry," in *Teaching Language and Literature, Grades Seven-Twelve*, 2d ed.; New York: Harcourt Brace & World, Inc., 1969.
26. Major, Clarence. *Dictionary of Afro-American Slang.* New York: International Publishers Co., Inc., 1970.
27. Mapes, Elizabeth. "Drama for Junior High School: *The Diary of Anne Frank*," *English Journal*, 57 (1968), 1307-11.
28. Matthews, Dorothy. "The Teaching of Drama in High School," *Illinois English Bulletin*, 56 (1969), 1-20.
29. Meadows, Robert. "Get Smart: Let TV Work for You," *English Journal*, 56 (1967), 121-24.
30. Mersand, Joseph. *Drama in the Secondary Schools.* Metuchen, N. J.: Scarecrow Press, Inc., 1969.
31. "The Modern Theatre or, The World as a Metaphor of Dread," *Time*, 88 (July 8, 1966), 34-35.
32. Moffett, James. *Drama: What Is Happening.* Champaign, Illinois: National Council of Teachers of English, 1967.
33. ———. *A Student-Centered Language Arts Curriculum: Grades K-13.* Boston: Houghton Mifflin Company, 1968.
34. Mueller, Richard J. "A Groundling's Approach to Shakespeare," *English Journal*, 53 (1964), 584-88.
35. Nelson, Jack P. "Greasepaint for Everyone," *English Journal*, 57 (1968), 391-92.
36. Nold, Ellen W. "Short Scripts and the Short Story," *English Journal*, 61 (1972), 377-80.
37. Ornstein, Robert. *Shakespeare in the Classroom.* Urbana, Ill.: Educational Illustrators, 1960 (available from National Council of Teachers of English).
38. Pearson, Hesketh. *G.B.S.: A Full Length Portrait.* New York: Garden City Publishing Co., 1942.
39. Peluso, Joseph L. *A Survey of the Status of Theatre in United*

States High Schools. Washington, D.C.: U.S. Department of Health, Education and Welfare, 1970 (Available from American Educational Theatre Association, Washington, D.C.).
40. Perry, John. "Adapting a Novel to the Stage," *English Journal,* 57 (1968), 1312-15.
41. Postman, Neil. *Television and the Teaching of English.* New York: Appleton-Century-Crofts, 1961.
42. Rabkin, Gerald. "On Teaching Drama," in Edward B. Jenkinson and Jane Stouder Hawley (eds.), *On Teaching Literature,* Bloomington, Indiana: Indiana University Press, 1967, 106-34.
43. Robinson, Barry. "Legitimate Theater: Students' Rite Off," *Media and Methods,* 4 (1967), 38-39, 42.
44. Schools, Leo. "Lifeboat," *Media and Methods,* 8 (1971), 86.
45. Sheehan, Peter J. "Theater of the Absurd: A Child Studies Himself," *English Journal,* 58 (1969), 561-65.
46. Smith, George, and Sauer, Gay. "Who Is Afraid of Godot?" *English Journal,* 57 (1968), 17-20.
47. Steichen, Edward. *The Family of Man.* New York: Simon & Schuster, Inc., 1955.
48. Steinberg, Charles S. "Television and the Teacher," *(nglish Journal,* 57 (1968), 1326-29, 1368.
49. Sweet, Bruce. "The Analysis of a Script: An Act of Love," *English Journal,* 56 (1967), 125-30, 134.
50. Turner, Darwin T., and Stanford, Barbara Dodds. *Theory and Practice in the Teaching of Literature by Afro-Americans.* Urbana, Ill.: National Council of Teachers of English, 1971.
51. Ward, Douglas Turner. "American Theatre: For Whites Only?" *New York Times,* Sec. 2 (August 14, 1966), 1, 3.
52. White, Charles A. "An Argument for a High School English Department Arena Theater," *English Journal,* 56 (1967), 131-34.
53. Wolf, Mary Hunter, and Miller, Victor B. "Theatre's Different Demands," Study developed in a Title III Program (ESEA) administered by Connecticut State Department of Education and the American Shakespeare Festival, 1970 (Available from ERIC).

R. W. REISING
Pembroke State University

3 Grammar

Ours is an age with a penchant for labels, each of them reflective of one dimension or another of contemporary life. To the man on the street it is commonly "the Jet Age," "the Age of the Computer," "the Nuclear Age," or, if he is musically inclined, "the Age of Aquarius." To the intellectual, depending on his critical perspective, it is most likely "the Age of Anxiety" (13), "the Age of Analysis" (44), or "the Age of Complexity" (21). Rubrics abound as the last half of the 20th century unfolds and social commentators strive to capture its spirit and its essence in a handful of syllables.

But for secondary school teachers of grammar there probably can be no question about the label most appropriate. With Peter F. Drucker they are bound to believe that ours is "the Age of Discontinuity" (9), an era which breaks with its grammatical ancestry and substitutes description and explanation for prescription and diversity for oneness. For them, linguistics, the scientific study of language, is the force which separates present from past and promises an ever-widening cleavage in the future. They are aware that, thanks to linguistics, two recently developed grammatical systems, structural and transformational-generative, are now available for classroom use and that still other systems—like Kenneth L. Pike's tagmemic grammar, Charles Fillmore's case grammar, Sydney J. Lamb's stratificational grammar, and M. A. K. Halliday's systemic grammar—may soon be perfected. They acknowledge with linguist Kenneth G. Wilson their tremendous debt to traditional grammars, which "have managed to examine the details of written English and to describe and classify them with splendid accuracy and thoroughness . . . [and] have supplied us with useful terminology for the discussion of many aspects of grammar . . . [and] the clearest and best accounts we have of some of the small but vexing problems we encounter when we try to describe the grammar of English"; but they also recognize with Wilson that such grammars answer relatively few questions about English (45) and that, therefore, if employed alone and unsupplemented, they serve neither language programs nor students well.

At the same time, however, teachers are aware that for the uninitiated, linguistics and its grammars can be frightening indeed. Their terminology and diagrams appear to be those of a secret society—or perhaps even communications from another planet. But there is little reason for alarm. What seems terribly cryptic is actually "little more than organized common sense," to use linguist Albert Marckwardt's phrase (26). Once one accepts the premises and goals of scientific language study, he is well launched toward understanding, at least in a basic way, what is involved. And there are many useful books and essays that he can call upon to expedite matters; the list appearing below in the section "Resources for Teaching Grammar" identifies some of them. Although other works listed represent fine introductions, *Linguistics: A Revolution in Teaching,* by Neil Postman and Charles Weingartner, is perhaps the best. In about 200 readable pages, it surveys the mysterious science that is not mysterious at all, and proves in a variety of ways that, more than anything else, it is a point of view, a way of looking at language. "What is Linguistics?" its authors ask. "It is conducting oneself in a particular manner—a scientific manner—when studying language," they convincingly respond (32, p. 16). Exploitation of such a belief in the classroom demands not a linguist familiar with every nuance of his discipline but a teacher ready, able, and willing to lead his students to honest answers to questions about what they hear, read, and write.

Most important perhaps, secondary school teachers of grammar in "the Age of Discontinuity" realize their job offers the possibility of greater rewards and satisfactions than ever before. Because of the insights which linguistics has supplied and those which it promises, they are in a position to provide a more accurate and more complete picture of how English works and what its possibilities are than their predecessors ever could. Simultaneously, however, they concede that many of the claims that have accompanied the arrival of the linguistic grammars, like some of those which have pursued traditional grammars down through the decades, are at best suspect and at worst totally invalid. Thus, they know they must carefully examine those claims, as well as some basic questions about grammar, before they can hope to treat grammar intelligently and creatively in the classroom.

WHAT IS GRAMMAR?

Almost everyone who has spent one day or more studying English believes he knows the meaning of "grammar." The word is "public property," as one observer notes, and thus there are as many definitions as there are users. To some it is a label embracing all information pertaining to language study—the terms, the rules, and so on. To others the word identifies a sort of language purity, while to still others it is "what remains of the study of English after literature, rhetoric, and public speaking have been drained off—the dregs of the course" (24, p. 1). Even among those who are professionally trained in language, the word can get slippery if they approach it with only their own language preferences, and no others, in mind. Because, as James Moffett suggests, the word is "so bedevilled with semantic confusion" (29, p. 155), it must be "nailed down" at the outset of any discussion in which it is to figure.

Although old, W. Nelson Francis's 1954 definition can prove more serviceable to teachers than others that have appeared subsequently. In its recognition of three different but related uses of the word, it provides a comprehensiveness and a validity acceptable to virtually everyone: "The first thing we mean by 'grammar' is 'the set of formal patterns in which the words of a language are arranged in order to convey larger meanings.... The second meaning of 'grammar'—call it 'Grammar 2'—is 'the branch of linguistic science which is concerned with the description, analysis, and formulization of formal language patterns.... The third sense in which people use the word 'grammar' is 'linguistic etiquette'.... These, then, are the three meanings of 'grammar': Grammar 1, a form of behavior; Grammar 2, a field of study, a science; and Grammar 3, a branch of etiquette"

(12). It is worth noting, as Francis and others point out, that by the time a child is five or six he has mastered just about all the syntactical complexities of his language; he is, in other words, skillful with Grammar 1 long before he ever enters high school. It is only Grammar 2 and Grammar 3, then, to which the high school English teacher has an opportunity to give his attention.

WHY GRAMMAR?

Grammar and aspirin have one feature in common: they cannot do all that people expect of them. Unless one places more faith in intuition and wishful thinking than in research and authority, there is absolutely no reason to believe that the study of grammar can satisfy all the demands that have been placed upon it down through the years. Ample evidence exists, for instance, to indicate that it does not discipline the mind (14, pp. 363-64); aid in the mastering of foreign languages (14, p. 369); or improve one's speaking ability (16). Furthermore, as W. W. West, Chairman of the Department of English Education at the University of South Florida, is fond of saying, there is no reason to believe that it helps one's listening skills either. Despite some who suggest otherwise because of their faith in linguistics (16; 3), it is unlikely, too, that grammar study improves reading ability or literary interpretation (10).

Yet there are good reasons why it remains, and should remain, a viable part of the high school curriculum. It belongs there because language is man's most important resource, the basis for his knowledge and the key to his power; and grammar study helps to explain why and how it works. "I know I can teach grammar, and I teach it for a good reason," proclaims James Sledd. "The proper study of mankind is man, and there is nothing so basic to our humanity as our language" (38). The examination of so major a facet of man's earliest and greatest invention certainly can be justified on humanistic grounds.

Grammar study also can be invaluable when viewed as an opportunity for students to learn how to learn. Every age, but none more than "the Age of Discontinuity," has an undeniable need for people who know and appreciate what is involved in the processes of inquiry, for people who understand "how answers are produced, how knowledge is generated, how learning is conducted" (32, p. 30). So important is the cultivation of this ability that Harvard psychologist

Jerome Bruner places it at the very heart of the educational enterprise at all levels. No student is too young to be excluded, he argues; in fact, "At the very first breath, the young learner should be given the chance to solve problems, to conjecture, to quarrel..." (4).

Yet, historically, high schools have been woefully remiss in this respect. More times than not, graduates have been followers, intellectually speaking, not leaders, able only to receive knowledge, not to pursue it. Grammar study, especially as outlined by linguists like Postman and Weingartner in *Linguistics: A Revolution in Teaching,* provides a long overdue and exciting opportunity for a shift in priorities. In a sense, it can demonstrate for other subjects how such a shift is possible. The built-in advantage that it possesses makes it a logical candidate for pedagogical leadership, for, as Samuel Jay Keyser indicates, "each student and each teacher constitutes, as it were, a ready-made laboratory in which it is possible to conduct instantaneous experiments in language" (20).

No longer do grammar classrooms need to be characterized by dull drills and parsing, by monotonous pigeonholing and underlining. With emphasis on *process* rather than *product,* inquiries into the forms, structures, and impact of language can convert them into lively, rewarding places—places where grammar study has a real reason for its presence. In the words of Keyser, "... it is possible to look at grammar as attempting to teach children how to make, critically examine, and reformulate hypotheses about language—using as evidence their own knowledge of English. In other words, grammar can be viewed as an opportunity for students to learn how to engage in rational inquiry..." (20).

DOES GRAMMAR IMPROVE WRITING?

Composition mastery has always been a goal of grammar study. So important a relationship deserves special, independent consideration, and thus no mention of it appears in "Why Grammar?"

When traditional grammar was the lone grammar taught, numerous researchers attempted to determine its value to composition skills. Franklyn Hoyt in 1906, Thomas H. Briggs in 1913, William Asker in 1923, Irvin O. Ash in 1935, Rosemary Smith in 1948, Nora Robinson in 1960, and Roland J. Harris in 1962 were among the many conducting experiments involving the relationship, and all concluded that grammar study contributes little to students' skills in writing (37, pp. 116–35).

Research involving structural grammar and writing abilty likewise indicates the former does little to improve the latter. Falk S. Johnson's study of 1960 suggests that students taught structurally prove to be no better theme writers than do those taught traditionally (37, pp. 142-43); and Roy C. O'Donnell's study of four years later also suggests that it makes little difference which of the two grammars is taught, that neither traditional nor structural grammar leads to effective prose (30).

Understandably, the most recent of the classroom grammars, transformational-generative, provides new hope for a breakthrough, and, therefore, some of its proponents, like Jean Malmstrom and Janice Lee, proclaim "that a knowledge of transformational-generative grammar does improve writing" (25, p. 60). Yet research is not on their side; claims as to its efficacy are at best premature. The most discussed experiment purporting to establish a tie between transformational-generative grammar and writing, conducted in 1964 by D. R. Bateman and F. J. Zidonis, has earned adverse comment because of its methodology (29, p. 165; 27, pp. 10-14); while the best done work on the possibilities of transformational-generative grammar in the classroom, conducted in 1969 by John C. Mellon, is punctuated in a variety of places by claims like "this study has nothing to do with writing or the teaching of writing" (27, p. 82). Equally significant, the title of Mellon's presentation at the 1972 NCTE Annual Convention leaves no doubt about his convictions on the subject: "Why a Knowledge of Transformational Grammar Does Not Lead to Better Writing" (28, p. 53).

Teachers in "the Age of Discontinuity" have good reason for teaching grammar, especially linguistically based grammar, but they should not do so in hopes of improving student writing. "There simply appears to be no correlation between a writer's conscious study of grammar and his ability to write," summarizes Mark Lester. "The claim is obviously false, for, if it were true, then all linguists would be great writers" (23).

HOW MUCH GRAMMAR SHOULD BE TAUGHT?

Topping the list of recommendations which J. N. Hook makes "about the role of grammar" in the high school curriculum is "there should not be too much of it" (17). Similar beliefs are voiced by Donald Sattler (35) and William West, who contend that the formal study of grammar should end at either the 9th or the 10th grade (42). West even goes so far as to recommend the elimination of "the study of grammar as a system from the curriculum of many terminal students" (41).

None of these men is, of course, opposed to grammar study. All, in fact, see it as desirable—but in its place. Grammar is *not,* and should *not* be, the total language program in any school which prides itself on providing the best possible preparation for its students. Other equally legitimate language concerns should also appear. History of the language, semantics, lexicography, etymology, kinesics, regional dialects, and social dialects are among the possibilities worthy of attention. Still others are those which Postman lists: the language of advertising, the language of news reporting, the language of politics, the language of religion and prayer, and the language of science (31).

Materials appropriate for study of these areas are now available. The "Domains in Language and Composition Series," published by Harcourt Brace Jovanovich, Inc., and featuring such titles as *A History of the English Language* and *Meaning of Language,* can be useful. Likewise, "The Language of Man Series," published by McDougal, Littell and Company, is potentially helpful because of such titles as *The Dialects of English, Understanding Body Language,* and *The Language of Advertising.* All of the books in both series appear in relatively inexpensive paperback editions.

It bears repeating that language study need not be and should not be synonymous with grammar study, old-fashioned or newfangled. Rather, it can and should focus on a variety of matters, all of them related because of their concern for viable language systems and situations. When a language program becomes multidimensional, when it recognizes and supports a myriad of bona fide language areas, it simultaneously places grammar study in realistic perspective and thereby gives it a vitality which previously it was bound to lack. No longer does it occupy so much student time and attention that boredom is inevitable; no longer is it so dominant a force that other major components of the curriculum, composition for instance, are either overlooked or shortchanged. Curriculum balance is the key if grammar study is to retain its potential for "turning on" and enlightening students.

The guide "Criteria for Developing and Evaluating Curriculum Guides," revised in 1972 by the Committee on Curriculum Bulletins, suggests that "probably no more than 10 percent of the total instructional time should be in grammar of any kind" (39). Such a recommendation makes sense. Obviously, it can be implemented most effectively and most easily in high schools with multiple electives programs. Under wise guidance, students can choose the grammar offering or offerings that best serve their needs. Too, nongrammar electives can, without distorting their purpose, contain some grammar components when they are appropriate.

But in a nonelective setting, the recommended percent does not necessarily have to increase. Grammar can be taught, as it were, incidentally or accidentally—that is, as assignments in composition and literature dictate, as logical and profitable extensions of them. Strengths and weaknesses in student themes can legitimately trigger grammar study, and, likewise, discussion of a Cummings poem or a Hemingway short story can be the catalyst.

A second possibility exists for those teachers in a nonelective setting who, although anxious to restrict grammar study to the desired 10 percent, believe that an orderly, cumulative approach is necessary throughout the entire school program. A sequential program for instruction in grammar can provide them with direction while simultaneously allowing them to avoid unwise repetition, a weakness which invariably kills student interest as well as wastes time. Although desperately in need of updating, Robert C. Pooley's sequence of 1958 represents a model into which changes for the good can easily be incorporated. Its major strength is that the grammar requirements imposed at each of the three levels of education can be accommodated without inordinate demands on either teacher or student time:

Grades 1-6
    No formal grammar
    Casual references to such terms as "sentence" and "subject"
    Emphasis on good usage habits; much writing
Grades 7-9
    Emphasis on the grammar of simple sentences
    Subject, verb
    Predicate adjective, predicate noun, before teaching direct object
    Simple adjective and adverb
    Compound subject, verb, and complement
    Phrase modifiers
    Indirect object, "a special kind of modifier"
    Adverbial clause as modifier
Grades 10-12
    Adjective clause, noun clause

Stress on subordinate elements
Expansion of sentence patterns
Emphasis on skillful use of phrases
Parallel structure
Intensive practical review, with analysis of own writing, in Grade 12

Hook praises the Pooley sequence because "it steers teachers away from the futile attempt to teach almost everything every year" (17). In other words, it steers them away from too much of a good thing.

RESOURCES FOR TEACHING GRAMMAR

The resources listed below can be valuable to secondary school teachers of grammar. They represent not a comprehensive list of materials on the subject but simply a useful one:

Aston, Katharine O. "Grammar—the Proteus of the English Curriculum," *Illinois English Bulletin,* 55 (1967), 1-30.

Aurbach, Joseph, et al. *Transformational Grammar: A Guide for Teachers.* Rockville, Md.: English Language Services (A division of Washington Educational Research Associates, Inc.), 1968.

Bach, Emmon. *An Introduction to Transformational Grammars.* New York: Holt, Rinehart & Winston, Inc., 1964.

Brengelman, Fred. *The English Language: An Introduction for Teachers.* Englewood Cliffs, N.J.: Prentice-Hall, Inc., 1970.

Chandler, William J.; Lipscomb, Clarence C.; and Tucker, M. Laurence (eds.). *An Approach to Teaching English Usage.* Raleigh, N.C.: Department of Public Instruction, 1969.

Crowell, Caleb E. *A Self-Instructional Orientation for Teachers.* New York: Holt, Rinehart & Winston, Inc., 1968.

DeLancey, Robert W. *Linguistics and Teaching: A Manual of Classroom Practices.* Monograph No. 9. Syracuse, N.Y.: The New York State English Council, 1965.

Dillard, J. L. *Black English: Its History and Usage in the United States.* New York: Random House, Inc., 1972.

Gleason, H. A., Jr. *Linguistics and English Grammar.* New York: Holt, Rinehart & Winston, Inc., 1965.

Grinder, John T., and Elgin, Suzette Haden. *Guide to Transformational Grammar.* New York: Holt, Rinehart & Winston, Inc., 1973.

Harsh, Wayne. *Grammar Instruction Today: A Combination Instead of a Choice.* Davis, Calif.: University of California, 1968.

Herndon, Jeanne H. *A Survey of Modern Grammars.* New York: Holt, Rinehart & Winston, Inc., 1970.

Hogan, Robert F. (ed.). *The English Language in the School Program.* Champaign, Ill.: National Council of Teachers of English, 1966.

Hook, J. N. "Grammar(s)—A Rationale," *Illinois English Bulletin,* 51 (1963), 1-11.

Jacobs, Roderick A. *On Transformational Grammar: An Introduction for Teachers.* Monograph No. 11. Oswego, N.Y.: The New York State English Council, 1968.

Laird, Charlton. *And Gladly Teche: Notes on Instructing the Natives in the Native Tongue.* Englewood Cliffs, N.J.: Prentice-Hall, Inc., 1970.

Lester, Mark (ed.). *Readings in Applied Transformational Grammar.* New York: Holt, Rinehart & Winston, Inc., 1970.

Linguistic Bibliography for the Teacher of English. Rev. ed.; Duluth, Minn.: Minnesota Council of Teachers of English, 1968.

Lipscomb, Clarence C., and Tucker, M. Lawrence. (eds.). *An Approach to Teaching English Grammar.* Raleigh, N.C.: Department of Public Instruction, 1970.

Lowry, Heath W. "A Glossary of Terms: Linguistics," *The Reading Teacher,* (November, 1968), 136-44.

MacLeish, Andrew. *A Glossary of Grammar Linguistics.* New York: Grosset & Dunlap, Inc., 1971.

Malmstrom, Jean. *An Introduction to Modern English Grammar.* New York: Hayden Book Company, Inc., 1968.

_____. *An Introduction to Modern English Grammar: Teacher's Manual.* New York: Hayden Book Company, Inc., 1968.

Miles, Leland. *Where Do You Stand on Linguistics: CEA Chap Book.* Rev. ed.; Fullerton, Calif.: College English Association, Inc., 1968.

Pei, Mario, and Gaynor, Frank. *Dictionary of Linguistics.* Totowa, N.J.: Littlefield, Adams & Company, 1969.

Pooley, Robert C., Director. *English Language Arts in Wisconsin.* Madison, Wis.: Wisconsin Department of Public Instruction, 1970.

Postman, Neil, and Weingartner, Charles. *Linguistics: A Revolution in Teaching.* New York: Dell Publishing Co., Inc., 1966.

Roberts, Paul. *English Sentences.* New York: Harcourt, Brace & World, Inc. 1962.

_____. *Patterns of English.* New York: Harcourt, Brace & World, Inc., 1956.

Seat, William, Compiler. "Linguistics Bibliography," *Illinois English Bulletin,* 54 (1967), 19-20.

Shane, Harold G. *Linguistics and the Classroom Teacher.* Washington, D.C.: Association for Supervision and Curriculum Development, 1967.

Shuy, Roger W. *Discovering American Dialects.* Champaign, Ill.: National Council of Teachers of English, 1967.

Sledd, James. *A Short Introduction to English Grammar.* Glenview, Ill.: Scott, Foresman and Company, 1959.

Stageberg, Norman C. *Using Grammar to Improve Writing.* Rev. ed.; Cedar Falls, Ia.: The Extension Service, State College of Iowa, 1966.

Thomas, Owen. *Transformational Grammar and the Teacher of English.* New York: Holt, Rinehart & Winston, Inc., 1965.

Tufte, Virginia. *Grammar as Style.* New York: Holt, Rinehart & Winston, Inc., 1971.

Tufte, Virginia, and Steward, Garrett. *Grammar as Style*. New York: Holt, Rinehart & Winston, Inc., 1971.

Yergin, Daniel. "The Chomskyan Revolution," *The New York Times Magazine,* December 3, 1972, 42-43, 112 ff.

TWO IN-SERVICE PROGRAMS IN MODERN GRAMMARS

During the fall of 1965, the English faculty of Ottawa High School in Ottawa, Illinois, decided they needed an introduction to modern grammars. With the help of their superintendent, who secured two graduate credits for each of them, 13 of the 20 English teachers on the staff embarked upon and completed a 15-week seminar in linguistics held at their school. Two university teachers, plus a high school English department chairman, were recruited from the area to serve as consultants at 3 of the 15 sessions that were scheduled.

"The mechanics of the seminar were relatively simple," explains Vernon Adams, chairman of the department involved. "We chose to meet on twelve Thursday evenings and three Saturday mornings during the second semester. The Thursday seminars were for two hours; the Saturday morning seminars were for three. . . . We had no chairman of our group, but volunteers served as the discussion leaders for an evening. . . . We agreed . . . to turn in a list of our readings at the close of the final seminar meeting. We sought no university-sponsored program with tests or papers to write. We simply wanted to learn" (1).

And learn the 13 did. Sledd's *A Short Introduction to English Grammar* was studied and discussed, as was W. Nelson Francis's *The Structure of American English*. "At some early meetings," Adams reports, "we divided into four 'buzz' groups during the first hour to give everyone a chance to bring out his individual questions. The final hour found us in one group, bringing questions and asking one another for further explanations" (1).

The advantages of so unorthodox a seminar were many. The freedom from pressure created in the participants an added impetus to learn. A rather extensive linguistics library, to which participants continued to add long after the seminar's end, was a second advantage; and a third was the improvement in staff morale that resulted. But most important was the advantage that became obvious in the classrooms of the participants. There, changes slowly inched their way in; materials on sentence patterns, phonology, and the like began appearing, and teachers started encouraging students to reach their own conclusions about language and grammaticality.

Adams concedes that "what we did is neither idealistic nor impractical. With careful planning, industry, and open-mindedness, English staffs in similar situations will have, at the very least, our success" (1).

Another idea for an in-service program that is different but neither idealistic nor impractical concerns the "In-Service Training Program in Linguistics." Available for purchase or rent through the Euclid English Demonstration Center in Euclid, Ohio, and specifically designed for use with high school English faculties, it consists of seven lectures: an introduction to linguistics, morphology (nouns, adjectives, verbs, adverbs, and pronouns), syntax, dialects, sentence patterns, and usage. The lectures come on tapes, are mimeographed, and include 176 slides. In just seven sessions, an English department can gain, thanks to the Euclid materials, a basic understanding of what is involved in linguistics and its grammars. Supplemented by readings and discussions, the program can provide even greater dividends.

SELF-INSTRUCTIONAL MATERIALS FOR TEACHERS

Two self-instructional books are worthy of special mention because of their value to teachers who, while unable to attend a class or a workshop in linguistics and modern grammars, nevertheless desire immediate and reliable reaction to their investigations of those subjects. *Where Do You Stand on Linguistics?* available from Donald A. Sears of the Department of English at California State College at Fullerton, consists of a "test" of 170 items calling for either "agree" or "disagree" responses. Costing $.75 a copy, with five or more copies available at $.60 each, it clarifies in layman's terms the major ideas of linguistics, helps the person taking the "test" to determine or clarify his attitudes toward linguistics and its classroom applications, and, finally, is bound to stimulate discussion and further investigation of the field. At the end of the 30 page pamphlet is a scoring key, not to be consulted, of course, until all 170 items have been completed. Also included is a useful linguistics bibliography, intelligently subdivided to accommodate several levels of linguistic sophistication.

Published by Holt, Rinehart and Winston, *A Self-Instructional Orientation for Teachers* is a self-instructional programmed course designed to introduce teachers to sentence analysis and diagramming according to the methodology of transformational grammar. The information in the 30-page booklet is presented in frames or steps, and answers to questions are immediately available. The program takes approximately two hours to complete.

Both the linguistics and the grammar booklets represent painless ways into what might otherwise be difficult subjects.

GRAMMAR AND KINESTHETIC KIDS

The vivacious Charlotte Brooke has a label for adolescents who live through their bodies. The Supervising Director of English in the Washington, D.C. Public School System terms them "kinesthetic kids," and contends that they, more than any other students, demand creative, imaginative teaching. Among the many strategies she recommends are two that relate to grammar. The first she calls "the living sentence," a device for illustrating how order figures in sentence construction. She first hands out eight cards to eight students, one to each student, and asks them to move about at the front of the room until they form an acceptably structured sentence. Movement and noise ensue—plenty of it—but eventually the eight students arrange themselves so that the following sentence appears for the rest of the class to discuss: "the tall boy ran slowly down the street." During the discussion, "slowly" comes in for special attention, the students realizing that it can function logically in several places in the sentence—but not in every slot imaginable. They thus learn for themselves something about the structuring possibilities of the language. They learn even more when, subsequently, each member of the class is handed a blank card, asked to write just one word on it, and encouraged to group with one or more card-carrying classmates to form a meaningful sentence. Sentences crop up all over the room, as do some nonsentences, and the class has an opportunity to analyze both.

Brooke's second strategy relates to the form classes of words. She assigns each student a blank card which he paints a color of his own choosing: red for noun, blue for verb, green for adjective, or purple for adverb. Each color thus identifies and represents one of the form classes of the language. Subsequently, the students arrange themselves in what they think are sensible sentences, and after the noise and the movement have ended, discuss the constructions that appear.

Teaching "kinesthetic kids" is demanding, but it can also be rewarding if a teacher works with and around the noise and the movement that are bound to be in the classroom — if, in other words, he teaches creatively.

GRAMMAR AND GRAMMATICALITY

At a 1965 NDEA workshop, Iris M. Tiedt, its director, set out to show all participants how they could prove to their students that they are "walking grammars." Her device was uncomplicated, a simple exercise that could easily fit into a conventional class hour. Its first demand called for an *E* next to constructions thought to be grammatical English sentences, a *non-E* next to those considered nongrammatical. Typical of the 10 constructions listed were "The story interesting to me was," "At him she the pillow threw," and "Mort couldn't finish the exam," none of which the native speaker of English would have difficulty in labeling. And this is exactly the point Mrs. Tiedt subsequently made. "You were able to select these sentences [the acceptable grammatical ones] because you are a speaker of English," she pointed out. "Any native speaker of English could select them. As a matter of fact, you were able to recognize English sentences long before you started to school, although you probably weren't aware of it."

After indicating that native speakers all possess a built-in ability to turn out sentences in their language, she inserted a second demand, this one calling for a rearrangement of seven groups of words to make sentences:

1. around the old corner the limped man
2. the fat sat smugly toad pad on his
3. his class could the new not boy find
4. vitamins you gives spinach
5. rocket air off the in went the
6. first Oswald finished was
7. permission you gave to go she

Again she conceded that native speakers doubtless had no trouble whatever making sense out of such nonsense; without thinking of any rules, she acknowledged, they could put words together to make English sentences.

Teaching inductively, therefore, she had illustrated for her audience that "the knowledge we have which enables us to make sentences of our language is called the grammar of the language, and we say a language has 'grammaticality,' which means it can be explained by a grammar." Her conclusion was that although students usually have the notion that grammar must be studied if it is to be spoken correctly, the little tests that she had imposed indicate that it demands no study at all. Students use it every day; they are indeed "walking grammars" (40, pp. 29-30).

In the fall of 1972, Mrs. Tiedt assumed the editorship of *Elementary English*. Under her guidance, one of the strengths of the journal has been its consistent attention to language and grammar teaching. Too, it now features a column called "Instructional Strategies," in which tips valuable to the grammar teacher appear regularly. Although primarily designed for teachers and supervisors at the elementary school level, *Elementary English*, thanks to the creative Mrs. Tiedt, often contains methodology useful on or adaptable to the secondary school level.

A BASIC LESSON IN TRANSFORMATIONS AND DEEP STRUCTURES

Teachers should not overlook two sentences, often cited by linguists, which can lead students to a fundamental appreciation of transformations and deep structures. "John is eager to please" and "John is easy to please" are, students will contend, basically similar constructions. They will be quick to point out that on the surface both contain the same grammatical elements in exactly the same order: noun, copula or linking verb, adjective, and infinitive phrase.

They will be willing to concede, however, that, even though diagramming does not reveal it, a difference exists. Common sense or logic, they will note, calls for its recognition. In one instance, they will explain, John is acted upon by forces outside himself which find him easy to satisfy, while in the other, he displays or demonstrates a quality, a willingness to do or represent something. Such an awareness will doubtless lead them to conclude that certain different but related sentences can be identified, but others cannot be; that certain transforms of the original sentences possess grammaticality, while others do not. "To please John is easy" is acceptable, they will contend, "To please John is eager" unacceptable; "John is eager to please someone" likewise acceptable, "John is easy to please someone" likewise unacceptable. The key to distinguishing between the original sentences, the students will eventually be forced to acknowledge, lies in recognizing that surface structures often reveal little and that deep structures, illuminated by and through transformations, often reveal a great deal. Only by untangling the knots that lie beneath the surface, they will conclude, do people manage to talk and comprehend.

Analyzing two sentences like those involving John will provide convincing evidence that, to be meaningful and accurate, grammar study must involve not merely identification of sentence parts but, more important, awareness of the presence and significance of transformations and deep structures.

CONSERVATIONAL GRAMMAR

An approach to grammar teaching developed for the elementary school level may prove, with appropriate adaptation, to be useful in secondary schools. Mrs. June Allen presses the case for *Conservational* Grammar, a grammar with an ecological dimension. All sentences, all transformations, all exercises concern the environment and the problems of pollution which threaten its existence. "Why not work with sentences that are *worth* transforming, that are worth *thinking* about?" Mrs. Allen asks. "Why not practice patterns whose *content,* too, is worth retaining? Why not learn ecology with English?"

Representative of the many suggestions which she provides is one that concerns bird feeders. Stocked with appropriate dietary preferences and placed outside classroom windows, they could be the stimulus for the manufacture, and the eventual use in sentences, of lively verbs, action words appropriate to capture the movements of hungry customers. "Dart," "snatch," and "scramble" are but three of the possibilities that would soon evolve. Students could subsequently learn to change the mood and the tense of the verbs as conservational observations allowed.

The littered earth and the polluted air and water could, similarly, trigger exercises. "Tell me these negative facts," requests the teacher, "using other words for 'ain't' ": Lake Erie ain't safe to swim in; the fish ain't alive; the air in New York ain't healthy to breathe (2).

Mrs. Allen also lists addresses of sources able to provide information potentially valuable in *Conservational* Grammar, among them the following:

Audubon Magazine, 1130 Fifth Avenue, New York, New York 10028

National Wildlife Federation, 1412 16th Street, N.W., Washington, D.C. 20036

Sierra Club, 1050 Mills Tower, San Francisco, California 94104

GRAMMAR

Ecology is and doubtless will continue to be important in "the Age of Discontinuity." Thus units or lessons involving *Conservational* Grammar loom as valid possibilities for involving students.

GRAMMAR AND FUN

Grammar and fun are not incompatible. In fact, they make a wonderful pair. Many authorities recommend the marriage, and even more teachers have used it to great advantage.

Teacher Janet Cote-Merow suggests that students make poster collages composed of examples from newspapers and magazines which illustrate grammar rules that have been learned. The activity demands that the students seek and discover their own examples of how the media put into practice what previously have simply been rules mentioned in class. There is an additional advantage, too, Mrs. Cote-Merow promises: the students end up doing quite a bit of newspaper and magazine reading (6).

More sophisticated perhaps are Vicki Hackett's suggestions. Her "Subject-Predicate Game" (15) is an activity involving players in four language arts areas: language study, creative thinking, speaking, and listening. Students first write simple sentences on slips of paper, then separate the subject from the predicate of each with a slash mark. Subsequently the subjects are lettered on lavender slips of paper, the predicates on blue slips, and all are placed haphazardly into a box. Each student then digs out a subject and a predicate at random, reads the pieced together sentence aloud to his classmates, and takes one minute, no more, to create an impromptu story, comic or otherwise, in which the sentence figures. Every story that is told thus has an audience, and usually it is an interested, appreciative one. The game can serve as a stimulus for creative writing, too, notes Mrs. Hackett.

Her "Word-Class Game" was created by students using Postman's *Discovering Your Language* as a textbook. It was designed to help them identify Class 1, 2, 3, and 4 words, as they are defined by Postman, and to encourage them to become aware of various kinds of words and their functions. The game requires a painted path, players' pieces, and cards of two colors, one containing simple sentences, previously produced by the gamemakers, the other either Class 1, 2, 3, or 4 and the number of spaces the player holding it must move. The game begins when a player draws one card of each color, and moves accordingly, forward if he answers correctly, backward if he answers incorrectly; the game ends when a player reaches the finish. Inside the game box, in addition to the rules, is a chart explaining the four word classes; players consult it to check on their answers as well as to refresh their memories and to aid their understanding. The game, Mrs. Hackett explains, can assist students to understand the role of syntax in determining the function of words (15).

Miriam Goldstein Sargon alleges that elective English and grammar fun go hand in hand. Because teachers in such programs are likely to be informed, curious, and enthusiastic about language, she maintains, they have a greater tendency to encourage students to play with language, to see what its possibilities are. "When youngsters play with language, then, what they do is their doing. They do not ask, 'Can I say this?' Sure, you can say anything. But is it a sentence of English? Well, there are sentences and there are sentences. Youngsters begin to experiment with their own sentences in the most daring, uninhibited, imaginative, and revealing ways."

The simplest of questions can trigger the desired experimentation in any classroom, contends Mrs. Sargon. "How do we know, for example, that 'you' is understood in a sentence like 'Come here'?" she asks. "Here's how today's youngsters figure out the 'why' and the 'how.' Instead of reading or memorizing or correcting sentences, they create their own. They experiment with sentences. They list all kinds, some very much like the given one: 'Help.' 'Dig that.' 'Follow me.' 'Help me.' 'Help yourself.' " Very quickly, she points out, they realize that the sentence in question follows the rules for forming other accceptable sentences that they have evolved: that like every other English sentence, "Come here" originally consisted of a subject and a predicate, that "you" must have been deleted to form the command or imperative sentence. "And how do they know it was deleted? Because the reflexive pronouns in the predicate are identical with the subject, as in 'You help yourself.' If you can omit the 'you' in 'You help yourself' to get 'Help yourself,' you can omit the 'you' in 'You come here' to get 'Come here.' Thus they have accounted for or explained the native speaker's linguistic intuition when he claims that 'you' is understood in imperative sentences" (34). In other words, through playing with language, as Mrs. Sargon illustrates, students can learn about it—and have some fun in the process.

The fun in testing the language's elasticity is also paramount in West's recommendations. "I believe," he says, "in helping students have fun with language," and he illustrates in a variety of ways. One of them focuses on the use of transformations to produce sentence variety. "Students will enjoy seeing how many transformed sentences they can make from a single sentence of their own," he says:

Basic sentence: John likes corn.
Yes-no question: Does John like corn?
Wh-questions: When does John like corn: Why does John like corn? How does John like corn?
Passive: *Corn is liked by John.
  Imperative: *John, like corn.
  Negative: John does not like corn.
Nominalization: (Place "that" before the sentence and finish the thought) That John likes corn . . . is surprising.
Infinitive nominalization: (Place *for* . . . *to* into the sentence) For John to like corn bothers his sister.
Gerundive nominalization: (Use *'s* and *-ing* in the sentence) John's liking corn surprises people.
Adjectivalization and deletion: (Replace one of the nouns in the sentence with the appropriate relative pronoun and embed the transformed sentence into another) Corn, which John likes, is rich in iron. John, who likes corn, is very strong.
Adverbialization: (By using the appropriate subordinate conjunction, relate the sentence to another sentence so that it tells how, when, where, why, and so on that the action of the main sentence occurs) Although John likes corn, most children do not. When John likes corn, the other children protest. If John likes corn, he will eat hominy.

The passive and imperative sentences appear with asterisks because they would not ordinarily occur in the language, West admits, and, consequently, not everyone would accept them as grammatical.

West believes, too, that Robert Allen of Teachers College, Columbia, has developed what is perhaps the simplest system for recognizing complete subjects. West urges teachers to lead students through the following six steps:

1. Isolate most of the English verb auxiliaries by having students ask questions answerable by "yes" or "no." Each begins with an auxiliary.
2. Have students find the auxiliary in any sentence in question. (The man *has* gone to work.)
3. If the sentence lacks an auxiliary, have students make it emphatic by adding a form of the verb "do." ("The man went to work" becomes "The man *did* go to work.)
4. Turn the sentence into a conventional yes-no question. (*Has* the man gone to work? *Did* the man go to work?)
5. If the original statement starts with something other than the noun phrase cluster subject, be sure students shift it, as they would in ordinary speech,

to the end of their question. (*When the court order came,* the men went to work. Did the men go to work *when the court order came?*)
6. Underline the material which comes between the two places in the sentence where the auxiliary has appeared. This material—with one exception, the "there is," "there are," and "it is" expletive constructions—is the complete subject of the sentence. All else is the complete predicate. If students attempt to shift the auxiliary of a subordinate clause as they transform the statement into a question, they will find the question does not sound like English. Thus ask them to try a second time (43).

Moffett places even more emphasis than does West on the desirability of a funlike, relaxed atmosphere when students grapple with grammatical considerations. In fact, to him naturalness is the key to the entire language arts curriculum, K through 12. Moffett contends that language arts at every level should be viewed not as a subject but as a means through which subjects, grammar included, are studied. For him language is thinking itself, and it is useless to break it into parts or pieces to be memorized or rules to be learned. Language production and experience, then, dominate the classroom that Moffett sees as desirable, and grammar study is not approached systematically but, instead, as need and situation demand. It appears under the guise of "sentence-expansion games, good discussion, rewriting of notes, collaborative revision of compositions, playing with one-sentence discourses, and verbalizing certain cognitive tasks" (29, pp. 180-81).

A Student-Centered Language Arts Curriculum, Grades K-13: A Handbook for Teachers, published in 1968 by Houghton Mifflin, outlines the program, and *INTERACTION,* published in 1972 by the same company, provides all the materials, including anthologies, recordings, and films, needed to implement it. An informal question-and-answer dialogue like the one below can be key, Moffett shows in both, in developing grammatical sophistication:

Appositive—I saw Mr. Smith. Who is he? The principal at Lincoln. I saw Mr. Smith, the principal at Lincoln.
Adverbial clause—We'll lose that game to Jefferson. Why? Because our boys haven't been training well. Because our boys haven't been training well, we'll lose that game to Jefferson.
Gerundive nominalization—I hope he doesn't tell me to stay after school. His telling me to stay after school won't bother me a bit, because I won't be here (43).

Likewise, the "Silly Syntax" game, variations of which appear at every level of the INTERACTION program, enables students to learn about options in word order. Similar to Mrs. Hackett's "Word-Class Game," it develops "sentence sense" in a natural, deductive way; players manipulate the sentence parts on their cards in an attempt to produce meaningful sequences. Skill in trading cards is important to success, and the fun results from the nonsense and surprise of imaginative sentence construction.

Every teacher of grammar, regardless of his temperament and goals, has reason and opportunity for "fun and games" in his classroom. They can turn students on to what otherwise might be dull investigations; they can enliven the study of grammar.

GRAMMAR AND THE BRITISH

Peter Doughty, John Pearce, and Geoffrey Thornton, the men responsible for *Language in Use,* are all British. Their book, therefore, exploits a view of language learning not often found on this side of the Atlantic. It provides a language-exploration program for grades 6 through 12 whose goal is an awareness which ultimately leads to competence; from awareness of what language is and how it is used, the authors posit, comes extension of language competence, both written and spoken.

"Pattern in Language," one of the 10 themes making up the book, consists of 13 units designed to allow students "to discover that language is patterned, ordered, and predictable; that reasons for doing one thing rather than another stem from the structure of language itself and are not an arbitrary requirement set up by teachers of examiners" (8, p. 89). As such it is perhaps of greater utility to grammar teachers than other themes. Its value—and creativity—is reflected in its fourth unit, "Patterns in Language," which explores pattern in the organization of language. The first assignment calls for division of the class into small groups, each of which puts a short, simple message into code; subsequently the groups exchange their coded messages and attempt to decode them. The second assignment involves the class in a discussion, first, of codes, possible only because there are predictable patterns in the language which can be exploited, and, later, of the coded messages previously developed—how their creators set about to devise them, how their classmates set about to crack them. The third assignment has the class, again in small groups, examining a selection of passages taken from languages unfamiliar to them. The aim of the assignment is to have students discover how much they can work out by studying the patterns in the language of the passages. Later each group reports to the class on their findings, some of which are likely to involve language features like word order, word classes, and punctuation. The fourth and final assignment of the unit concerns comparison and contrast of features found in English with those obvious in other languages examined. Like the other 109 units making up the loose-leaf book, this one is totally student-centered, and while there are numerous suggestions for teachers working with it, no prescribed responses appear (8, pp. 97-98).

Available from Ginn and Company, *Language in Use* contains an unusual approach to language learning, one that can lead to creative teaching in this country as well as in England.

GRAMMAR AND INQUIRY

Keyser is among the many people who believe that grammar should be viewed as an opportunity for students to learn how to engage in rational inquiry. With the help of school personnel in Needham and Gloucester, Massachusetts, he has demonstrated that such study can be profitable as well as enjoyable at both the elementary and the secondary school levels. Among the several lesson plans from which he has worked is one whose goal is to try to indicate differences between syntactic and semantic aspects of English noun plurality and to attempt to get students to formulate generalizations about the nouns under discussion. Initially the teacher, aware that syntactic and semantic number do not always go together, asks his class to consider pairs of sentences featuring nouns that can be counted. Appropriate would be sentences like "One chair is by the window" and "Two chairs are by the window." Once the students understand that the difference between the two types results from a singular noun and the singular "is" in one and a plural noun and the plural "are" in the other, the teacher introduces a pair of scissors and invites the class to discuss them. One of the sentences certain to be uttered very quickly is "The scissors are on the table," after which the teacher can ask about the appropriateness of "are" to team with one item, scissors. Students will not be reluctant to point out the two parts of the scissors to justify the plural verb, but the teacher will be equally unreluctant to note that neither part makes up the scissors but only both together. Class discussion will subsequently center on other objects of two parts which function as a unit and which, although taking plural verbs, can be either singular or plural.

Later the teacher can lead the class to probe the relationship between syntactic and semantic number in words like "class," "band," and "team," citing as evidence the behavior of those words with verbs such as "scatter," "disband," "disperse," and "surround," all of which usually require a plural meaning for the subject although the syntactic number can be singular. The point with such nouns is that the syntactic number results from the unit in question whereas the semantic number results from the individuals making up that unit. Awareness of the distinction between, and possibilities of, syntactic number and semantic number can eventually lead the students to construct and discuss nonsentences similar to "The boy who had been changed by magic into a swarm of bees dispersed," which suffers from, first, the conflict between the fact that "boy" is syntactically and semantically singular and thus cannot occur with a verb like "disperse," and, second, the fact the relative clause beginning with "who" provides the boy with precisely the necessary semantic property required in order to disperse.

One of the conclusions to which students can be led as a result of the lesson is that they know, but are not aware that they know, a distinction operative in English with a potential for numerous new and creative constructions, including ungrammatical ones. Such a discovery reflects Keyser's faith in the possibilities of inquiry if it is encouraged and exploited at every level of education. "Indeed," he prophesies, "it is conceivable that this kind of inquiry might culminate at the highest level in a theoretical course in linguistics in which the facts of language which have been brought out in earlier grades are then viewed as evidence for one linguistic theory over another" (20).

Comparable enthusiasm for the possibilities of inquiry, discovery techniques in grammar teaching comes from Miss Jane Morrisey, a teacher in New Rochelle, New York. Typical of her lessons is one whose goal is to assist students to formulate a generalization about the order of modification before a noun headword modified by a determiner, a number, an adjective, and a noun. Initially, she writes four clusters on the chalkboard: tall the three tree oak; nine peas those old giant; small cakes our birthday four; smart six my girl friends. Her first question after doing so is, "Do the four clusters make any sense? her second, "If not, will someone volunteer to make sense out of the first cluster?" Eventually she has students rearrange all four on the chalkboard, and proceeds to ask them how they were able to determine meaningful sequences. Subsequently they examine the rearrangements together and decide that all four contain the same language components, which are then classified in boxes on the chalkboard in the following order: determiner, number, adjective, noun, noun. She next queries the students on the word in each rearrangement that they think most important to it, and she labels their choice "the headword." She is thus in a position to pose several related questions like "What kinds of words have we discovered modify the headword?" "How did we reach this conclusion?" "Why didn't we work with the original clusters?" and "How did we put the clusters in order?" On the basis of responses provided by her students, she is able to move them to hazard a conclusion about word order and, later, to formulate possibilities for a descriptive rule to explain order of modification, all of which are written on the chalkboard, discussed, and clarified. She concludes the lesson by assigning as homework the construction of 10 additional clusters like those examined; creating that number in the required sequence —determiner, number, adjective, noun, noun—will serve to reinforce what the students have seen for themselves during the class period, Miss Morrisey believes (32, pp. 83–85).

Inquiry teaching cannot work miracles, but it can and does allow students to reach their own conclusions and to sharpen their intellectual tools. Too, it provides grammar study with a legitimate reason for being in the classroom.

GRAMMAR AND BLACK ENGLISH

Historically, the teaching of grammar to speakers of black English has been marked by constant frustration and only occasional success. Well-intentioned teachers have more times than not been armed with ignorance of black language and culture and with methodology that students find demeaning. Typically, for instance, they have attributed so-called natural rhythm to blacks, believing it a genetic characteristic. Similarly, they have commonly been unaware of the role nonverbal behavior plays among blacks, who communicate differently from other races with their body movements (19).

Pedagogical technique has often been no more enlightened. In order to teach black children that sounds convey meaning, language arts teachers have frequently used gimmicks like toy whistles and rattles, unmindful that the typical two-year-old knows what sounds mean—for his own culture (7, p. 273).

GRAMMAR

The belief that black English is without grammar has been still another popular misconception. But, thanks to linguists, white as well as black, it has recently, and very fortunately indeed, been exploded. James L. Dillard is perhaps the best-known of the many authorities who provide convincing evidence that black English is a language in its own right, not only with its own history but, equally important, with its own laws, structure, and literary — as well as practical — value. "It probably came from the West Coast of Africa," he states, "almost certainly not directly from Great Britain" (7, p. 6).

Kenneth R. Johnson and Herbert D. Simons provide further clarification. "Black dialect is systematic. That is, it is not a collection of sloppy, random, erroneous sounds and grammatical structures which the speaker carelessly utters. Instead, when the phonological and grammatical deviations from standard English heard in the speech of many blacks are contrasted with the points in standard Englsh, it is clear that these deviations are consistent and systematic. Black people are not making just any noises, but particular noises" (19).

Mrs. Dorothy Z. Seymour puts reverse spin on the same point and thereby provides a telling message for grammar teachers to ponder. "Let's turn the tables on Standard English for a moment," she suggests, "and look at it from the West African point of view. From this angle, Standard English: (1) is lacking in certain language sounds, (2) has a couple of unnecessary language sounds for which others may serve as good substitutes, (3) doubles and drawls some of its vowel sounds in sequences that are unusual and difficult to imitate, (4) lacks a method of forming an important tense [the habitual, used to express action which is always occurring], (5) requires an unnecessary number of ways to indicate tense, plurality and gender, and (6) doesn't mark negatives sufficiently for the result to be a good strong negative statement" (36).

Teachers hoping to work effectively with speakers of black English must, therefore, rid themselves of the notion that that dialect is deficient or impoverished. They must see it as just as worthy of respect as any other language. They must recognize, too, that many blacks use only that language, while others employ standard English as well as black English, the social situation and audience of the moment determining for them the type of English that is appropriate. "Correctness," then, looms as a relative term for informed teachers, who must deem standard English unwise whenever its audience cannot comprehend all that is being said (19). Equally important, they must strive to educate all their students, especially whites perhaps, to the fact that since every language is a vehicle of identification, an index of a speaker's culture, black English merits neither mockery nor vilification. Its rejection, like the rejection of any language, is tantamount to rejection of the people speaking it.

In "the Age of Discontinuity," teachers must also make every effort to gain knowledge about black language and culture. A good starting point is Dillard's *Black English,* published by Random House, a readable book containing an abundance of information and insights. Given special attention in it is William A. Stewart's TOEFL method for teaching standard English as a second dialect, a method based on the belief that students must internalize the rules of standard English if it is to be mastered. "The technique consists of intensive practice to the point of overlearning," Dillard explains (7, p. 269), and demands that teachers utilizing it neither condemn the other language the students speak nor forget that it possesses equal viability and richness.

Dillard, too, favors Network Standard Dialect, rather than the various "educated" local dialects, as the second language for speakers of black English. "The door to nationwide integration is still open" (7, p. 287), and it can remain open, he believes, if the consensus standard dialect is taught.

Black English is a controversial, emotion-packed subject, not without huge social and economic significance. Teachers of grammar must be committed to constantly searching for more information about it, while remaining flexible and innovative in their classroom techniques.

GRAMMAR AND FIELD RESEARCH

Grammar study need not be confined to the classroom. In fact, it has by its very nature every right to go beyond it to "the real world," as students, unfortunately, are fond of calling everything outside the school, to that world, in other words, not populated solely by students, teachers, and administrators. When grammar study does invade and become indistinguishable from "the real world," it assumes a vitality and a reality that are desirable; it becomes, in short, relevant.

An Approach to Teaching Usage, produced by the Department of Public Instruction in North Carolina, outlines class or group projects which can ultimately lead to a valuable *Guide for Appropriate Usage.* One suggestion calls for taping, and subsequently analyzing, usage heard on local radio and television stations. Inter-

GRAMMAR

views with several people can be compared and contrasted—those with a lawyer, a farmer, and a businessman, for example. Another suggestion focuses on usage on the high school campus. Students can render judgments on the basis of tapes made at a variety of sites, among them the football field, a chemistry lab, and a social club meeting (5, p. 27).

More meaningful perhaps, and certainly more popular, is field research involving all three facets of dialect study—not merely grammar but also pronunciation and vocabulary. Mrs. Carol Hughes involved her Annawan, Illinois, students in a dialect study of their area, Henry County, and reports that even those who normally disliked language study became enthusiastic when given an opportunity to go out into the field rather than into a book to gather information. Her class selected 24 informants of varying ages and occupations, and, using their own questionnaire, gathered responses to 30 items, 10 on grammar and a like number on pronunciation and vocabulary. Those designated to be on grammar appear below:

1. She will (look after, tend, mind, take care of) the baby.
2. She is (fixing, making, getting) supper.
3. I (reckon so, guess so, suppose so).
4. It's a quarter (of, to, till) ten.
5. We named the child (for, at, after, from) him.
6. It goes (clear, clean, plum) across.
7. He is sick (to, at, in) his stomach.
8. It's (rather, kind of, sort of, middling) cold.
9. It's (almost, nigh, well-nigh onto, near, pretty near) midnight
10. He (caught, took, take, katched) cold.

Mrs. Hughes admits that her students included some items under grammar that perhaps more logically belonged under vocabulary and that they should have given some attention to plural formations and verb tenses (18). Nonetheless, the questions they developed under her guidance represent a commendable first effort; they enabled both teacher and students to increase their knowledge of language habits found in the area—and to enjoy themselves in the process.

The Annawan study was not sophisticated; dialectologists, as well as grammarians, doubtless would not be totally pleased with it. Yet it proved valuable to those who were involved with it, just as any similar study, inspired by an equally creative teacher, can be rewarding to its participants. For the teacher who wishes to have his students embark on dialect, or simply grammar, fieldwork but who believes that he lacks the necessary background to provide sensible guidance, *Discovering American Dialects,* written by Roger W. Shuy and available through the National Council of Teachers of English, represents a useful resource. In less than 70 pages, it provides much expert advice and a horde of sound, practical suggestions. Field research in grammar and related studies is worth undertaking, and Shuy indicates how it can be pursued most profitably.

GRAMMAR AND THE FUTURE

In 1921 Edward Sapir, perhaps the most respected linguist of recent time, proclaimed that "All grammars leak" (33, p. 38), and there is no reason to assume that his pronouncement is any less valid today than it was when first conceived. No grammatical system thus far developed, and none in the offing, can hope to account for every construction and every quirk of the language. English is too rich and its formations too numerous and complex to allow for "a perfect engine of conceptual expression" (33, p. 38), to use Sapir's metaphor.

Yet, in the imperfections as well as the strengths of each grammar—and of all of them colllectively—lies the real pedagogical challenge. Secondary school teachers of grammar in "the Age of Discontinuity" have an opportunity to lead their students to a myriad of awarenesses about the grammatical makeup of their language—among them, certainly, the belief that there is no "Great Grammar Book in the Sky," created by a divine being for all mortals to obey, and, too, that because all grammatical systems are man-made, all are subject to defect. Likewise, the success which all of the grammars enjoy, and the linguistically based ones most, in revealing and explaining the power and the subtlety of the language merits even more classroom time, skill, and commitment.

"New appraoches to grammar, beyond generative-transformational grammar, are anticipated," suggests Edmund J. Farrell on the basis of responses which a panel of experts in English submitted to him for compilation in *Deciding the Future: A Forecast of Responsibilities of Secondary Teachers of English, 1970-2000 A.D.* (11, p. 157). It is easy to concur. The work of men like Pike, Fillmore, Lamb, and Halliday is truly promising, and there is good reason to expect that it will in the years ahead provide teachers with even more information and insights than they presently possess. The future is indeed bright. In the words of Charlton Laird, "We have outgrown the old grammar; we have not yet grown into a new one. We have, I am sure for good and all, shaken ourselves loose from a grammatical stagnation, from a grammatical purblindness that kept us for decades from seeing anything much except what our ancestors had seen, at least some of which utilized little but linguistic myopia. If we do not yet have an entirely new grammatical statement, we do have great improvements in our grammatical approaches and we are developing an openness of mind that cannot but be good" (22, pp. 67-68).

REFERENCES

1. Adams, Vernon. "In-Service Program in Modern Grammars," *Illinois English Bulletin,* 54 (1967), 1-4.
2. Allen, June. "The Case for Conservational Grammar," *Elementary English,* 47 (1970), 684-86.
3. Briggs, F. Allen. " 'Grammatical Sense' As a Factor in Reading Comprehension." Tampa, Fla.: University of South Florida, 1968. Mimeographed.
4. Bruner, Jerome. "Growth of Mind," *American Psychologist,* 20 (1965), 29-33.
5. Chandler, William J.; Lipscomb, Clarence C.; and Tucker, M. Lawrence. *An Approach to Teaching English Usage.* Raleigh, N.C.: Department of Public Instruction, 1969.
6. Cote-Merow, Janet. "Enliven Grammar," *Scholastic Teacher,* (October, 1972), 37.
7. Dillard, J. L. *Black English.* New York: Random House, Inc., 1972.
8. Doughty, Peter; Pearce, John; and Thornton, Geoffrey. *Language in Use.* Boston: Ginn and Company, 1971.
9. Drucker, Peter F. *The Age of Discontinuity.* New York: Harper & Row, Publishers, 1968.
10. *Encyclopedia of Educational Research.* New York: The Macmillan Company, 1950.
11. Farrell, Edmund J. *Deciding the Future: A Forecast of Responsibilities of Secondary Teachers of English, 1970-2000 A.D.* Urbana. Ill.: National Council of Teachers of English, 1971.
12. Francis, W. Nelson. "Revolution in Grammar," in Virginia P. Clark, Paul A. Eschholz, and Alfred F. Rosa (eds.), *Language.* New York: St. Martin's Press, 1972, 111-28.

13. Glasrud, Clarence A. *The Age of Anxiety.* Boston: Houghton Mifflin, 1960.
14. Greene, Harry A., and Petty, Walter T. *Developing Language Skills.* 2d ed.; Boston: Allyn and Bacon, Inc., 1963.
15. Hackett, Vicki. "Games in the English Class," *English Journal,* 61 (1970), 100-3.
16. Hook, J. N. "English Language Programs for the Seventies," in Raymond D. Crisp (ed.), *Designs In English.* Urbana, Ill.: University of Illinois, 1972, 62-74.
17. _____. "Grammar(s)—A Rationale," in Raymond D. Crisp (ed.), *Designs in English.* Urbana, Ill.: University of Illinois, 1972, 30-40.
18. Hughes, Carol. "A Classroom Survey of Dialects," *Illinois English Bulletin,* 67 (1970), 20-25.
19. Johnson, Kenneth R., and Simons, Herbert D. "Black Children and Reading: What Teachers Need to Know," *Phi Delta Kappan,* 53 (1972), 288-90.
20. Keyser, Samuel Jay. "The Role of Linguistics in the Elementary School Curriculum," *Elementary English,* 47 (1970), 39-45.
21. Kohl, Herbert. *The Age of Complexity.* New York: The New American Library, 1965.
22. Laird, Charlton. *And Gladly Teche: Notes on Instructing the Natives in the Native Tongue.* Englewood Cliffs, N.J.: Prentice-Hall, Inc., 1970.
23. Lester, Mark. "The Value of Transformational Grammar in Teaching Composition," in Mark Lester (ed.), *Readings in Applied Transformational Grammar.* New York: Holt, Rinehart & Winston, Inc., 1970, 201-9.
24. Lowery, Josephine P. *This Is Grammar.* New York: Charles Scribner's Sons, 1965.
25. Malmstrom, Jean, and Lee, Janice. *Teaching English Linguistically: Principles and Practices for High School.* New York: Appleton-Century-Crofts, 1971.
26. Marckwardt, Albert H. "The Structure and Operation of Language," in Robert F. Hogan (ed.), *The English Language in the School Program.* Champaign, Ill.: National Council of Teachers of English, 1966, 31-41.
27. Mellon, John C. *Transformational Sentence-Combining: A Method for Enhancing the Development of Syntactic Fluency in English Composition.* Champaign, Ill.: National Council of Teachers of English, 1969.

28. *Minneapolis, '72.* Urbana, Ill.: National Council of Teachers of English, 1972.
29. Moffett, James. *Teaching the Universe of Discourse*, Boston: Houghton Mifflin Company, 1968.
30. O'Donnell, Roy C. "The Correlation of Awareness of Structural Relationships in English and Ability in Written Composition," *Journal of Educational Research,* 57 (1964), 464–66.
31. Postman, Neil. "Inventing an English Curriculum," in Howard C. Zimmerman (ed.). *Ideal Designs for English Programs.* Toledo, Ohio: The University of Toledo, 1968, 20–25.
32. Postman, Neil, and Weingartner, Charles. *Linguistics: A Revolution in Teaching.* New York: Dell Publishing Company, 1966.
33. Sapir, Edward. *Language.* New York: Harcourt, Brace & World, Inc., 1921.
34. Sargon, Miriam Goldstein. "Johnny Is Neither Eager Nor Easy to Please," in *The Humanity of English: NCTE 1972 Distinguished Lectures.* Urbana, Ill.: National Council of Teachers of English, 1972, 115–34.
35. Sattler, Donald. "From Dream to Blueprint—A Paradigm for a Secondary School English Program," in Howard C. Zimmerman (ed.), *Ideal Designs for English Programs.* Toledo, Ohio: The University of Toledo, 1968, 43–47.
36. Seymour, Dorothy Z. "Black Children, Black Speech," *Commonweal,* 95 (1971), 175–78.
37. Sherwin, J. Stephen. *Four Problems in Teaching English: A Critique of Research.* Scranton, Penn.: International Textbook Company, 1969.
38. Sledd, James. "Who Is Subverting Whom?—Grammar or Gramarye?" *English Journal,* 49 (1960), 293–303.
39. Strong, William. "New Criteria for Curriculum Guides," *English Journal,* 61 (1972), 1342–49.
40. Tiedt, Iris M., and Tiedt, Sidney W. *Contemporary English in the Elementary School.* Englewood Cliffs, N.J.: Prentice-Hall, Inc., 1967.
41. West, William W. "A Curriculum Design," in Howard C. Zimmerman (ed.), *Ideal Designs for English Programs.* Toledo, Ohio: The University of Toledo, 1968, 26–30.
42. West, William W. "Recommendations for a Language Program." Tampa, Fla.: University of South Florida, 1970. Mimeographed.
43. West, William W. "Relevance from All the Grammars." Tampa, Fla.: University of South Florida, 1970. Mimeographed.

44. White, Morton (ed.). *The Age of Analysis.* New York: The New American Library, 1955.
45. Wilson, Kenneth G. "English Grammars and the Grammar of English," in Leonard F. Dean, Walker Gibson, and Kenneth G. Wilson (eds.), *The Play of Language.* New York: Oxford University Press, 1971, 102-25.

JAN A. GUFFIN
North Central High School, Indianapolis

4   Writing

It may be natural for us to *want* to write, but it is not natural for us to write. In fact, of all the language arts, writing is the most unnatural. We learn to listen and speak in almost complete unawareness, but we learn to read and write in almost complete awareness. This may explain why the analysis of listening and speaking skills is a comparatively recent phenomenon and why reading and writing skills have remained under the academic microscope for almost as long as they have been taught. One might guess that having remained under such close scrutiny, the arts of writing and of teaching writing would be fairly clearly understood by now, but this is not so. For all our talk about why we write, what we do when we write, and how well we write, we have reached relatively few solid conclusions. But the fact that the academic air is so full of notions concerning these matters doesn't mean that the teaching of writing is a polluted subject. On the contrary, the increasing demands on the profession to be more scientific suggest strongly that the teacher of writing establish thoughtful rationales for his task, plan multiple strategies, and above all, have an open mind.

WHY WE WRITE

The question of why we write probably never looms larger than when we face a sizable stack of ungraded papers. Answers to the question are legion; and although it may be expedient to have a couple handy for the curious student, it is more important that the teacher arrive at some answers that are for him personally and professionally meaningful. A few of the better answers which have been proposed on this issue range from the simple explanation that "One of man's fondest pleasures is that of verbalizing his thoughts and feelings, of communicating them to other people" (36, p. 451); to the pragmatic, "It is a practical necessity because all students have to do considerable writing in other courses [than English] too, as on papers and tests, and still more in college" (31, p. 98); to the philosophical, "... in the written communication of his thoughts and feelings man finds somehow a portion, however small or fragmented, of immortality" (36, p. 451).

In establishing personal rationales, however, we have to think about more than just writing; we have to think about *composition* too, a word which Edward Lueders urges teaches to take seriously: "... any writer—regardless of his purpose and particular medium, the successful student as well as the professional—deals in the act of relating parts to the whole which identify in the term *composition*" (22, p. 104). His statement is as important philosophically as it is practically, for as we continue to de-compose and represent the world in scientific terms, our need to compose experience in human terms is imminent. In spite of the hundreds of ready-made, wash-and-wear procedures we go through each day, our decisions are not always disposable. Our need to reach decisions in an orderly way and convey them sensibly to those around us is contingent on the act of composing. In this sense, composing and writing are among the surest acts of affirmation in a democratic, economically affluent, culturally explosive age.

WHAT WE WRITE

Labels are sometimes convenient, sometimes comfortable, and sometimes troublesome. Instead of offering "Writing for Those Who Wish to Become Doctors," "Writing for Those Who Wish to Become

Businessmen," or "Writing for Those Who Wish to Write," most high schools find it convenient to offer courses in "expository writing," "creative writing," or just plain "composition." Also some teachers may feel comfortable to know that they are teaching exposition and therefore won't have to bother with the freewheeling artist; or that they are teaching creative writing and therefore won't have to bother with all those stuffy rules of the expository writing class; or that they are teaching composition, where they can do what they please. It should be clear why labels, in spite of their convenience or their comfort, are sometimes troublesome. Pity the poor soul who may someday find himself teaching a course entitled "Composition: Creative Exposition."

Such an idea makes more sense than fun, however. If we consider our age as " . . . a time of soaring interest in education; of a greatly increased production of books, periodicals, newspapers, house organs, and other printed material for mass distribution; of the flood of business and personal correspondence, of direct mail advertising, and of advertising copy of all kinds; of an almost universal dependence upon duplicating processes and the preparation of copy for mimeograph and ditto and photoduplication" (22, p. 105), we can readily see the need for incorporating *both* expository and creative elements into whatever writing course we find ourselves teaching. This does not mean that we should necessarily dispose of such labels, but neither should we let them get in the way of understanding some of the fundamental issues which confront every teacher of writing.

HOW WE TEACH

Every teacher of writing eventually shapes his course and develops his teaching techniques in relation to various priorities: those established by the school or department in which he works; those dictated by the needs and interest of his students; and those he establishes for himself through what he learns from working with students, talking to fellow teachers, and reading professional literature. Cutting across all these priorities and affecting them at different times with different emphases are a host of other concerns directly related to teaching and related to teaching writing directly. The remainder of this chapter will deal with these concerns as well as with a series of approaches to teaching a variety of writing tasks.

CREATIVITY

English educators, especially since the Anglo-American Conference at Dartmouth in 1966, have placed increasing emphasis on a humanistic approach to the teaching of English, and within that framework, have directed significant attention to the development of creativity in students. This new respect for creativity lacks the element of faddishness sometimes attached to previous trends in English education, partly because it is coincident with a sense of need in American society and with a more empirical understanding of creativity as a part of the intellect. J. P. Guilford, one of the pioneers in the analysis of creativity, suggests that "There is undoubtedly in this country, and possibly also in others, an undercurrent of need felt for increased creative performance and a desire to know more about the nature of creativity itself" (3, p. 142). As reasons for this national interest in creativity, he cites the growing demands for inventive thinking in science and technology; boredom, which arises from our having to behave less and less like human beings in our jobs; and the space-age appeal to our imaginations.

Thanks to the work of such men as Guilford, Getzels, Jackson, Terman, Torrance, and others, we now have scientific evidence that creativity is not an amorphous, freewheeling quality that functions as part of an unorthodox personality, but an identifiable part of the intellect which, with its attendant skills, can be measured and *can be taught*. It is beyond the scope of this chapter to survey all the findings of these men, but those factors most clearly related to the teaching of writing can hardly be ignored.

Definitions of creativity abound. Perhaps one of the best is that of Carl Rogers, who, without respect to the social value of the creative product—i.e., "good" or "bad" creativity—describes the creative process as " . . . the emergence in action of a novel relational product, growing out of the uniqueness of the individual on the one hand, and the materials, events, people, or circumstances of his life on the other" (3, p. 71).

More important to the teacher than definitions, however, is the kind of behavior which seems to identify a creative individual. Such an individual may be characterized by his tendency to think *divergently* instead of *convergently;* to rely less on the aspects of cognition and memory (most frequently measured by IQ tests); to approach learning situations in unstandardized ways; and even to appear off-beat or inferior at times in his thinking (16, pp. 185-87).

In relation to these qualities, Frost and Rowland suggest that "...*the failure phenomenon of many children, specifically the culturally disadvantaged, represents a failure of schools and teaching rather than failure of pupils* ..." (16, p. 185). They also add that "At the present time we probably have more dropouts *in* the schools than out of them, meaning that many creative people attend but may in fact be uncommitted to and largely uninvolved in pre-set, standardized goals and school-determined methods of attaining them" (16, p. 187).

Admittedly these are severe implications for the language arts teacher, especially the teacher of writing, who, with sometimes unmanageable class sizes, naturally favors learning environments which are not disruptive. But such matters have to be dealt with if the teacher is genuinely interested in the creative potential and expression of all those he teaches. And unless he clearly understands the factors which both inhibit and encourage creative expression, the teacher himself can become one of the greatest barriers to creative growth in his students.

Robert Strom identifies the following factors as most inhibitive to creative expression: (1) social expectation, including peer censure; (2) tests based on detailed memorization; (3) stereotyped sex roles; and (4) discouragement of fantasy and imagination (40, p. 83). Especially important here is the element of peer pressure. In a study of American, Greek, and Canadian children which measured attitudes toward divergence through written imaginative stories, Torrance found that American children revealed the greatest source of peer pressure. The forms of this pressure included ridicule, laughter, coercion, and isolation. American Negroes attending nonsegregated schools responded to pressure in the form of hostility, violence, ridicule, and coercion (40, p. 83).

The factors most contributive to creative expression include (1) a respect for unusual questions and ideas, (2) an atmosphere where thinking is made a legitimate classroom activity, (3) frequent periods of nonevaluative learning, and (4) an attitude of the teacher toward the student as primarily one of support (40, p. 83).

Another consideration for the teacher of writing is the relationship between creativity and level of IQ. A traditional misconception is that the two are closely enough related to suggest that one who does not possess a high IQ is not likely to be creative. The word "high" here is itself relative, but some distinctions can still be made. Getzels and Jackson, exploring whether the highly intelligent student is also the highly creative one, reached important conclusions in the areas of scholastic achievement, motivation for achievement, perception by teachers, and values.

They found that "... despite a 23-point difference in IQ between the two groups, both scored superior to the total population," and that "The creative group would probably be termed 'over-achievers' in educational settings." They also discovered that the high achievement of the creative group was not attributable to high achievement motivation; that teachers, rating students according to the degree they enjoy having them in class, rated students with high IQs as more desirable than the average student, and creative students as less desirable than the average student; and that "... the high-IQ students appeared to be highly success oriented, whereas the highly creative students did not" in terms of the values held by each group (16, pp. 184–85).

In another study, Catherine Cox of Stanford University studied 300 acknowledged creative geniuses and estimated their probable IQs on the basis of early mental traits. She concluded that the IQs of such people as Molière, Heine, Balzac, and Sir Isaac Newton were probably in the range 120–130, less than many of today's college freshmen (40, p. 79).

What all of this means to the teacher of writing should be fairly clear. It will be helpful to all concerned if we often remind ourselves to value the ideas of students first for their quality and to worry second about the correctness of their expression; to tolerate sometimes unorthodox reactions among our students; to regard our less intelligent students as well as our intelligent ones as having creative potential; to view creativity as a "real" part of the intellect; and to keep, as has been suggested, *an open mind.*

THE SLOW LEARNER AND OTHER SUCH NAMES

Also mentioned earlier was the hazard of labels, and nowhere are they more hazardous than in trying to describe students with special learning problems. One can ignore the professional and social caterwauling over such terms as "the culturally disadvantaged," "the culturally deprived," or "the culturally deficient," however, and still realize that for a variety of reasons, some students simply don't learn so quickly as others. It may be natural, after all the September planning, to be impatient when the class doesn't meet the December deadline we had so neatly set; but then maybe our plans are too rigid anyway. A more realistic concern may be the diversity of language experience which can exist in a single American classroom.

Martin Joos, in *The Five Clocks,* comments that "It is still our custom unhesitatingly and unthinkingly to demand that the clocks of language all be set to Central Standard Time," and that we still feel shame if our clock is out of step with the "English Department's tower clock" (18, p. 9). His point is especially relevant to the writing class, where in his terms, the considerations of age, style, breadth and responsibility of usage all help to determine what an individual does with language. The teacher in this class will therefore necessarily not be a keeper of time, but of time, time, time. . . .

Merely because a student learns slowly, however, one may not automatically assume that he has problems with his language. In learning to write, he will go through the same mental processes as his average or rapid classmate. According to Robert Strom, he will simply need more time, goals which are proximate, and activities which do not require a sustained effort for success. Strom found in working with slum children who had learning problems that " . . . their curiosity does not express itself in well-phrased query; they initially manifest little desire to work independently; and they seem to experience difficulty in putting ideas down on paper" (40, p. 82).

William Jenkins underscores this idea by noting that disadvantaged children have wider receptive powers than expressive ones and therefore need to express themselves as much and as often as possible (2, p. 363). And James N. Britton, discussing children from linguistically deprived homes, explains that "We need to test out in writing what we can do with the written forms, what meaning we can derive from the written forms, what meaning we can communicate in the written forms. The written language forms a gateway to most further learning," especially so for these children, " . . . because here will be the first and perhaps the greatest opportunity of coming to terms with this language which will prove so valuable later on" (7, p. 40).

Whether we are working with students who learn slowly, those who lack broad cultural exposure, or those who have narrow linguistic backgrounds, we can draw some conclusions about teaching writing from the observations of these men. First, all of these students will profit from writing activities which are frequent, brief in nature, nonevaluative, near to speech, and as creative as the interests of the student will allow. They should also probably involve a balance between structured and unstructured writing tasks. And finally, such assignments should culminate as often as possible in presentation to real audiences.

For these students, as well as for others, an imaginative teacher will take advantage of daily resources in devising such writing assignments. The atmosphere in school is as likely to change as the weather, and especially dreary days or especially bright days lend themselves to brief written reactions. Student gatherings—assemblies, pep sessions, elections—as well as discussions of controversial issues which arise from time to time are equally valuable. They not only provide the student with practice in fluency, but give him an important chance to organize his thinking and verbalize his feelings. And by all means, what the students write in such situations should be read—*then and there*. At times, the class discussions which grow out of such exercises may provide the opportunity for a longer, more formal assignment which the students would truly enjoy writing.

Another possibility for brief, nonevaluative expression may lie in the world outside the school. An occasional half hour spent writing about something he had to do, something he wanted to do, or something he voluntarily did for someone else over the weekend, may be a good way to get a student's mind working and his hand moving on Monday morning.

No less valuable for this kind of student are assignments which are more directed than free. This may be the kind of student who is rewarded by, even dependent on, the certainty of an occasional dictation. Such exercises not only test his ability to record accurately but also to listen with precision. Frances Conway has described an assignment which she uses to fill the empty spaces at the end of English class meetings that is a pleasant and profitable variation on the dictation assignment. Both she and the students play roles, she as a telephone caller or someone else with a problem; they as the recipients. Among the situations she describes are those of a waitress taking an order for a family of eight on Easter Sunday; a cashier answering the phone for a store which makes deliveries; a mechanic making a work order for a lady who gives vague directions; and an executive giving orders to a secretary for his travel itinerary (9, pp. 983, 986).

The other side of this technique is explained by Kenneth Koch in *Wishes, Lies, and Dreams*. In teaching New York City children to write poetry, he sometimes finds that children who have serious problems with fluency do well to compose orally; in effect, dictating their thoughts to him. He prefers this technique to the tape recorder for two reasons: (1) the time it takes for him to write provides the student with additional time to think, and (2) when the poem is read, the student is not distracted by the occasional noises which the recorder picks up along with the language (21, pp. 46-48).

Whatever the strategy, whatever the assignment, the importance of a real audience for the writing of the slow learner cannot be overemphasized. Using pictures from *The Family of Man* to stimulate the writing of creative short stories, Rollyn Osterweis stipulates to students that the stories must not only match the picture, but also must be meaningful to someone who hasn't seen the picture. The students provide ther own audience by testing their stories against others who haven't looked at the same picture (33, pp. 93-95).

We sometimes like to think that slow learners are far enough out of the mainstream of American high school students to occupy only a corner of the English curriculum; instead, they occupy a very significant part of the language arts enrollment. In 1965, one in every five children was classified a slow learner, and it is this group that results in the most school dropouts (40, p. 83).

EVALUATION

If a study were ever made to determine the dropout rate of teachers of English, it would no doubt show a high correlation between the demands for the teacher to assign grades to student writing and the frustration attendant on such a task. Of all the problems associated with the teaching of writing, that of evaluation is the most persistent, the most perplexing, and the most problematical.

In spite of the fact that for over 50 years attempts have been made to design a standardized test which will provide a valid measure of one's ability to write, research in this area remains skimpy. Clarence Derrick (10) lists the following four tests as those most in fashion in 1964:

Cooperative Sequential Test of Educational Progress, better known by its acronym, *STEP*. The portion used to test writing is known as the *STEP Essay.*
College Entrance Exam Boards Writing Sample (CEEB)
Advanced Placement Tests in English, by *CEEB*
General Composition Test, by *CEEB*

Derrick explains that the STEP test is inexpensive and efficient to implement because it is locally graded, but its results show fairly low reader and score reliabilities. He describes the use of the CEEB Writing Sample as little more than a public relations gesture, since the essays were not sent to colleges, no score was reported, and the college merely used them at its own discretion. The Advanced Placement Tests he regards as a luxury item and predicts that because of the expense in administering and grading, they will eventually price themselves out of the market as numbers increase. And the General Composition Test, he notes, has produced less reliable results than Scholastic Apititude Test scores or College Board's English Achievement Test. His conclusion is that all such tests should be renounced as tests of *writing,* and should be accepted only for the *skills* they measure (10, pp. 496-99).

Mr. Derrick's comments preclude a trend since the time of his writing to hold all standardized testing in some disfavor, and his conclusion is generally acceptable to most teachers of writing today. Too often, we probably deceive ourselves by thinking that we are measuring a student's ability to write through the use of such tests, when we are really doing no more than tabulating his proficiency in skill areas.

Used judiciously, however, such tests may provide valuable indexes to skill levels. A recent study by McDaniel and Pietras used creative writing samples by disadvantaged 6th-grade children in conjunction with standardized test scores to study the correlation between language arts skills and the ability to write effectively. Their conclusion: "We would like to say, based on our data, that we can profitably view disadvantaged children as we have been viewing children for years. Test scores help identify given levels of developed skills, and such skills are related to effective writing" (27, pp. 181-86).

Aside from the problems of standardized testing, it may be a credit to the creativity of the teacher that he has devised so many strategies for grading individual written work. These strategies range from giving no letter grade and some written commentary to giving two letter grades and no written commentary, with many variations between these two extremes. Some of these variations include having students grade the writing of their classmates; having them correct the writing of their classmates; having them grade or correct, in conjunction with the teacher; having them submit a series of writings, from which the teacher will grade one or two; and having the class grade or examine a sample composition on overhead projectors or through duplication procedures.

Again, research is not too helpful. One study concluded that there was no significant improvement in sentence structure of 7th-grade writers when three different evaluative measures were used: teacher correction; class correction through a formal presentation; or self-correction (5, pp. 735-47). Another found no significant difference between peer and teacher correction for compositions among 9th-grade students (5, pp. 735-47). What seems to work best at this point is whatever technique proves to the greatest satisfaction of both students and teacher. For helpful insight on how one teacher turned first-day routine into a profitable discussion of grading procedures with his students, read Richard Adler's article on "Exploring the Grading Process with Students" (1, pp. 11-16).

In recent years, the growing concern of teachers for arriving at realistic measurements of their students' work has reached national proportions, and at the Annual Meeting of the National Council of Teachers of English in 1971, the Board of Directors adopted an official policy on grading. This policy is designed to improve the student's understanding of instructional aims and his ability to assess his own growth; it is aimed toward the long-range goal of gradeless teaching. All teachers should read this policy in full, as well as the history of its development, in *Measure for Measure: The Tenth Report of the Committee on Classroom Practices* (Urbana, Illinois: The National Council of Teachers of English, 1972). This will acquaint the teacher with the present sentiment of his major subject-matter organization, and also aid him in fashioning his own scheme for evaluating student writing.

WRITING AND RELATED SKILLS

Ole Sand, quoting a National Education Association survey for the schools of the sixties, indicates that "Priorities for the school are the teaching of skills in reading, composition, listening, speaking (both native and foreign languages), and computation . . . " (14, p. 117). Traditionally, high school departments of English have entertained reading, writing, and speaking as a triadic base for the development of their curricula. They have only recently included listening as a fundamental concern for the development of their programs. This inclusion has been coincident with a complete reexamination of the relationship of all these skill areas and with a general movement in the schools toward a total, humanistic curriculum as opposed to a child-centered program. The rethinking of these problems has clearly indicated that the relationship among the four basic skill areas in the language arts is so close that their separation is merely an academic matter.

The impact of linguistics on the teaching of writing is still too recent to reveal many certainties, but the impact has been great both in terms of forcing us to consider the phenomenon of language and its relationship to the writing process. And from the encounters with the linguists, at least one certainty has permeated the ranks of English teachers: "Recent studies have confirmed what should have been plain enough from the results over the generations, that the connection [between the study of grammar and the ability to write effectively] is negligible. Apart from its possible value as a mental discipline or as knowledge interesting for its own sake, the teaching of grammar has been chiefly a waste of time" (31, p. 68).

Many school programs and textbooks still include nonfunctional grammar study, however, partly because of habit and partly because most teachers favor having materials available for teaching whatever grammatical concepts will functionally improve a student's ability to write good sentences.

It is also generally agreed today that the effectiveness of a student's writing is closely connected to the amount and quality of reading he has done. Studies by both Evelyn Barbig and Robert Lacampagne indicate that students who produce the best writing among their peers not only read more widely, but do so voluntarily (6, pp. 677-90). It seems obvious that enthusiastic readers bring to the writing situation a sensitivity to the possibility of language and an awareness of its power that the unenthusiastic or poor reader cannot know.

In fact, Shuman has suggested that " ... perhaps we have no greater job as teachers of composition than that of doing all that we can to encourage reading at every opportunity" (37, p. 400). However, we cannot really encourage reading as we should unless we are enthusiastic readers ourselves, and as writing programs tend to focus on the individual expression of students, this demand increases for the teacher. More than ever, he needs to have at his disposal as many references as possible to the interests which his students bring to the writing class.

As our interest in speaking and listening has increased, and as we have reached a more realistic understanding of language and how it is used, the relationship between speaking/listening and writing has become clearer to the teacher and more important to the writer.

Again, experiments with speaking-writing sequences have been less conclusive than we might hope for, but have not been unsuccessful in motivating students to write more freely, to reproduce their thoughts with somewhat greater clarity, and generally to compose more thoughtful papers. The use of tape recorders, role-playing, and small group discussion prove useful in encouraging students to talk their way into a writing assignment, often with an expanded frame of reference and a more favorable disposition.

WRITING AND LITERATURE

For many years, the writing course in American high schools has been shaped around the literature students have studied, and undoubtedly some of these courses have been highly successful in teaching students to write and to enjoy and understand literature. However, those who especially enjoy teaching writing or those who recognize a strong need for writing among their students, often point to the central weakness in such a format: the course becomes largely a literature course, with most of the time devoted to reading and discussing selected works, and very little time devoted to writing assignments. This is especially true in courses which combine the teaching of composition with the use of a literature anthology. The teacher may favor the security and the expedience of the reading text and thus assign few written tasks, or become a slave to the curriculum guide which indicates that a given portion of the anthology should be covered by the end of the course.

A second weakness often cited in such an approach is that the writing tends to become almost exclusively centered on literary topics, mainly because of the study of the literature, but also because such classes in the upper grades often contain students who are college bound, and the teacher honestly believes it is his duty to teach an academic kind of expression for the freshman English course.

These weaknesses are relative, of course, to the kinds of students one teaches. Highly motivated college-bound students may indeed find satisfaction in writing literary analyses, particularly if their interest in literature is genuine and if they are capable. In terms of the whole population, however, this hardly seems a feasible objective for a writing class and more often than not produces a deadly kind of prose which leads to such questions on the part of teachers as: "Of those sixty out of a hundred young people who finally show up in

Freshman Composition class, how many will ever need or wish to write again except for those interminable term papers?" (31, p. 97)

Still within the framework of the read-write approach to the teaching of writing, but markedly different from the literature anthology/composition format, is the composition course built around the reading of nonfiction. In such courses, students are often asked to read essays or articles from magazines as a springboard to written assignments on the same or related subjects. A difficult problem for the teacher of such a course lies in selecting material for reading and discussion which truly interests students and motivates them to write, or in choosing collections of essays which do not become quickly dated. Publishers have in recent years provided dozens of readers built around social or political problems of national interest. In the hands of a skilled teacher, such books can be used toward expanding the interests and the writing abilities of his students; in the hands of a careless teacher, they can become jumping-off points for sociological or political debates and little else.

None of the weaknesses mentioned here need appear in a literature-based writing class, however, whether that which is read is fiction or nonfiction. In spite of the critics of these courses, many students enjoy writing in some way about things they have read. Not only does such writing allow the student to sharpen his perspectives on his reading, but also to express his own view toward some aspect of a work. Writing parodies is popular with almost all students at some time in the development of their writing ability; writing dialogue is not only fun for many students but often increases their understanding of character; composing rejoinders to the writer of an essay provides not merely a chance to spout off one's own steam, but a valuable, even if unconscious, exercise in rhetorical analysis as well. And all of these exercises can be used in the literature-based writing course.

All levels of society have become more socially aware and to some extent more philosophically engaged by impending world issues during the past decade. Partly because of this, nonfiction now enjoys a popularity previously unknown in this century. Many high school students enjoy using such literature in exploring those thinkers who have been especially instrumental in shaping a world view, either in the past or the present.

When this is the case, two slim volumes by Robert Downs, former president of the American Library Association and head of the University of Illinois Library, may prove invaluable. *Books That*

Changed America (12) and *Books That Changed the World* (13), available in both hardcover and paperback editions, give clearly written, objective views of such major thinkers. The respective articles in these books rarely exceed 10 pages, are suitable for both average and above-average readers, and are highly useful both in terms of expanding the students' understanding of important world thinkers and of providing the basis for a wide variety of writing assignments. Such timeless essays also allow the teacher to acquire related material over a period of time from magazines and periodicals which enhance Downs' treatment of his subjects.

Another important consideration for the literature/composition teacher is the writing curriculum which precedes his own course. This is particularly true in courses where teachers assign a frequent number of papers to be written on teacher-designed topics. What may seem to the teacher to be a stimulating and exciting topic on which to write may amount to nothing more than a dull repetition of writing topics from courses during previous years. Often in the study of fiction, for example, such topics as "The Ideal Hero," "The Major Flaw in the Character of . . . ," or "The Downfall of . . . ," abound in uncomfortable frequency, and although they may be justifiable and rewarding one time, they may become boring and difficult to handle the second and third times around. With all that literature offers in the realm of idea, it is difficult to understand why such assignments must appear so often.

One good way to avoid falling into such a trap is simply to make a class exercise out of designing a series of composition topics on a work which has been studied. Students almost always enjoy having their ingenuity challenged in such a way, however unaware they may be of the levels of thinking they take themselves through in performing such exercises. The results almost always contain surprises, many of which may prove far more imaginative than what the teacher is able to think up himself.

Probably the single most important thing for a teacher in these courses to remember is that, in most cases, an overwhelming distance exists between the level of usage found in the literature the students read and the level of usage of the students themselves. Part of the writing teachers's responsibility is to help close this gap, and this *decidedly* does not mean bringing the student's level of usage to that of what appears in the literature.

What it does mean is that in whatever writing experiences take place, the teacher must *begin with the language of the student* and encourage him to broaden and shape his language to suit the level of idea with which he is working and the audience he is addressing.

This may mean that the teacher will have to assign more writing of a personal than a literary nature, eventually enabling the student to fuse his personality and the literary ideas about which he writes. Ideally, his personality should present itself in whatever he writes.

Herbert Muller, writing about the Dartmouth Conference, notes that "The British inclined to trust to the aid of literature to keep students interested in writing, and in composition to the stimulus of personal, creative writing... [whereas] the Americans were more concerned about the practical necessity of training in exposition, the kind of writing students have to do in other courses, and later on in professional memoranda and reports" (31, p. 102). This is not surprising when one considers that the British student does considerably more creative writing throughout his schooling. Thus as he approaches a greater amount of factual writing in the upper grades, he may unconsciously impose more of his "self" in all that he writes.

It is ironic that in our country we take such pride in our record of experimentation and creativity in science, yet persist in believing when we get around to writing about such things, that we must necessarily develop a prose style which is both unexperimental and unimaginative. Wouldn't an occasional "whoosh," "zoom," or "splash" be refreshing in such literature?

TEXTBOOKS

Textbooks exist because teachers demand them. Teachers demand them for a number of reasons—they are convenient, relieving the teacher of a certain degree of planning; they are expedient, providing for the class an organized format in exploring different kinds of writing experiences and information that is neatly categorized; and they are safe, allowing the teacher confidential information which prevents awkward debates with students over right and wrong answers.

None of this means that textbooks are bad. It may mean, however, that they are often misused, especially composition textbooks. The best question to ask of such books is always whether they are designed primarily for the student, containing a writing *program* which is aimed at taking him through different kinds of developmental writing experiences; or primarily for the teacher, containing basically information which he needs to know in working with what his students produce.

James Moffett criticizes most composition texts on the bases of six kinds of classified information which they often include: (1) "... advice, exhortation, and injunction,... the how-to-do-it part, the cookbook material"; (2) expository information, "... the definitions and explanations of rhetoric, grammar, logic, and semantics"; (3) exercises; (4) "... the presentation of samples of good writing to serve as models"; (5) "... writing stimulants ... closely related to models because sometimes these prompters are also reading selections"; and (6) "... assignment directions themselves" (30, pp. 201-9). His criticism is not merely vituperative. He does not deny each of these aspects as harmful in themselves, but warns that their irresponsible or thoughtless use often leads to a kind of oversimplification in the teaching of writing which actually promotes rather than solves problems.

The point is a valid one but is characterized by an irony of which Moffett himself is fully aware: "I believe the teacher should be given a lot of help for the very difficult job of teaching writing. A lot of what is in textbooks should be in books for teachers, and is in fact partly there to educate them, not the students. The real problem, as I think many educators would admit, is that too many teachers cannot do without textbooks because they were never taught in schools of education to teach without them" (30, p. 209).

Undoubtedly, schools of education could improve in the area of training to which he refers, but the problem is not exclusively theirs. A significant number of composition teachers receive minimal training in schools of education. Rather, they come to their own classrooms by way of college English departments, which are only remotely concerned with "how" students learn to write. As English majors, most new composition teachers have had practically no training in the teaching of writing. They have written many papers of their own, which may partially explain the plethora of "The Major Weakness in the Character of ... " type assignments, but which will hardly serve the needs of an inexperienced teacher.

In addition, the textbook problem has been compounded by the recent trend among publishers to offer large numbers of texts of a specialized variety, often largely motivational in nature. Such books will often be designed around a single aspect of writing, such as "personal writing," "style," "rhetoric," "point of view"; or around particular gimmicks for stimulating students to write, such as pictures, dialogues, or films. Again, these texts may prove helpful in *enhancing* certain composition courses, but they are of limited help in establishing confidence for an inexperienced teacher who may still be grappling with a workable terminology to use in commenting on his students' writing.

As the teacher gains confidence in handling the material of his course, he will probably rely less and less on formal textbook instruction. But as a beginner, he is in a position to do little else. He will learn most quickly and develop his own effective techniques by viewing judiciously whatever text he has, asking as many questions as possible of his fellow teachers, reading as widely as possible in professional journals, and taking advantage of in-service training in the teaching of writing.

THE LANGUAGE OF WRITING

All writing eventually obtains an identity which, in order to be discussed, requires some kind of transactional language. Despite the well-meaning intentions of the teacher who records such comments as "good general discussion," "interesting style, but mechanics need some attention," or "aside from organizational problems, a pretty good discussion of the subject," students will quickly and rightly dismiss such jargon as meaningless. It will remain meaningless as long as the student is forced to rely on his own often vague notions of what "style" means, for example, or as long as the teacher is unable to define in mutual agreement with the student, just what *he* means by such words.

This language of writing is further complicated by the way it is treated in many composition texts, by its relationship to the technical language of literature, and by the changing hues of meaning which some of its terms acquire from time to time. Typically, writing texts treat the terminology of writing in one of two ways. In books which focus on a series of programmed or sequential assignments, this language will appear in subordinate positions within given assignments, usually in the middle or at the end of the assignment directions. Books which focus more clearly on the technical aspects of writing will introduce a term as a concept, then build an assignment from or around it. In either case, the language remains in sufficient isolation to be of little benefit to the student.

In the first of these formats, for example, a term such as "point of view" may appear in a chapter on writing description, and "style" in a token chapter dealing with creative writing at the end of the book. The student, and sometimes the teacher, fails to remember that everything he writes is characterized by both. In the second format, a chapter dealing with "point of view" may include a variety of writing activities built around this term, but when the student has finished that chapter and moves to the next one, which may focus on "methods of development," he again fails to make the essential connection.

A second obstacle to workable terminology is the relationship which the language of writing shares with the language of literature. One might correctly argue that since literature is writing, there should be no difference, but he may be hard pressed to defend his point when a student points to a passage in his writing text which describes "mood" as the attitude of the writer toward his verbs, i.e., indicative, subjunctive, etc., and a passage in his literature book which claims "mood" as a "general feeling which the author creates in a story by the details he selects." Imagine the confusion which results from a teacher's wanting the student to work on changing the quality of his verbs, and a student's thinking that in order to improve the "mood" in a piece of writing he will have to concentrate on a different quality of descriptive word.

Finally, such language achieves meaningless proportions through the shades of meaning which some terms acquire as they come and go out of fashion. The two best examples of the moment are probably the words *creative* and *rhetoric*. These words are enjoying wide current use, with such a broad range of professional and social referents that they may mean nearly anything. Thus, both a student and a teacher may feel perfectly comfortable with them for opposite reasons. Also important here is the student who may have met these terms in a speech class. Not long ago, one student confidently asserted that "Oh yes, she had studied 'torical questions when they did their demonstration speeches."

All of this is by no means to suggest that effective writing or growth in writing is contingent upon a mastery of such transactional terms. Rather, it is to indicate the problems a teacher faces in trying to establish a basis for dialogue with his students about what they have written. Perhaps an ingenious person could achieve the same thing by ignoring these terms altogether and working out a color code, by which the student would understand that when his "green" is out of order, he has failed to make some important considerations concerning his audience. But why complicate the matter by devising an entire scheme of new language? The old will be sufficient if it is clearly understood.

In fact, it may be necessary to add no more than two new words. For the teacher who is struggling to make sense of a pile of old and new textbooks, the curriculum guide, a stack of professional journals, and old college notes, it may be helpful for him to think of any piece of writing as having certain properties after it is once composed. These properties vary less in kind than in degree from expository to creative writing, in spite of how they may be treated by the writing and the literature textbooks. Because these properties literally "constitute" writing once it is written, it is convenient to refer to them as "composition constituents," thus avoiding the confusion which results from trying to group such terms under "organization," "mechanics," "structure," or whatever else. Toward a more cogent expression of what one feels should be done to improve or change a piece of writing, the composition constituents scheme, which deliberately uses traditional terminology, may prove helpful.

COMPOSITION CONSTITUENTS

1. Subject analysis
   - a) focus (the boundaries of the subject; setting)
   - b) thesis (burden of proof or major idea explored)
   - c) refocus (major points within the boundaries of the subject which support item [b])
2. Substance (the meat, commonly the body or bulk of the writing)
3. Audience
4. Length-proportion (both determined largely by the analysis of the subject)
5. Point of View:
   - a) speaker or narrator
     1. first person
     2. third person omniscient
     3. partially omniscient
   - b) distance or angle
     1. physical
     2. psychological
     3. technical
        - (a) person   (e) mood
        - (b) number   (f) tone
        - (c) tense   (g) voice
        - (d) case
6. Handling of the substance
   - a) mode
     1. narrative
     2. descriptive
     3. expository
     4. argumentative
     5. lyrical
     6. dramatic
   - b) method
     1. details
     2. examples
     3. comparison
     4. cause/effect
     5. definition
     6. dialogue
     7. scene
   - c) movement (or plot)
     1. chronological
     2. spatial
     3. logical
        - (a) deductive
        - (b) inductive
7. Structure
8. Coherence
9. Unity
10. Mechanics (spelling, punctuation, grammar, usage)

STYLE

RHETORIC

Such an attempt to reconcile the language most often used in expository composition and general literature texts may seem at first too arbitrary, perhaps too simplistic. To some degree it is both. To equate "movement," a term often used in discussing expository prose, with "plot," usually restricted to an analysis of fiction without pointing to the intricacies of conflict, climax, resolution, etc., may be stretching a point; or to couple the expository "thesis statement" with the fictional "major idea explored," may be unfair. In each case, considerable qualification is needed. But to demand such qualification here is to ignore the purpose of the groupings in the first place. A beginning teacher should have a functional enough understanding of all the terms to make the proper distinctions for himself, but it should help him to see juxtaposed those words which often create confusion between student and teacher.

Aristotle, Quintilian, or even a modern scholar of rhetoric might shudder to see all of these constituents (among which are scattered some aspects of classical rhetoric) bracketed toward the emergence of style and rhetoric. But if one can accept style, in its broadest sense, as the "imprint of the writer's self on what he writes," he will see that such an imprint occurs through the characteristic handling of all these constituents. And if a general definition of rhetoric as " . . . largely an instrument to increase the range of rational choice in speech and writing" (32, p. 15), or as the "fullest and most calculated development of thought," will suffice for the teacher of writing, he will see that rhetoric, too, depends on the orchestration of these factors.

The beginning teacher who relies too heavily on this arrangement of the language of writing may himself eventually oversimplify his analysis of what his students write; the teacher who objects too strenuously will probably never discover a strategy that is altogether certain; the teacher who can use it as a point of departure for meaningful conversation with his students about the craft and the art of writing will save himself an enormous amount of precious time.

FLUENCY

Fluency, according to Paul Roberts, " . . . we can define as simply the ability to get your ideas on paper in a reasonable length of time" (35, p. 3). And, of course, one immediately asks, "How many ideas does any person have?" and "What is a reasonable length of time?" Actually neither is too important to the person who simply cannot make his hand move across the page in a smooth, continual way, recording without hesitation his ideas as they occur to him. An uncomfortable number of low performance grades in our schools may be traced to the problem of fluency in writing, perhaps because the reasons for a lack of fluency may be manifold. The physical and psychological environments in which students write; the embarrassment (and sometimes the reprimand) attendant on a poor handwriting; confusion of subject matter; the fear of an inaccurate response; and above all, poor spelling are among those factors most contributive to the problem.

Too often teachers mistake a problem in fluency for ignorance or inability, mainly because they are not trained to look for signals. Furthermore, the causes may be so remote that the teacher is never able to determine them precisely. But he can at least alert himself to the possibility of this problem by paying special attention to the following kinds of written work: underwritten, overwritten, and haltingly written.

In the present context, an underwritten paper is one in which a student is able to produce a mechanically perfect token, say 100-150 words in 10 minutes or less. This student may actually have a number of ideas at his disposal, or an impressive amount of correct data, but practically all of it is lost in his preoccupation with correctness. So conscious is he of the appropriateness of his usage, grammar, or form that he cannot avoid sacrificing what he thinks or knows for "right" writing. Unfortunately, his self-consciousness can often be traced to the expectation of teachers, previous or present. The same kind of paper may be produced by the student who suffers too great a preoccupation with high grades, wherein the teacher may in no way be responsible. Indeed, the student's home may be as much to blame as any other agency for such inhibitions. Finally, this kind of writing is often found among students who are forced to make dramatic shifts in usage, particularly students from dialect homes. J. L. Dillard mentions such a group of students in an anthropology class. Those who felt free to express themselves in their natural dialect made noticeably better scores than those who felt the need to transpose their ideas from their dialect to standard English (11, pp. 276-77).

The overwritten paper may indicate just as serious a fluency problem as the underwritten paper. This paper is characterized not just by a greater amount of prose than that produced by others in the same writing situation, but by a greater amount that is punctuated almost entirely by commas and contains a number of words used erroneously or nonsensically. Overwritten papers may also be those which demonstrate an unusual quantity of prose, all of which is practically illegible. Students who write such papers often do so for the same reasons which cause their classmates to produce underwritten papers, but they unconsciously look at their problem through the opposite end of the telescope. These students may have suffered at the hands of teachers who placed too great a premium on quantity, thus forcing the student to extend his ideas to unmanageable proportions, or to pad with meaningless or erroneous words. Some students who tend to punctuate only with commas are actually disguising their fear of incorrect punctuation or sentence completion in the hope that quantity will impress the teacher sufficiently that he will overlook mechanical weaknesses. And finally, the paper which is 90 percent illegible may have been written by the student who is afraid that his natural fluency will not produce sufficient quality for teacher expectations, and he too has found a way of overcompensating.

Finally, fluency problems may be indicated by papers which are haltingly written. The earmarks of these papers include great leaps in thought; excessive paragraphing; or the omission of important words, sometimes whole phrases *next to misspelled words.* Sometimes the student in this case will create illogical leaps in thought because of his reluctance to express part of what he is thinking. Thus he will hesitate to censor such ideas, then proceed, often with detail that is actually part of a new idea or that refers to an idea two or three sentences back. This kind of hesitation may also lead to excessive paragraphing, especially four or five paragraphs in a row which contain no more than one or two short sentences. When this happens, the student has really deliberated long enough to produce an appropriate paragraph, but has not recorded all he has been thinking. Unconsciously he begins a new paragraph as if he *had* recorded this thinking.

The paper which omits important words or whole phrases next to misspelled words probably contains the most characteristic signal of poor fluency. Consider the following examples, typical of this kind of paper:

1. The counterversal speakers [in favor of the new law] defeated themselves with the audience.
2. I was so embrassed [when I dropped the hamburger] I didn't eat lunch anymore for a month.

In both cases, the student has realized his difficulty with the words "controversial" and "embarrassed," and has pondered over them so long that when he resumes his writing, he unconsciously omits some of what he intended or needed to say.

Even the most fluent person is not able to record all that passes through his mind, for the hand and the mind simply do not work at the same speeds. But the more fluent one becomes, the more chance he has for exploring the possibilities of his thought, the possibilities of language, and the increasing effectiveness of his expression.

Fortunately, when a lack of fluency is the result of the errors described here, it is one of the most correctable of writing problems. If a teacher can be sensitive to such problems, develop a rapport with the student which will allow an honest description of the problem, and give him a bit of reassurance, the student will often increase his fluency very quickly. If the student who "underwrites" can be assured that he will not be severely punished for an occasional mechanical error, he will generally begin to express himself more freely. The "overwriter," if he can believe that the teacher will accept the quality of his ideas, will gear himself down to plain, direct speech with amazing quickness. And the student who worries over his inability to spell correctly may be reassured to know that about half the writing of the normal adult will consist of a repertoire of about 100 basic words (2, p. 365).

If the student is to grow in the short time that he is with any one writing teacher, however, the analysis and correction of fluency problems should begin almost immediately. Early in the course, for example, the teacher might ask the students to do a timed writing, which necessitates only very clear directions—(1) to write about three things which bother, amuse, interest, or concern (any one of these is sufficient) the student, and (2) to write as fast as possible until the teacher says to stop. After the students have written for 8 or 10 minutes, the teacher can collect the papers, scan them for the kinds of writing described above, and perhaps identify students with fluency problems.

Once he has identified such students, the teacher can usually rely on two kinds of writing activity to help correct the problem: free, nonevaluative writing, done frequently and for short periods of time; and timed dictations, also frequent and also short. The nature of the fluency problem will help determine which kind of activity is most appropriate, and with minimal consideration, this is usually obvious.

JOURNALS

One of the most popular forms of free or nonevaluative writing during recent years has been the journal. "Popular" doesn't necessarily mean good, but whether the journal is used to a minor or major extent in the teaching of writing, it seems to serve a useful purpose; namely, that it enables the student to practice the physical and mental processes of writing.

In its simplest form, the journal is merely a running commentary by the student on any number of subjects, some suggested by the teacher to stimulate a reaction among the students, others completely the result of what the student happens to be thinking about at a given time. When used in this way, the journal often becomes a part of class routine, the students writing daily or at least periodically for 5 or 10 minutes during some portion of the class hour.

Some teachers like to collect the journals at intervals, read them, even comment on what has been written. Others prefer never to read what the student has written unless the student requests it. Used even in this simple way, the journal is helpful in at least two ways; it creates an ongoing writing situation for the student in which he can increase his fluency and have some fun with ideas and with language; and it helps the teacher fill awkward end-of-the-period gaps, when the business of the day has been completed. Generally students enjoy this kind of journal writing, although some may need to be shown its value if they feel that what they are writing is never going to be read by another person.

The uses of the journal are by no means confined to this simple approach, however. In fact, they are limited only by the imagination of the teacher. In more ambitious ways, journals are sometimes used as a basis for class discussion, an inroad to future writing assignments, or as a bridge between personal and expository writing. In connection with this last approach, they may even serve as practice in one kind of reading skill.

The journal can be a valuable aid as a basis for class discussion. In this case, the students are asked to share their journals with other members of the class. Having made several entries, the students pass their journals around the class or dump them in a pile on a table from which each person takes one to read thoughtfully for 20 minutes or so. As they read what others have written, they are asked to concentrate both on what has been said and on how it has been said. Written comments are welcome, including both comments on the content and the writing itself. After the journals have been read, the teacher asks for suggestions for discussion topics which emerge from the journal writing. A list is made on the chalkboard, the students vote on one or two they would most prefer talking about, and a discussion follows.

A good follow-up to this kind of activity is to ask students to write again in their journals following the discussion. The teacher may wish to collect the journals after this writing, to skim for ideas which were not expressed verbally or to look for significant changes in the point of view of one student or another. If the class is very much engaged by the topic under discussion, the teacher can carry it even further by compiling a profile of the salient points of discussion from the journals after skimming the postdiscussion writing. And of course, there is the possibility that all this might culminate in either a creative or expository paper on the topic.

One point which teachers often overlook in using the journal is that students are also interested in what teachers think about when they are not concentrating on run-on sentences or misspelled words. Could not a teacher also keep a journal and submit it for student reading, just as the students submit theirs to the class? It may prove a good way of enhancing interest and generating thought.

Another approach to the use of the journal involves the student's keeping track of his thinking for future reference. Here the student is usually invited to write in his journal at any time he feels the need for recording an interesting observation, idea, or reaction he has experienced. Later he is asked to use his journal as a professional writer often uses a notebook; it contains the genesis of ideas for expansion, modification, or refinement. When students use the journal in this way, they are often surprised at what they recorded a month previously. In some cases, they realize that a single idea has asserted itself in their thinking without their being aware of it; and when they give it additional thought, they may be motivated to create a piece of writing around this idea. At other times, they will wonder that they ever conceived of such claptrap, and discard it immediately.

Again, the exchange of journals among members of the class may prove worthwhile. Often, upon reading a classmate's writing, a student will be able to suggest ideas worthy of further development that the writer himself is unaware of, or he may be moved to borrow from what a classmate has written to use for his own composition purposes.

When the journal is to be used as a basis for further writing

ASSIGNMENTS

Depending on one's approach to the teaching of writing, "assignment" may be a dirty word. Indeed, some teachers feel that for a student to grow honestly in his writing, he should not be given prefabricated or canned tasks to follow, that he will generate his own assignments as he increases the amount of writing he can produce. In such an approach, the teacher acts as reader, prompter, critic—both a catalyst and helpmate to the student as he explores the possibilities of his own expression. For successful implementation, however, this approach usually calls for a master teacher and a fairly small class.

Most teachers still find that some kind of help in devising meaningful writing activities is needed by the student to expand his general frame of reference. It is also an aid to the teacher in terms of organizing his course. This help is usually expressed in the form of an assignment. The teacher in search of good writing assignments may do well to make three considerations: common pitfalls in designing assignments, short-range assignments, and long-range assignments.

From his work with student teachers, Edmund Farrell, assistant executive secretary of the National Council of Teachers of English, has derived the following helpful list of "don'ts" for the teacher making assignments:

1. Avoid assignments which can be answered by "yes" or "no."
2. Avoid assignments that lead to short, often fragmentary responses: "How did you feel when you finished . . . ?"
3. Avoid assignments that lead to idle speculation or that may be treated frivolously: "Factors which might have caused Shirley Jackson to write such a story."
4. Avoid assignments which are vague or which assume knowledge students may not possess: "Elaborate on the symbolism in 'The Lottery.'"
5. Avoid assignments which, by posing numerous questions, provoke incoherency.
6. Avoid assignments which a student may regard as too personal.
7. Avoid assignments which pit a novice writer against a professional (15, p. 429).

Short-range assignments are usually those which can be written either on the spot, that is, within the space of a class hour, or those which the teacher calls for in a day or so. Many of these assignments may be formulaic in nature, outlining for the student a system to follow, or offering him a preconceived idea of the dimensions of the assignment. The *haiku, cinquain,* and *sestina* enjoy wide use in this respect, primarily for their deliberate yet simple structure and brevity. Also popular in prose assignments of this sort are short direct paragraphs which create a dominant impression of character, depict a specific situation, or describe a given setting. The more self-reliant the student writer becomes, the less need he may have for such exercises; but students with very limited writing experience often profit from the feeling of accomplishment that comes with a finished product, no matter how awkward or rough it may appear to an experienced reader. Exercises of this type also are convenient space fillers between longer assignments, when some students have completed work ahead of their classmates and lack something else to do.

Long-range assignments, of course, are those which extend over days or weeks and may involve many steps before they are actually completed. Long-range does not have to mean "one piece of writing of great length," however. Students often enjoy long-term activities which involve assembling several short pieces in sequential or thematic order. Also they enjoy mixing writing forms in such assignments — prose and verse, perhaps, unified by monologues or dialogues. In long-range planning, it will prove helpful to the student if he is allowed to accumulate a sizable number of writing samples before he is asked to assemble them in a major assignment. Thus he has the privilege of looking critically at what he has written, choosing what he feels is his best work, perhaps revising some which doesn't meet his present standard.

Some classes profit greatly from doing "class" assignments on a long-term basis. Here, students usually pool writing from the folder of each person in the class; read all that is contributed; suggest topics from their reading for the class to build a total project around; appoint some members of the class as an editorial board, others as proofreaders, and still others as typists. Ultimately each member of the class assumes a particular responsibility in the final product, yet each is engaged in some important aspect of the total writing process. This is also an excellent way for students to see the intricacies of publishing material.

HOMEWORK

The question of how much, if any, or what kind of out-of-school assignment should be made to students has raged for nearly as long as homework has been part of the American school pattern. Few people deny that the high school student will necessarily perform some work at home which is relative to his major assignments in the classroom. But the controversy does not center on such work; it centers on the traditional exercises or drills which students long ago recognized as inconsequential, either in terms of what they seemed to be learning or in terms of the regard paid to such tasks by the teacher himself. Few students today are willing to settle for 15 check marks in the teacher's grade book as the constituent of a high performance grade. This is not to say that students unconditionally resist periodic evaluations, for some regard them as security measures against poor examination grades. Slow learners especially may find the idea of skill tasks done at home and submitted for a grade somewhat rewarding, because it indicates to them that they are indeed making progress in their subject.

Most students, however, have come to resist traditional homework to a point of simply not doing it. And teachers in many schools have begun to reconsider the matter not only in the light of student resistance, but also in relation to new ideas about intelligence, learning, and the importance of healthy attitudes on the part of the student. Moreover, overcrowded schools in many parts of the country have been faced with such critical scheduling problems that some students attend school only during a portion of the day when their classes meet. Increasingly, study halls are being eliminated, class periods are being shortened or modified toward greater efficiency, and in general, a greater premium is being placed on the efficient use of everyone's time.

More flexible scheduling has also provided the student with more time away from school, which allows many of them to hold jobs, and only the highly motivated, self-sufficient student can manage the pressure commensurate with the many activities which govern his life. In short, there is little time.

Part of the rethinking process among educators which has altered administrative plans, fostered new teaching techniques, and reconsidered the interests and needs of the student, has focused on the problem of homework, and a new view entertains the issue with a different question than previously asked. Instead of "What should the student be asked to take home?" we are now beginning to ask, "What can the student bring to school?" What, among the dozens of occupations or preoccupations which face the student each day, can he bring to *enhance* the in-class learning situation? How can he begin to integrate the many things he thinks about, is stimulated by, worries over, or dreams of with the concepts which we presumably are trying to teach in the classroom itself?

In a recent issue of *Illinois Schools Journal,* Marlow Ediger is credited with saying that " ... students may profitably engage in activities involving 'interviewing; making models, charts, tables, and graphs; visiting a place of interest; collecting pictures relating to a unit being studied in school; and listening to a program or news broadcast on radio or television' " (38, p. 208). Later in the same article, the authors, R. Baird Shuman and Henry Sublett, Jr., suggest that "Where coordination is ideal, a student's outside work in one of his courses should contribute to what he is learning in every other course" (38, p. 209).

In perhaps no other course the student takes is he more likely to make good use of his daily out-of-school activities than in a composition class. Here he is free to draw from the experiences he has with others in his job, in the home, or among friends. He can select from the broad range of media those observations he feels contribute in some meaningful way to what he is writing. He can choose from a countless variety of printed matter—billboards, magazines, newspapers, handbills, menus, road markings, driving instructions, safety regulations—hundreds of details to support or embellish the major points in a piece of writing.

Furthermore, a resourceful teacher can turn some of these observations into challenging and engaging out-of-school assignments. Writers of billboard advertisements probably have more fun with language than any English teacher in the country. Why not challenge him by joining the students in noting especially clever uses of language, misleading or careless language, or language that could make its point with twice the power and half the number of words?

Or the teacher might hold 30-minute gab sessions on Monday morning to find out what kind of activities students were engaged in over the weekend and eventually ask the class how such experiences might be incorporated into what they are writing. He might also find out what students read when they are not in school and capitalize on their reading interests in the writing class, not merely by asking them to react to content, but also by asking them to assess the quality of writing which they find in popular magazines. Or he might discuss films with students, and relate them to what has appeared in student journals or other free writing activities.

The teacher might also ask students who have jobs to describe to the class their most unusual customer, their nicest customer, or their most annoying customer. Or he may at some time suggest that they share their impressions of behavior in shopping centers; what unusual behavior have they noticed at a local mall.

Instead of asking students to watch a television show merely because it appears to be educationally sound, perhaps the teacher should inquire about television viewing habits and tastes, encourage the students to think critically about what they have watched, and consider how a good writer might handle the subject more effectively.

Shuman and Sublett also noted that "Well-planned, long-ranging out-of-school assignments can make some students experts in fields of their own interests and can, at the same time, contribute dramatically to their progress in school" (38, p. 210). These kinds of assignments can either be built around subjects or topics which interest the student keenly because of what he already knows, or they may take the form of inquiries, allowing the student to pursue ideas he has never had the chance to investigate thoroughly.

One teacher accomplished this by allowing his students to correspond with a group of peers in a different part of the country. As a group, the class decided to focus their own letters on the following four points: (1) personal introduction, (2) information on their city or town, (3) information about their school, and (4) personal interests. The result was that both New Englanders and Californians wrote themselves into new understandings of themselves and past the stereotyped pictures of their peers they had previously accepted (8, pp. 984-86).

Obviously, the list of possibilities for assignments which enable the student to grow and to sustain his interest in learning at the same time is interminable. Why, with any thought on the part of the teacher, and any meaningful exchange between him and his students, should there ever really be a problem in this area?

GROUP WORK

Not too many years ago group work was fairly uncommon in American schools, especially at the high school level. In the past 10 years or so, at least two important factors have contributed to the popularity and widespread acceptance of this kind of teaching/learning strategy: a change in attitude on the part of educators toward lockstep learning, and increasing class size in most secondary schools. As we have revised our thinking about learning rates, realizing that not all students progress in the same manner at the same pace, we have broken away from the traditional lockstep format which characterized schools in this country for most of this century.

Within the classroom this has allowed a greater variety of learning situations, and psychologists and teachers have discovered that students often learn as much from each other as they do from a teacher who stands at the front of the room and talks to them. The small group process has been the first step in the departure from that format, and current research indicates that students not only acquire as much information through this strategy as they formerly did, but also that they increase essential communication skills, more quickly overcome psychological barriers to learning, and clarify their value systems through discourse with peers and adults.

Also, in recent years, teachers have been assigned increasingly heavy teaching loads, often with class sizes exceeding 30 or 35 students. With such unwieldly numbers, the teacher feels hard pressed to keep his class meaningfully organized and everyone busy at some constructive activity.

The small group process, in its various forms, has been a logical move on the teacher's part toward a more expedient way of solving these problems. Such a change demands a sometimes radical revision in the teacher's own thinking concerning his role in the classroom; but when he is able to view himself as an adjunct to learning rather than a provider of knowledge, he can generally make the necessary transition painlessly.

Considerable literature is available which deals with the group-process concept, and an attempt to review it is not appropriate to this chapter. However, a few general comments and suggestions, drawn from the publication of the Institute for the Development of Educational Activity, Dayton, Ohio, may prove especially helpful to a beginning teacher or to one who has not tried such techniques before. Below are two short lists, the first enumerating points for the basic understanding required of a teacher who plans to use small groups; the second listing the most basic principles of operation of the small group:

Features of the Basic Understanding of the Teacher

1. The teacher relinquishes his role as the center of attention and becomes an associate in the learning process; consequently, this means more rather than less involvement with students.
2. The teacher must develop clear and explicit instructional objectives.

3. He must perceive the nature of the subject matter, understandings, and skills that he wishes to encourage by the use of this technique.
4. He must learn how to frame the questions and the tasks assigned to the group so that they aim in the desired direction.
5. He must be careful not to preclude unexpected outcomes that also can provide valuable learning for the students.
6. He must understand the various roles that the individual may play within any small-group situation.

Basic Principles of Operation of the Small Group

1. The normal size of the dicussion group should be from 5 to 8 students.
2. The teacher should make certain that the chairman understands his role.
3. An attractive room environment, proper furniture, and good acoustics aid greatly in the production of better discussions.
4. The time of the discussions should be planned so that the group will adjourn when interest starts to drop off. Most experiments suggest that 15-30 minutes is a fairly good median.
5. Participants should be provided with basic fact sheets if the topics will be better discussed with such information available.
6. The teacher should plan a topic that will stimulate thinking and help the student realize that many right answers exist representing a variety of viewpoints.
7. Students should formulate, or be provided with, clearly defined objectives for each small-group discussion (17, passim).

The small group can serve many purposes in the writing class, the most conventional ones being to stimulate student thinking through discussion; to provide an immediate audience for what has been written; and to enable students to evaluate the papers of their classmates. Probably the most frequent form of this approach as a vehicle for student discussion is that described earlier in this chapter under the heading of "Journals." Students break into small groups, discuss a topic briefly, compile their findings, compare results, sometimes resume discussion either in the small group or among the class as a whole, etc. Often the result is more spirited writing, less groping on the part of the student for the dimensions of a subject, and more details at his ready disposal.

To some extent, the use of the small group as a means of providing an audience for what students have written has also been treated here. However, some additional comments may illustrate less customary variations which prevent the awkward repetition of merely dividing into groups to read and discuss. One variation which students enjoy, mainly because it often proves to be both challenging and creative, is to restrict the discussion in all groups to a single alternative writing form for what they are reading.

For example, if students are reading a set of short papers by their classmates, the teacher might ask them to read only with the possibility in mind of adapting what they are reading to an appropriate form for a speech, a poem, a play, etc. Students themselves often overlook real possibilities in their own work and the problems involved in remaking a piece of writing to suit a different purpose.

An alternative for the small-group discussion is to ask students to consider the piece of writing on which they happen to be working in terms of a different age level audience. If they are reading poetry which classmates have written, for example, they may be encouraged to specify what changes would have to be made in order to convey essentially the same point of a poem to an audience of six year olds, a group of factory workers, a school board, or a group of college professors. Students find this kind of activity profitable, since they often direct their writing to their own age level, and although this in itself has many advantages, it may sharpen their perspectives on the writing process itself to entertain different audiences. In many cases, this is asking too much of individual students; they need the kind of exchange which the small group will provide.

Finally, the small group process lends itself to the evaluation of writing by members of the class. This can become troublesome and repetitive, however, if the same format is used too often. The conventional approach here is merely to have students read and comment on what their classmates have written, and sometimes this proves helpful, particularly if the students are unusually perceptive. It may also help improve mechanics, since the range of ability level in terms of "correctness" will vary greatly within the same classroom. But the students often tire of this process, finding that the same comments appear with too much frequency, largely because the student reader can't think of original or stimulating things to say.

In this respect, it is helpful to ask two, even three students to read the same paper, assign it a grade, and not disclose that grade until all have completed their evaluation. Then the students should compare the grades they have given the same paper. Often the discussion which emerges among three or four classmates, defending their own evaluation against another's, elicits more constructive criticism than does a single reading by one student and the teacher. Obviously, to make this most beneficial, the writer should be present when the evaluation of his work is being discussed by his graders.

This is not to suggest that the grade arrived at by those discussing the paper should be a final one. It may only be used as an indicator to the writer of the chances for his paper at a given stage. Perhaps rewriting will take place before the paper is ever formally submitted for a grade.

One more point should be made about group work in general. More and more people are realizing that for too long we have allowed the elementary teacher and the secondary teacher to remain in separate professional camps. In many areas, especially in that of the small group process, the elementary teacher can provide valuable insight for the secondary teacher who may be less experienced in the approach. Some of the most creative and significant group activity takes place in the elementary classroom, and there is no reason to believe that many of the learning strategies which are used there are not equally valuable for the secondary classroom.

One should read what master teachers such as Hughes Mearns, or more recently, Kenneth Koch and Stephen Joseph have accomplished with young children, working in sometimes purely spontaneous ways with rather sizable groups of children. Two helpful books by Mearns include *Creative Power* (29) and *Creative Youth* (28). Those by Koch and Joseph include *Wishes, Lies, and Dreams* (21), and *The Me Nobody Knows: Children's Voices from the Ghetto* (19).

STUDENT PROFILES

The word "profile" may at first have too clinical a ring to it for some teachers, since it often carries the connotation of a cumulative record of the student's performance on a series of tests, or a longitudinal record of his growth. In a sense, these meanings apply to the word in the context of a writing class, but are secondary rather than primary. Here, the word refers to a profile that is first collective, then individual. A quick and versatile tool for the teacher, an often enlightening vehicle for the student, the profile may be used to indicate the scope of reactions among the students to a particular issue; to indicate multiple points of view in a single writing assignment; or perhaps most importantly, to enable the student to see himself in relation to his peers in an examination situation.

The simplest use of the profile involves merely asking the students to respond in writing to a given issue or problem before discussing it; collecting the papers; and recording the one or two major reactions from each paper. This is less time-consuming than it may appear, for when this is done, the teacher is reading for specific material, and does not have to linger over any one paper. Recording the class data is also a task which may be done by an able student in the class, or a student office helper.

When the profile is complete, the teacher presents it to the class, either by reading it to them or preferably presenting it in duplicated form; asks them to consider its aspects; and begins a discussion. Any number of writing problems may present themselves on the way to resolving student opinion, which may never be resolved, by the way; or which, on the other hand, may be too uniform even to discuss for any length of time. At the discretion of the teacher, the profile used in this way is generally both expedient and fun.

It may be equally useful in illustrating for the class the range of approach and technique used by student writers for any one assignment, providing all or at least a significant number, have written on the same topic. In this instance, the teacher will want to skim papers, usually separating those which seem most original, most unoriginal, or indicative of a certain strength or weakness which he feels the class would profit by considering.

Again, a few selections are duplicated and distributed to the class for discussion and evaluative comment. If the teacher has not tried this approach, he will likely be surprised at the insight which is provided through class discussions of such material. It is usually more valuable in such cases if the papers are printed anonymously; therefore, during a discussion the writer may have the privilege of hearing his work praised by a person with whom he is not well acquainted, or in some cases, hear his work severely criticized by his best friend. In either case, it is often to his advantage to hear an honest response. Students seem to take readily to this strategy. It is particularly good for a shy student who may be reluctant to show his work to other people for fear of rejection. He may need the kind of praise which the profile can provide for him.

Perhaps one of the most valuable ways to use the student profile in a writing class is to compile a cross section of responses on an essay examination to enable the student to view his performance in relation to other ability levels represented on the same test. Lawrence Blondino (4) has used nearly the same approach with success in the teaching of literature by offering his students what he calls "the class answer," to make them more aware of the range of responses and potential for analysis (4, pp. 1032-35), but it seems even more essential in a writing class, or in any class where some uniform testing through writing takes place.

For one thing, students often feel that a teacher reads essay responses capriciously, relying too much on the student's ability in oral work, the clarity of his handwriting, or the personal effect he has on the teacher. And in truth, teachers often do rely on just such things. Because it is difficult for a teacher not to be effected by these factors, the profile justifies itself fully. By presenting to the student what, under these circumstances, must be a more thoughtful reading of his response, the teacher establishes a much more negotiable atmosphere for determining results in essay tests.

The most expedient way to handle this form of the profile is to represent the full range of class ability on any one question. For example, when reading the tests, the teacher arranges the responses in three stacks—high, low, and average. He then goes through them again, refining the first reading by further separating extremely high and extremely low papers. He looks also in this reading for what may be termed a "maverick" response, i.e., one which clearly does not respond to the question asked on the test, or does so in an acceptable but perplexing way, thereby presenting problems in evaluation. He then reproduces one response from each stack, including any maverick papers, arranging them in random order to avoid an oversimplified reading by students—that is, merely accepting the first as best, the last as worst, and numbering them from one to five or one to six.

The teacher should not return the tests until a lesson using the profiles is completed. After making any comments of a general nature about the test, the teacher should distribute the duplicated responses and give the class 10 to 15 minutes to study them carefully. He should instruct each student to rank the responses from "high" to "low" by rearranging their numbers in the margin. He should insist that no discussion occur, no sharing of individual rankings to ensure that each student is thinking for himself. When the students appear to be finished, the teacher may ask for a rapid-fire recitation of the results. He should simply instruct each student to announce the new high-to-low order of the responses according to his evaluation. A typical recitation might begin:

First Student: #3, #1, #5, #4, #2
Second Student: #3, #1, #4, #5, #2
Third Student: #3, #1, #5, #2, #4

And so on. When all students have given their evaluations, which takes no more than four or five minutes, the teacher might ask what response seemed to appear consistently high among the student rankings, what appeared consistently low, etc. Then individual members of the class may by asked to defend their scoring of the essays.

Students tend to be honest in this kind of situation, and generally a consensus is fairly evident from the beginning. Sometimes, a great deal of discussion is needed, and sometimes the class consensus may not agree with the way the teacher has them ranked. This may call for another reading of the exams, if the situation is critical enough. But what has anyone to lose through such honesty?

The student not only has the opportunity to share in the thinking of the class on the matter, sometimes even to defend his own paper; he also has a chance to see why indeed his paper must be a middle-range response, and therefore accepts the grade of "C" it bears. And the teacher has a chance to perfect his own talent in evaluating such writing as responsibly as possible.

REVISION

Most professional writers no doubt regard revision as a foregone conclusion. Composition textbooks urge and reurge it. Teachers tell their students to write and revise, write and revise. Maybe this explains why students seldom do revise. Maybe too, they lack an appreciative audience and therefore don't believe that what they have written is worthy of revision. And since fewer and fewer teachers enforce revision as a class or individual exercise, maybe they too question its value in student writing. Or maybe there is a mistaken notion in the air of just what revision means.

Indeed, simply to tell a student to rewrite something he has already written with some care without giving some specific suggestions for improving the quality of his writing is perfectly meaningless. Equally so is asking a student to "rewrite" a paper meaning in actuality for him to "clean up" a paper mechanically, with the side hint that "these things have to meet the demands of publishers," especially when the student knows full well that his chances of publishing that particular writing are hopeless. Most worthless of all, of course, is asking a student to rewrite a paper as a punitive measure, which, unfortunately, does still happen.

Shuman has made a clear distinction between two major aspects of writing—what he calls the "technology" and the "art" of composing. "The technology of composing involves such areas as spelling, punctuation, and general mechanics. The art of composing involves primarily the development of a sensitivity to words and ideas, to people and events, to objects and ideas" (38, p. 392). These are valid distinctions to make in the context of any discussion of writing, but particularly so here, since so much of what has become a traditional pattern of revision in high school classes has focused on the technology instead of art.

If we accept the word "revision" literally, it must mean not merely a "reviewing" or "reseeing," but a "new" or "second" *vision*. To repair the technological aspects of a piece of writing constitutes only a minor part of the new vision; surely the art must have its place too. And there are only three or four ways that we may expect this to happen in anyone's writing: either through a highly developed sensitivity to the irregularities in writing which allow one to know intuitively that something is wrong, and better yet, put his finger on it; through a systems approach, where we analyze each aspect of a piece of writing on an individual basis, not unlike checking the car over before vacation; through the advice of a critical reader; or through a combination of all of these.

For students, the most direct route, of course, is merely to accept the advice of the teacher, make whatever changes are called for, and forget the matter. The direct route in this case is far from the best. If the student can share in an honest exchange with the teacher, however, sharpening his manner of seeing his subject by refining his feelings through sincere reexamination, he may make more progress toward real revision. But this is not an easy thing to accomplish, when 34 others need the same kind of attention.

Abbreviating this kind of exchange and expanding that with peers through the small group process may be of some help here. At least the student is increasing the possible number of reactions to his writing and thereby the possible number of observations which may prove helpful in seeing what he has written in a truly different way. But even the most genuine remarks on the part of the teacher and his fellow students are going to be of minimal value, if when he resumes his writing, he honestly has little more to go on than "It seemed a little weak in this area," or "You need more descriptive words to make your point."

All of which takes us back to the literal description of a piece of writing. And again, the student does not necessarily have to be able to recite definitions of "mood," "point of view," or "coherence." But the teacher does. Above all, he needs to be able to detect in a piece of writing those aspects, which when altered in some way, will make a significant difference in its total posture. In other words, he needs to be sufficiently rehearsed in the "language of writing" to apply its meaning to his reading of student papers.

When he is, he will be able to recognize that the student has perhaps unconsciously made two or three awkward shifts in point of view, not only through changing his subject, but by inconsistencies in tone as well. And when he is aware of such inconsistencies, he is able to say something like: "The portions I've bracketed here are good, but very different from the rest of the paper. Try rewriting these as inserts, addressed to a child in a child's language and see the difference it creates in the total paper." Or, "You seem to be flirting with a truly creative definition of a male chauvinist here, but consider its placement in the total paper. How will your entire paper be changed by relocating and expanding this paragraph in particular?"

It may well be that by asking such questions or making such suggestions, the teacher will enable the student to arrive at new ideas or different conclusions which are even better than those we can offer. So much the better. The point is that the student, through this emphasis on the "whole" writing, can begin to view his writing in a dynamic way instead of sacrificing his enthusiasm and critical thought for an immediately "clean" paper in terms of mechanics. If he is helped toward this ability, he will want to see his paper free of technological inconsistencies, for he will be proud of what he has produced.

GENERATIVE WRITING

In nearly every writing program in the country, the problem of sequence both within the total writing curriculum and within a given writing course, surfaces from time to time, usually just long enough to provoke a quick reiteration of fundamentalist ideas from two basic camps: those who see no particular value in structuring the writing programs of high school students, and those who see no value in anything but a particular structure. As in other areas of the teaching of writing, research on whether or not students benefit significantly from carefully designed sequences of learning activities is inconclusive enough to permit both points of view a fairly regular audience in professional journals.

Most teachers will agree that the problem of sequence in the total curriculum is superseded by the problem of sequence within a given course. When faced with students who clearly possess or lack the skills outlined in a curriculum guide, teachers in good conscience will attempt to make adjustments in their own courses which will enable the student to begin the course where he should in terms of his own readiness. Knowing where to guide the students from that point in relation to a meaningful experience during the several weeks of a particular course, however, can present sometimes overwhelming problems for the classroom teacher.

Stephen Judy, who favors what he calls a "naturalistic" approach to the teaching of writing, feels that writing is learned rather than taught, and that students will derive appropriate structures and levels of meaning in their writing when free of artificial impositions of a teacher or textbook (20, pp. 213-18). In this context, he sees students writing from their own experiences, creating their own audience by examining the papers of others, and treating the classroom itself as a publishing center. The role of the teacher in this situation is that of a resource person as opposed to a formal instructor. This means, of course, that the teacher must possess enough bibliographical awareness to be of real help to his students in advising materials for their use, and such an awareness includes not only resources available in the school library, but also those in current or back issues of popular magazines.

James M. McCrimmon, on the other hand, feels a need for a more explicit structure in helping students develop their writing ability. He especially emphasizes the importance of sequence in teaching rhetorical structure, and has outlined a cumulative sequence for writing in the 7th through 9th grades. This sequence begins with lessons in specification, moves to those which deal with comparison and contrast, and finally to those which treat classification in writing (23, pp. 425-34).

Ken Macrorie, in his books *Uptaught* (25) and *Telling Writing* (25), and in articles such as "To Be Read" (24, pp. 686-92), strikes a middle ground in working with students who produce writing on a spontaneous and natural basis, but who increase their awareness and their ability through a series of steps which take them from writing about their own experience in a free and unstructured way; through self- and class evaluations of what they have written; to the literal preparation of some of their writing for publication in the school community.

The brief descriptions of the ideas of these three men indicate a wide range of approach, yet provide a beginning teacher with some basis for conclusion too. First, all three men are highly successful teachers, not merely theorists who "imagine" that writing should be taught in such and such a way. This alone should illustrate that no one approach is *the* approach. Secondly, as divergent as they may appear, all three treat writing as an ongoing process for the student; it is unlikely that any one of these men would ever treat what a student had written capriciously, terminating one assignment and urging another without helping the student to see where his writing is taking him in terms of developing his ideas with increasing expertise.

The beginning teacher, as he has the chance to experiment with different approaches, will develop what, in relation to his classroom situation and his own ability, will be a workable and satisfactory approach in terms of sequence. As he does so, it may be helpful for him to keep in mind that whatever assignments he devises, whatever methods he develops for working with those assignments, he is primarily concerned with techniques which will enable the student to "generate" himself to new levels of ability, including the areas of both ideas and skills.

Toward this end, he must, in his planning, force himself to think conceptually as well as specifically. For example, instead of satisfying himself with a specific assignment which seems sufficiently glamourous to evoke a set of interesting papers, he must also consider what possible changes can be rendered on that set to produce yet another good assignment and either reinforcement or development of particular skills.

Kenneth Koch illustrates this point nicely by showing the sequence of poems which he developed with his New York City youngsters. Instead of just asking the students to write poems which dealt with "wishes" they had, he followed this assignment with a poem which focused on the making of a comparison, then a poem focusing on "noises," then one focusing on "dreams," and finally, one which contained "wishes, comparisons, noises and dreams together" (21, *passim*).

This kind of overall thinking may be extremely difficult for the beginning teacher to achieve at first, particularly if he is working with a textbook which is separated into chapters and does not incorporate what the student has written in one assignment into what he is asked to write in another. If this is the case, the teacher may do well to devise recapitulative activities which ask the student to use old writing in new ways. One good way to handle such assignments is to ask the students to choose two pieces of writing which he has done previously, preferably two of opposite character, place them side by side, and concentrate on how they can be fused and directed to an entirely new audience.

Suppose, for example, that the student has written a brief testimonial kind of paragraph which begins with "I, John Jones, am an active person," and proceeds to prove this point by enumerating the many things he does which make him active. At some other time, he has written a short piece describing an unusual incident he has experienced, one of a sensational nature perhaps, that has caused him to think about the meaning of his existence. How can he now use those two papers in producing a third, longer paper which is directed toward a different audience, producing a different impact.

Students may at first view such assignments as impossibilities and may require help from the teacher in deciding on an audience. And the teacher himself must believe that a new paper can be produced. Once the assignment is launched though, and the student begins to see that he can indeed use his own previous experiences in building a larger context for his writing, he is likely to discover a wide range of possibilities for future expression. The creative process of making something new of something salvaged from earlier writing is also likely to stimulate his interest and his pride in his own thinking.

TECHNOLOGY AND WRITING

Educators vary in their assessment of the place of technology in teaching for the future. Some, like Sidney Tickton, believe that although we will see a substantial increase in the use of technological equipment in the classroom in the coming years, it is still unlikely to provide the major portion of instructional programs by 1980 (14, p. 82 ff.). Others, like Neil Postman, believe that its impact will be great enough to cause us to revamp English programs completely in another decade. Specifically, he imagines that we will have to consider the importance of what he calls "media ecology," the study of media as environments. This may include as a part of the English program the analysis of technology's effect on institutions such as the church, school, marriage, voting, patriotism, and justice; the assessment of the mass media effect on public issues; and the derivation of characteristic art forms of both today and the future (14, pp. 161-68).

Regardless of the degree of impact which technology will have on teaching in general over the next 10 years or so, we all know that eventually it will be great and that its implications for the teaching of writing are manifold. Already the tape recorder, video tapes, the use of music, and films are gaining wide use among composition teachers.

Probably the two most characteristic uses of the tape recorder recently have been as a vehicle for the teacher correction or commentary of student writing and as instruments for talk-write approaches to the teaching of writing. In the first instance, the teacher merely uses the recorder instead of a red pen in communicating his feelings about a piece of writing. The student listens to the comments made by the teacher, and attempts to revise his writing in accordance with the suggestions made. As such a device, the tape recorder has proved helpful in some situations. It is a definite time-saver for the teacher; however, its value here is relative only to what the teacher has to say. If it is nothing more than a substitute for penciling in grammatical errors in the margin of student papers, its use is of questionable value. If it is the basis for richer dialogue between student and teacher, it may prove indispensable.

In talk-write programs, the tape recorder is often used to enable a student to capture on tape his initial reactions to a topic, listen to himself thinking aloud, and refine his thoughts as they are transposed to paper. This approach has the advantage of allowing the student to record his ideas faster than he could by hand and therefore giving himself not just an additional step in the thinking process before he writes, but also perhaps a larger number of details to select from in refining his ideas.

More imaginative uses of the tape recorder are also available to the teacher of writing. One especially good technique for use in creative writing is to use the recorder as a means for doing "sound" narratives, then transcribing the sound into "written" narratives. Here, the student produces a story through the use of a catalog of sounds which he himself makes or records. When the story is played back to a class of students, they are asked to reproduce in writing the sequence they have heard on tape, or to create narratives which they feel reflect the sense of what has been recorded.

Video tape machines are becoming available to more and more school systems and also offer promising uses in the teaching of writing. In many schools, their use is complicated by the fact that only one recorder is available for use by all departments, and scheduling its use is sometimes awkward. However, if the writing teacher has it available for a few days in succession, he can devise a number of activities which students enjoy and can profit by. Video taping class discussions, skits, guest speakers or performers, or other kinds of presentations may provide students a chance to review and discuss what they have seen, and comment on it in writing either by way of creative or expository assignments. Teachers often feel uncomfortable with such equipment, particularly if they are not experienced in its use; however, this should not prevent its being used. Students themselves are often knowledgeable about such hardware and can be of great assistance in using it efficiently.

Music has long been a popular device in writing classes for stimulating students to write, and promises even greater possibilities as more and more students become interested in playing instruments, composing songs, and in many cases, performing in public. Typical uses of music include the analysis of song lyrics, sometimes rewriting them, composing song lyrics, setting poetry to music, writing mood pieces based on listening exercises during class, and creating words to match instrumental arrangements.

The richest resource in the use of music is the students themselves. Since they are immersed in popular culture in a way that most adults are not, they can often provide materials from their own collections which are as valuable as those the teacher might provide and are generally in line with the interests of the class as a whole.

This is not to suggest, however, that the use of music should be confined to that which is found in popular culture. Often, if used strategically, classical music can be just as effective with high school students in provoking creative thinking and writing. One of the best resources for the teacher here is Henry Pluckrose's ingenious little book, *Creative Themes* (34), which includes 12 major themes integrating art, music, poetry, fiction, etc. Some of the themes include: "Fairground and Markets," "Magic and Fantasy," "Space," "God and Heaven," "Ice and Snow," "Masks, Maps, and Natives." At the end of each chapter, he has included helpful lists of resources related to each theme. They should prove invaluable for working with both younger and older students.

Recent interest in the use of film in the classroom has evoked some imaginative treatment in the writing class. Hundreds of short, often nonverbal films are now available at nominal prices, or through film divisions of public libraries, and teachers are discovering that students respond enthusiastically to them, partly because they compete in both imagination and in quality to television fare. Many such films are being made by students themselves, especially on college campuses around the country.

An outstanding feature of these films is that because of their length, they can often be viewed two or even three times in a given class period. This allows the teacher to experiment with them in more creative ways than if he were forced to have only one showing. For example, a 10-minute film might be shown three times during the class hour—first, with the sound track turned off so that students concentrate on the visual message only; second, with both picture and sound, to note the differences created by the addition of music; and third, with both picture and sound, but with a focus on possible narration for the film. Students respond quickly to such possibilities when they have the opportunity to view the film in succession, with some time left for discussion either between showings or immediately following the successive ones.

Films are also very useful in free, nonevaluative writing exercises. The student is asked to view the film and react in writing immediately without discussion. He may view it again, adding to what he has said, or changing it as new ideas occur to him through a second viewing. Discussion may also prove helpful here, as through an exchange of ideas, class members may enhance their original thinking or contribute to that of someone else.

The following list of films is only a token indication of all that is available for classroom use. These are films, however, which have proved successful in many schools, and will at least provide the unfamiliar teacher with an idea of the range of subject matter treated in such films. The list also includes the name of the film distributor, who is usually listed by address in audio-visual or film catalogs:

1. *Claude*. Pyramid Films, 1969. 3½ min. color.
   Claude is uncommunicative and seemingly unaware of his parents' fault-finding and their oft-repeated statements that he will never amount to anything. One day Claude pushes a button on a secret box he constantly carries, and everything changes.
2. *The Critic*. Learning Corporation of America, 1963. 4 min. color. A satirical comment on audience reaction to art films.
3. *Drummer Hoff*. Weston Woods, 1969. 6 min. color.
   Using animation and easy, brisk verse, the film describes the building and firing of a cannon. Each brightly uniformed soldier furnishes parts of the remarkable machine, but Drummer Hoff "fires it off."
4. *The End of One*. Learning Corporation of America, 1970. 9 min. color.
   The camera watches seagulls scavenge for food from a garbage dump. At a distance a lone frail bird limps along a polluted stretch of beach, dying, while his fellows continue their raucous competition, unconcerned and uncaring.

5. *Kind-hearted Ant.* Contemporary/McGraw-Hill Films, 1969. 10 min. color.
   The kind-hearted ant's behavior unintentionally disrupts the harmony and order of the ant hill.
6. *Let the Rain Settle It.* Association, 1969. 12 min. color.
   Explores the basis of satisfactory race relations, using an incident in which a breakdown of a car brings a white boy into the house and life of a black boy.
7. *Notes on a Triangle.* International Film Foundation, 1966. 5 min. color.
   Animation of a single geometric form. A white triangle is divided into many complex designs, which constantly take on new forms.
8. *The Question.* Contemporary/McGraw-Hill Films, 1969. 10 min. color.
   An animated film in which a little man seeks the answer to the meaning of life in religion, politics, science, money, psychology, and war, and eventually finds it in love.
9. *Vicious Cycles.* Creative Film Society, n.d. 7 min. color.
   This is a spoof of the Hell's Angels type of motorcycle clubs, utilizing the live action/stop motion "pixillation" photography technique often used by Norman McLaren.
10. *The Wall.* Contemporary/McGraw-Hill Films, 1967. 4 min. color.
    A critical commentary on the people user, the person who watches while others struggle to make the breakthrough and then takes advantage of their struggles.

RESOURCES

It has been suggested at various points throughout this chapter that probably the best resources for the teacher of writing will be found immediately in the writing classroom, in the interests and experiences of the students, in the material everyone contributes from his own busy life. In addition, the following materials or those of similar nature, are those which any school should attempt to include for the teacher of writing so that he may have at his disposal more ideas to stimulate his own thinking and a means of keeping abreast of professional progress in this important area. These materials are drawn selectively to represent as wide a range as possible of composition theory and practice without draining a school or departmental budget:

Burton, Dwight L., and Simmons, John S. (eds.). *Teaching English in Today's High Schools.* 2d ed.; New York: Holt, Rinehart, & Winston, Inc., 1970.

Dillard, J. L. *Black English: Its History and Usage in the United States.* New York: Random House, Inc., 1972.

Hook, J. N. *Writing Creatively*. Boston: D. C. Heath, & Company, 1963.
Jenkinson, Edward B., and Seybold, Donald A. *Writing as a Process of Discovery*. Bloomington, Ind.: Indiana University Press, 1970.
Jones, Alexander E. *Creative Exposition*. New York: Holt, 1957.
Joos, Martin. *The Five Clocks*. New York: Harcourt Brace Jovanovich, 1961.
Joseph, Stephen (ed.). *The Me Nobody Knows: Children's Voices from the Ghetto*. New York: World Publishing Company, 1969.
Koch, Kenneth. *Wishes, Lies, and Dreams*. New York: Chelsea House Publishers, 1970.
Lewis, Richard. *Miracles; Poems by Children of the English-Speaking World*. New York: Simon and Schuster, 1966.
Macrorie, Ken. *Telling Writing*. New York: Hayden Book Company, 1970.
———. *Uptaught*. New York: Hayden Book Company, 1970.
Moffett, James. *Teaching the Universe of Discourse*. New York: Houghton Mifflin Company, 1968.
Pluckrose, Henry. *Creative Themes*. London: Evans Brothers Limited, 1969.
Postman, Neil, and Weingartner, Charles. *Linguistics*. New York: Dell Publishing Company, 1966.
Sohn, David A. *Film: The Creative Eye*. Dayton, Ohio: George A. Pflaum, 1970.
Squire, James R., and Applebee, Roger K. *Teaching English in the United Kingdom*. Champaign, Ill.: National Council of Teachers of English, 1969.
Tate, Gary, and Corbett, Edward P. J. (eds.). *Teaching High School Composition*. New York: Oxford University Press, 1970.
Torrance, Ellis Paul, and Myers, R. E. *Creative Learning and Teaching*. New York: Dodd, Mead and Company, 1971.

WRITING WRITING

The medium of writing is the miracle of language, and surrounded by the possibilities of language, the teacher of writing can be sure of only one thing—he can be sure of nothing. Gertrude Stein puts the matter another way: "The only thing that is different from one time to another is what is seen and what is seen depends upon how everybody is doing everything. This makes the thing we are looking at very different and this makes what those who describe it make of it, it makes a composition, it confuses, it shows, it is, it looks, it likes it as it is, and this makes what is seen as it is seen. Nothing changes from generation to generation except the thing seen and that makes a composition" (39, p. 311).

Maybe there is one other thing the teacher of writing can be sure of. Miracles happen when we expect them most.

REFERENCES

1. Adler, Richard. "Exploring the Grading Process with Students," in Allen Berger and Blanche Hope Smith (eds.), *Measure for Measure: The Tenth Report of the Committee on Classroom Practices.* Urbana, Ill.: The National Council of Teachers of English, 1972, pp. 11–16.
2. Allen, Dwight W., and Seifman, Eli (eds.). *The Teacher's Handbook.* Glenview, Ill.: Scott, Foresman and Company, 1971.
3. Anderson, Harold H. (ed.). *Creativity and Its Cultivation.* New York: Harper and Brothers, 1959.
4. Blondino, Lawrence. "The 'Class Answer' as a Teaching Device," *English Journal,* 57 (1968), 1032–35.
5. Blount, Nathan S. "Summary of Investigations Relating to the English Language Arts in Secondary Education: 1968," *English Journal,* 58 (1969), 735–47.
6. _____. "Summary of Investigations Relating to the English Language Arts in Secondary Education: 1969," *English Journal,* 59 (1970), 677–90.
7. Britton, James N. "Writing to Learn and Learning to Write," in *The Humanity of English.* Urbana, Ill.: The National Council of Teachers of English, 1972.
8. Brokowski, William W. "A Composition Strategy That Worked," *English Journal,* 59 (1970), 984–86.
9. Conway, Frances G. "Dictation: The Last Few Minutes," *English Journal,* 59 (1970), 983, 986.
10. Derrick, Clarence. "Tests of Writing," *English Journal,* 53 (1964), 496–99.
11. Dillard, J. L. *Black English: Its History and Usage in the United States.* New York: Random House, Inc., 1972.
12. Downs, Robert B. *Books That Changed America.* New York: The Macmillan Company, 1970.
13. _____. *Books That Changed the World.* New York: The New American Library, Inc., 1956.
14. Eurich, Alvin C. (ed.). *High School 1980.* New York: Pitman Publishing Company, 1970.
15. Farrell, Edmund J. "The Beginning Begets: Making Composition Assignments," *English Journal,* 58 (1969), 245–48.
16. Frost, Joe L., and Rowland, G. Thomas. *Curricula for the Seventies.* Boston: Houghton Mifflin, 1969.
17. Institute for the Development of Educational Activity. *The Small*

Group Process. Dayton, Ohio: Institute for the Development of Educational Activity, n.d.
18. Joos, Martin. *The Five Clocks.* New York: Harcourt Brace Jovanovich, Inc., 1961.
19. Joseph, Stephen N. (ed.). *The Me Nobody Knows: Children's Voices from the Ghetto.* New York: World Publishing Company, 1969.
20. Judy, Stephen. "The Search for Structure in the Teaching of Composition," *English Journal,* 59 (1970), 213-18, 226.
21. Koch, Kenneth. *Wishes, Lies, and Dreams.* New York: Chelsea House Publishers, 1970.
22. Lueders, Edward. "Teaching Writing Today—Composition or Decomposition?" *English Journal,* 56 (1967), 103-8.
23. McCrimmon, James M. "A Cumulative Sequence in Composition," *English Journal,* 55 (1966), 425-34.
24. Macrorie, Ken. *Telling Writing.* New York: Hayden Book Co., 1970.
25. ———. "To Be Read," *English Journal,* 57 (1968), 686-92).
26. ———. *Uptaught.* New York: Hayden Book Company, 1970.
27. McDaniel, Ernest, and Pietras, Thomas. "Conventional Test Scores and Creative Writing among Disadvantaged Pupils," *Research in the Teaching of English,* 6, no. 2 (1972), 181-86.
28. Mearns, Hughes. *Creative Youth.* New York: Doubleday, Page, and Company, 1926.
29. ———. *Creative Power.* New York: Dover Publications, Inc., 1958.
30. Moffett, James. *Teaching the Universe of Discourse.* New York: Houghton Mifflin Company, 1968.
31. Muller, Herbert J. *The Uses of English.* New York: Holt, Rinehart, & Winston, Inc., 1967.
32. Ontario Institute for Studies in Education. *Rhetoric: A Unified Approach to English Curricula.* Toronto, Ontario, Canada: Ontario Institute for Studies in Education, 1970.
33. Osterweis, Rollyn. "Pictures as Inspiration for Creativity," *English Journal,* 57 (1968), 93-95.
34. Pluckrose, Henry. *Creative Themes.* London: Evans Brothers Limited, 1969.
35. Roberts, Paul. *Understanding English.* New York: Harper Bros., 1958.
36. Shuman, R. Baird. "The Righteousness of Right Writers," *The Clearing House,* 41 (1967), 451-57.

37. _____. "Composition in a Time of Flux," *The High School Journal,* 52 (1969), 390-400.
38. Shuman, R. Baird, and Sublett, Henry L., Jr. "Home Study or Busywork?" *Illinois Schools Journal,* 50 (1970), 206-11.
39. Stein, Gertrude. "Composition as Explanation," in Leonard and Virginia Woolf (eds.), *The Hogarth Essays.* Garden City, N. Y.: Doubleday, Doran and Company, 1928.
40. Strom, Robert D. *Teaching in the Slum School.* Columbus, Ohio: C. E. Merrill Books, 1965.

BERTRAND F. RICHARDS
Indiana State University

5 Spelling, Punctuation, and Vocabulary

The first statement that must be made by way of introduction to this chapter on spelling, punctuation, and vocabulary is that in all actuality they are not separate entities but important parts of language. The second statement is that while it is convenient to deal with these aspects of language as isolates, they are closely linked. Spelling and vocabulary are but different segments of the same thing. A word is not *known* until both its sound and its physical representation are mastered along with its meaning.

The term "language" itself is misleading. Language is an abstract something utterly foreign to students who fail to realize that it is actually a form of behavior, a process, and an activity in which almost every human being is constantly engaged. The field of study becomes more meaningful if we reserve the term "language" for a more specific usage and refer to this continuous process of communication as *Languaging*. This term (borrowed from Postman and Weingartner in *Teaching as a Subversive Activity*) by its verbal nature predicates a continuing activity. Language is a way of communicating. Languaging is the art of putting thought or experience into language.

As English teachers dealing with language and composition, we rail against cant and jargon; yet, where in the universe can one find an atmosphere more clouded with cant and jargon than in the typical English classroom? Where else do students encounter the highly specialized and confused nomenclature of the various grammars? We accept as our responsibility the task of making our charges competent in the process of languaging, still all we provide them with is a set of terms and a body of principles couched in these terms which they never meet with once they have left our classrooms. That which is "learned" but never used is soon obscured among memory patterns, often beyond conscious recall.

One of the greatest contributions of modern linguistic science is the recognition of the simple fact that language is made up of two systems, the *phonemic* and the *graphemic,* and that the graphemic system is only an attempt to give permanence to the phonemic system. Or, not in the jargon to which we have just objected, writing exists only to record and to give permanence to speech. This point, while arguable, is essentially true. As sophisticated, educated adults we most frequently write without conscious awareness that we are setting down what we are saying, but this is what we do although we have suppressed the act of speech at the audible level.

The problem of this chapter is to present some creative approaches to the teaching of spelling, punctuation, and vocabulary in the secondary schools. The process would be much simplified if we could assume that we were first teachers for our students. But such is not the case. For once the admonition, "Begin at the beginning," does not apply, for we cannot go back to the beginning. Our students are adolescents and the beginning for them was somewhere in their distant pasts, 8 to 14 years ago.

By the time they reach high school, kids have theoretically learned to spell and to punctuate; they have mastered a vocabulary of sorts. We may be dissatisfied with the botched-up job that has been done, but it has been done. It is too late now to start at the beginning, to act as if our students had never had instruction in language. In a true sense, the teaching of spelling and punctuation to high school students is remedial teaching.

While students have had instruction in the language arts, we can assume that in most cases they have not had instruction in languaging. The ability to language may be equated with a means of extending power over experience. But by dealing with aspects of language totally unrelated to the everyday needs of students, we deny them this power. Practice in languaging, in bettering his versatility in communication, is what the high school student needs.

As teachers we too frequently demand that our students conform to a standard which does not actually exist in their real world—the standard of textbook English. In dealing with our student writer, we should be much interested in his saying something important in the standard of his own English, which certainly does exist, and in encouraging him to make gradual improvements in that standard.

Before starting on anything like a creative approach to languaging, assume a positive approach to your teaching and attempt to get your students to view the problems in languaging in the same positive manner. It is indeed our salvation that kids *know* far more than they *don't know*.

It is work, but well worthwhile, to grade a set of first papers in which the "rights" are counted and the "wrongs," while not ignored, are given little emphasis. The top of a student's paper might look like this:[1]

Spelling		Punctuation		Vocabulary	
Total words,	250	Total marks,	52	Total words,	250
Right	246	Right	49	Right use	249

It is sometimes a revelation and quite reassuring to students to be told that their right ways of communicating far outnumber their wrong ways. The tasks of improving these languaging skills seem less insuperable, and students are more willing to accept them when they know that at the outset their chances for success are roughly 69-1.

If we could go back to the beginning, we should take every advantage of the findings of modern linguistic science and teach spelling as it should be taught—for what it really is. Instead of teaching that letters have sounds, we should teach that sounds are basic to speech and that letters are signs chosen arbitrarily to represent sounds in writing or printing. Instead of teaching that the letter *a* has the following sounds: as in "pay," "pad," "paw," "parry," "papa" (both *a*'s), and so on, we should teach that there is a sound /o/ which is constant, but which is represented by letters or combinations of letters of the English alphabet. We can, and linguistics does, call these written representations of sounds *graphemes*. Some of those for /o/ are:

---

[1] If you are too busy to count the total words—and you will be—ask each student to count the number of words in his paper and record the number at the top of the first page.

SPELLING, PUNCTUATION, AND VOCABULARY

o	as in	no
o..e	as in	note
oe	as in	hoe
oh	as in	oh and ohm
oo	as in	brooch
ou	as in	pour
ow	as in	slow
ot	as in	peridot
os	as in	dos-a-dos
ough	as in	thorough
au	as in	landau
eau	as in	eau de cologne

There are others, of course. But many are of foreign derivation, and many are questionable. How many of the above combinations really are representations of /o/ and how many involve silent letters? What about "though" and Vincent van Gogh? What about "brooch" and Hendrik Willem van Loon?

We should admit to students that English spelling is both erratic and difficult, but we should also maintain that it is not impossible and is more reasonable than it seems. There is no need to take our students through the intricacies of phonology and phonetics, but there is no harm in their knowing that a substantial number of words are spelled as they are by scientific and logical principles. There are also many for which there seems to be no rhyme or reason.

Spelling is a part of writing and nothing else. You do not spell *words;* you say them. It is only when man attempts to record these shaped, transient puffs of agitated air that spelling is born. The sounds of speech are the basis of language. The recording of them is our attempt to do the best job we can with a rather inadequate tool.

This tool is the English alphabet and its accompanying punctuation marks. It is inadequate in that it has only 26 letters to represent some 40-odd sounds. The remarkable thing is that it does manage to represent them, sometimes in strange and devious ways.

While we must accept our students with whatever spelling equipment they bring with them, we can take time to explain the *why* of English spelling. Never let them believe that their 26 letters govern or produce certain sounds; the reverse is true—in English certain sounds govern the marks that can be used to represent them.

Spelling must be inseparably linked to vocabulary. The sound /kæt/ can be spelled either c-a-t or k-a-t, but only the first spelling belongs in the vocabulary as representing the name of a four-legged, purring feline. In like manner, the differentiation between "steel" and "steal" or "leaf" and "lief" is almost purely a vocabulary matter; all these spellings are correct.

If the interest of students can be aroused to the point that they will listen to the historical development of English spelling, much can be done to help them understand how English spelling came to be in the mess it seems to be in today. But at the same time it will help them to realize that there is more reason and plan behind our orthography than appears at first glance. Some of the irregularities become slightly more regular.

This chapter cannot, of course, trace the history of English orthography. But there are a few salient facts which can change the attitude of students toward spelling.

First, students should know that English is an admixture of languages, almost all of them derivatives of a long-lost parent language, Indo-European. This common ancestry explains the fact that the differing languages of successive waves of the invaders of Britain could mix and merge into Anglo-Saxon, the mother of English. It also accounts for the fact that Anglo-Saxon could so readily borrow from other tongues with the same Indo-European parentage—principally Latin, French, and German.

The second fact is that for almost 400 years English was an underground language. Kids are pleased to hear that English was outlawed—to know that it is natural for them to talk and to spell like a bunch of outlaws. The underground period was that following the Norman Conquest in 1066. English was outlawed; no schools or schoolmarms taught English. The law of the jungle prevailed and only the strongest, most useful parts of the language survived. This survival that English endured accounts for the fact that the language today is so remarkably strong and flexible. English expresses nuances of meaning with ease where other languages labor mightily or fail completely. While English gained much in utility in its schoolless period, its spelling suffered. People spelled words as they sounded *to them*.

Perhaps phonetic spelling is the best spelling, but to be effective it requires a phonetic alphabet, and that the English alphabet is not. The citizenry of medieval England labored, just as our present-day scholars labor, to make 26 characters represent 46 or so sounds.

The third salient fact is that printing was introduced into England too soon. Mechanical printing gives a degree of permanence to the graphic representation of language far beyond that of the pen or of the brush. When the press came to England in 1476, the outlaw period was over; but English schools in English had not been established long enough for scholars to have come to an agreement on what characters or combination of characters of the 26 should be used to represent the specific sounds of speech. Who knows? Had they been given time enough, scholars might have changed and expanded their alphabet to a perfectly phonetic one, and all our problems would be over. We would spell each word exactly as it sounds. But printing was introduced when it was, and printers and typesetters became the martinets who decided what the *correct* and *uniform* spelling of every English word should be. The matter was further complicated by the fact that few of these early printers were even English. They were Flemish or Dutch or German or French or whatever, and they attempted to apply foreign rules for spelling to rebellious English words.

The final fact which can be presented to students is so closely related to the introduction of printing that it is almost inseparable from it. Inseparable as far as modern spelling is concerned, that is. This fact is that phenomenon known as the Great English Vowel Shift.

Probably because it was an outlaw language, a working language of the streets and other noisy places, and not a language of quiet cloisters and cultured courts as it had been, English began to change. Its new role demanded that it be spoken with greater volume and with stronger emphasis. For this or for some other reason, the inhabitants of England began to change from the ancient pronunciation of long vowels which had closely resembled that of modern Italian to a pronunciation formed with the tongue higher and farther back in the mouth. As a result, other vowels were forced out of their normal positions and were also formed still higher and farther back. This is the change known as the Great English Vowel Shift. But in 1476, when William Caxton introduced printing into England, this shift was not complete. The attempt to render in type words employing the old, the new, and the changing pronunciations accounts in large part for the incredible number of sounds our printed symbols for the vowels of the English alphabet are capable of indicating. Had printing only waited for the English vowel system to stabilize! As it was, printing perpetuated an orthography in a state of flux. And, strangely enough, in spite of all the progress we pride ourselves on, the established spellings of words have resisted almost every effort made in the name of progress to change them.

There have been changes. The useless "ue" has almost disappeared from "catalog," Americans at least have changed "-our" to

"-or" in words such as "honor" and "color," and the final "e" has all but been eliminated from "develop" (possibly because by the most common orthographic rule its presence would demand the pronunciation /develoap/). For the most part, spelling has resisted change, and English orthography is crystallized in fonts of type and the bullheadedness of typesetters. This standardization is neither wholly good nor bad. It is senseless that we cannot simplify spelling and make it reasonable. But it is not practical. The insurmountable task of translating only the indispensible books and documents of the language into the new spelling prohibits any far-reaching attempt to reform spelling. And we must remember always what spelling really is—a permanent representation of speech. In the act of going from the printed signs to the reproduction of speech which is reading, the variances of traditional spelling offer many clues to meaning. "Tonight's the night" cannot be confused with "Two knights the knight" although the speech pattern produced by each string of printed symbols is identical.

The act of reading is always an act of decoding—the graphemes of writing or printing must be translated to the phonemes of speech. Granted that for much of our reading activity the process of deciphering is almost automatic and certainly almost unnoticed, the process is there. To ensure the best possible communication, it is desirable that the decoding remain as automatic and as unnoticed as possible. Orthographic standards do exist among the great majority of the English-speaking peoples of the world. Any deviation from these standards either slows the task of deciphering or calls attention to the process, thus destroying the automatic quality so necessary for effective reading and successful communication.

CREATIVE APPROACHES TO SPELLING

What possible creative approaches can there be to the teaching of spelling? Frankly, there are none. Spelling is a discipline and a difficult one at that. The teaching of spelling has engrossed pedagogues and classroom teachers alike for generations. Probably every method conceivable has been explored and reexplored. What can be presented are some creative approaches to the *learning* of spelling.

Students will participate actively only in what they perceive as important to them or in what they are convinced may become important to them as their education progresses. And this "may become important" must be clearly understood as an immediate time: tomorrow, next week, or at most next semester. Kids do not comprehend "important" as connected with some such vagueness as "later on" or "in adult life." They know, if we do not, that their life is "adult," that they are living it now, and that importance can be assigned only to *now* or to the discernible now of sometime soon. Therefore, if they are of driver-training age, such words as "alternator," "carburetor," or "signal" have both importance and immediacy and will be learned, whereas "syzygy," "concomitant," or "calculator" will not be established because one might conceivably in some mist-shrouded future become an astronomer, an educator, or an accountant.

Most students can learn anything they want to learn; they can and do learn many things they do not particularly want to learn but need to know. Look at the way they take to driver-training. They do not avidly *want* this information, but they *need* it in order to be able to drive a car—which they most certainly do want to do. Even little kids dream of the day when they will be old enough to drive, but driver-training in the fifth grade would meet with only a little less resistance than grammar in the fifth grade, and driver-training for an adult who has been driving, but poorly, for years and who encounters a judge tired of his numerous accidents, is not the fascinating subject it is for the anxious teen-ager.

The real problem of creative approaches to spelling (and punctuation and vocabulary) in the high school is one of making kids *want* to spell correctly or of convincing them that they need to learn spelling—that they will be better off if they do. It is difficult to get today's nonconformist students to accept correctness in spelling which demands conformity in the highest degree.

Any attempt to achieve the goal of seducing students into a positive attitude toward spelling must be student-centered, not teacher-directed. The following materials are suggestions as to how this happy state of affairs can come about. Remember that they are only suggestions not intended to be followed slavishly. Any creative teacher can improve on them, especially if he poses the problem to his own creative students and allows them to develop the methodology which will work best for them.

A Manifesto

We buhleave that the importants of spelling is overemfazied in thuh Inglish klassroom. The only think that madders is that we are abul to put down in writting the thawts that our in are heds. Just so peeple can make out watt we are trieng to say is all that kounts. It is rong to seperate good students from bad simpley on the way thay spel. You kan draw a paralell betwien the nied fur acceracy in speeking an the necesity for coreckness in riting, but rememmer that we probably perfer to right as we speek.

Almost every English teacher who meets with a new class will encounter a marked resistance to the study of spelling. This resistance may be subtle—the students simply make no effort to attain correct spelling; they listen politely or with boredom to the harangues and admonitions and do nothing. Their resistance may be open—they will question the necessity for correct spelling, "As long as we get our meaning across does it really matter that our spellings do not agree with those of the dictionary?"

Before the teacher answers this question, he had better think quite seriously about it. Does it matter? He, of course, is convinced that it does, but has he considered deeply enough about *why* it matters that he can give his students reasonable arguments and persuade them that correct spelling is worth its effort and is vital to success in school and in life?

The wise teacher will avoid preaching and authoritative prescription. He will abhor the old rigamarole that poor high school spellers can only hope to become poorly paid secretaries and office boys. He will instead let his students investigate the question of spelling. He will challenge them to try to convince him that they are right about spelling, but he will insist that in all fairness they will allow him to persuade them that spelling is worth its salt.

Then, suppose that they come up with the "Manifesto" given above. The teacher must consider it objectively and without bias. He will admit that none of the misspellings really obscure the meaning. "Seperate" cannot mean anything but *separate,* nor can the misplaced *l* in "parallel" cause the word to indicate anything other than straight lines equidistant apart. (Of course, you may draw a parallel between lines equidistant apart and redundancy.)

The teacher can claim that the manifesto is less efficient as communication, especially for a majority of readers, in that it takes longer to read and comprehend it than the version given here with standard spelling.

We believe that the importance of spelling is overemphasized in the English classroom. The only thing that matters is that we are able to put down in writing the thoughts that are in our heads. Just so people can make out what we are trying to say is all that counts. It is wrong to separate good students from bad simply on the way they spell. You can draw a parallel between the need for accuracy in speaking and the necessity for correctness in writing, but remember that we probably prefer to write as we speak.

The students who composed this masterpiece may come to recognize from the corrected version that there are faults in syntax, diction, and style which were obscured in the original manifesto—perhaps there is one advantage to poor spelling. The mind was too busy with translation to catch the full import of what was being said. It is important to note that the reader of the first manifesto in his successful attempt to grasp the meaning of the words restructures them with their proper English spellings. This process takes time. One should also note the differences between reading the passage himself and hearing it read. Except for "students" and possibly "madders" and "probably," the difficulties erase themselves. The students are right; their spellings probably are a better mirror of actual speech in all that madders.

Granted that there were no possibilities of mistaken meaning because of the misspellings in this document, students might be asked if they can think of sentences where a misspelling can obscure or even change meaning. These examples might help.

A freshman girl, a sweet and innocent little thing, writing of her ambition in life set down that she wanted "to meet a nice young man and get *marred*."

And her boy friend admitted in his composition that "the Key Club plans to make money Saturday by washing *widows*."

A student writing an evaluation of a class criticized the teacher, "You never know what to expect; his grading is so *erotic*."

Another, "Silas Marner suffered from *melon colic* seizures."

And, "Lucy lived only for the promise of a *haven* where she could lead an *immoral* existence."

With its converse, "If Welfare doesn't send me more money, I will be forced to lead an *immortal* life."

The list could go on endlessly. Every English teacher is familiar with the boners and bloopers of student compositions. They have been collected in book after book and in column after column of magazines and newspapers. Every teacher could, and many teachers do make their own collections of ludicrous errors to regale their friends and associates and, all too often, to shame their students.

The point to be made here is that the teacher may start to convince pupils that spelling does count by sending them sleuthing for errors—not their own—to bring in and report to the class. Suggest to them the fruitfulness of newspapers, especially the want ads, as a hunting ground. Can they explain why, as one progresses upward in the publishing hierarchy, such misspellings become less abundant? Might they not draw a conclusion applicable to their own care in finishing compositions?

In the beginning of this chapter, attention was called to the close link between spelling and vocabulary. How often are words marked misspelled when the fault is word-choice rather than letter arrangement? In the examples given above, only the omission of *i* from "married" resulting in "marred," the *n* from "window" resulting in "widow," and the *e* from "heaven" resulting in "haven" are true spelling errors. "Melon colic" is an unintentional pun, but it is as good a phonetic transcription of sound as is "melancholic" — perhaps even better, and the poor student, having only heard a word alien to his vocabulary, might have thought Silas to be afflicted with stomach pangs rather than sadness. The confusion between "immoral" and "immortal," neither word misspelled, is simply a transposition of meanings.

The lack of distinction between similar words which bothers us teachers so much when we grade themes is no bother to students at all. The boy who writes

I will not go out in this weather, weather you want me to or not

(He may even write "whether—whether" or "whether—weather") probably does not understand what we mean when we mark *nonsense* on his paper. His speech makes no distinction between /w/ and /hw/. And the girl describing the Halloween parade can see nothing wrong in writing

The judges could not decide which which deserved the prize

(or "witch—witch" or "witch—which"). Nor will she be likely to discover her error when she reads her sentence aloud — both pronunciations are the same in her vocabulary.

Confusion among words of similar sound and spelling but with different meanings is common. "Connie went skiing on her weak end." "Harry found his stake rather tough." "Not having any Simoniz, Amy put furniture polish on her clothes and wiped the car." Careless teachers are likely to mark such errors *SP* and let it go at that to the puzzlement of students.

If only every teacher could draw — what funzies he could have!

But remember that in every class there is at least one student who can draw. *Draw*

A picture
A pitcher
A statue
A statute
A picture of a pitcher
A picture on a pitcher (don't neglect the tattoo)
A pitcher on a picture
A picture of a statue with a pitcher
A picture of a statue of a pitcher
A statue of a pitcher with a picture of a statute
Julie throwing the pitcher out
The umpire throwing the pitcher out
The pitcher hanging on a nail
The pitcher hanging from a noose
(Don't neglect Connie skiing on her weak end)

This drawing can go on *ad infinitum* (and *ad nauseum*) but it can also be fun, and kids can come up with much better suggestions for pictures than you can. At the same time they will learn never to confuse "picture" with "pitcher."

From their own activity in the running battle with you as a teacher over the importance of spelling, the students most likely will convince themselves that correct spelling is important — at times. You may also become convinced that they are right and that spelling need not matter — at times.

SPELLING AND COMPOSITION

This chapter is not about composition; and yet, spelling is an integral part of composition. When a youth writes, it is vital that he get his ideas down on paper before they escape him. To insist on mechanical correctness during the heat of creativity or the burden of clear exposition is worse than a disservice to the pupil — it is a crime.

The use of his best English should, of course, become habit with every writer. The words he really knows should flow quickly and correctly from his pen. He should not allow himself to write "skull" when "school" is in his firm possession. When he has finally mastered "separate" and "definite" he should not permit himself to slip back into "seperate" and "definate" even though thoughts and ideas are gushing so rapidly that his pen cannot keep up with them. But this discipline must be truly self-discipline. His desire to make his best English habitual must be the goad; teacher insistence will never turn the trick.

It is after the first writing is done, when the ideas and concepts are securely captured in pencil or pen on paper, that attention can be paid to correct spelling, punctuation, and other mechanics. The trouble is that too many students consider this first, white heat writing as the final product. They may make a neater copy to hand in, but they seldom *edit* their papers.

"Edit" was italicized above quite purposely, for it is a key word in the elimination of spelling errors from compositions. No one likes to find and correct errors. But students will take great pride in considering themselves as editors. If the teacher sets up publication as the real goal for all writing, then students will work diligently toward correctness. The teacher may well, as a creative approach to the teaching of English, establish the class as a publishing house.

Again, the concern of this chapter is not with composition, but an important part of editing is the elimination of mechanical errors. Students should not at first edit their own papers. The errors they made were not made willfully or knowingly. They wrote what they believed to be right, and it is extremely difficult for them to find their own mistakes. Of course, we are not speaking of that first draft which flowed unrestricted from the creating mind. We assume that the paper handed in is at least a second copy from which the errors of haste and carelessness have been eliminated.

Kids with their writing are like mothers with their babies; they cannot see their faults. But others can! That is why it is possible for a classmate (or a group of classmates) to find quite readily the errors which the writer could not see at all, simply because to him they were not errors.

A blessing it is that not all people misspell alike. Even on a test over the 50 most commonly misspelled words, no two students will make identical errors. Even Gary, who copied from Barbara, will be smart enough not to let his paper look exactly like hers. You may be amazed to find that while individuals make errors galore, the class will spell every word correctly. That is, "privilege" was only missed by 6 out of 25, "business" by only 2, and 3 got "ameliorate" right the first time around.

Utilize this collective knowledge in editing against spelling. Perhaps a good plan would be to have single editors — students exchanging papers and working on them. But the minute an editor is not sure about a word, let him call out for help. You will have a noisy classroom, but who ever proved that learning can take place only in complete silence?

Sometimes it is advantageous to have students edit in groups, to have editorial committees. Group editing, as any other group activity in the classroom, requires careful watching; too often one or two in the group carry all the work load. Others do not contribute or may even obstruct the group project. Keep groups small; in fact, pairs of students often work more effectively than larger units. Two editors working together can be most efficient—one reading and the other questioning.

Early in the game, students should learn that it is no crime not to know, nor to admit that one does not know. But it is sinful to be unwilling to take the effort to find out. Students should be free and quick to appeal to other students, to the teacher, and, above all, to the dictionary if there is the slightest doubt in anyone's mind as to the spelling of a word. Naturally, if you are appealed to, or if you happen to be around when a word is being questioned, you might ask why the word is difficult to spell. If you can give a logical explanation of a seemingly erratic spelling such as "yeoman" or "euphony," by all means do.

Even though editing carries less stigma and is more acceptable to students than grading or correcting, the novelty of it will soon wear off unless you as a teacher take steps to see that it remains an important and meaningful activity. Set up the class as a publishing house, and make it for real. Promise the students that their best work will appear in print, and live up to your promise. At its worst, *print* may mean only typewritten pages with numerous and increasingly illegible carbon copies. It may mean (progressing upward) dittoed copies, mimeographed pages, or beautifully Xeroxed specimens. The ultimate goal is real printed pages from a print shop—complete with an attractive cover and publication data. But whatever your budget will permit, make sure that the publication appears.

As is true of any publication, its success depends on how widely it is read. It is not enough that circulation is limited to your classroom. The efforts of your students must be read by a much larger audience. Parents, of course! And grandparents! A whole host of relatives! Let students know early that copies will go to the administration and to other faculty—that will keep them on their toes. And be sure that there are enough copies that kids may pass them around freely to other students, not just to their classmates but also to their friends.

Almost every student believes (although it is not true) that whatever is printed is perfect. Tell them that you expect the same degree of perfection in their publication, and let them know from the start that this perfection is their own responsibility—not yours. You expect them to work so painstakingly that when the volume appears they can say, and rightly, that any errors that are found are those of the typesetter or the printer. Such activity takes English out of the classroom and into the real world. Students are engaged in an activity which is interesting, worthwhile, and of immediate concern to them. The training they receive is bound to make them better spellers or, at least, to possess the know-how to assure perfect spelling in a paper if they are convinced that it is worth the effort.

OUR SPELLING BOOK

Get students to write their own spelling book. While grading one another's papers, have the graders list all misspelled words, both the misspelling and the correct one, on a slip of paper to be handed in (unidentified). Assemble and duplicate a class list. Tell the students that their goal is the shortest spelling list on record. With each new writing, the same practice will be followed; but words which are not missed by anyone in the class will be removed from the original list. Of course, new misspellings must be added to the original list. Set as a goal for the semester or for the year *Our Spelling Book* with completely blank pages.

Kids may start to cheat by intentionally not finding misspellings in themes they grade, but this practice will not last long if the project is recognized as their own. You, as teacher, on your reading of the papers will locate errors which students have missed. If they are few, ignore them; they will be caught on subsequent papers. If they are many, after the original list is compiled, inform the students, "I am sorry, but I must add the following words to your list. Try not to make me add any more next time."

If *Our Spelling Book* is an activity that you as a teacher are going to impose upon them, forget it. Let the students do the work—all of it. Let them prepare the original list. Let them type the

SPELLING, PUNCTUATION, AND VOCABULARY

ditto master or cut the mimeograph stencil. Let them act as judges; does "judgement" go on the list or not? What about "alright" and "develope"? They must not make their decisions flippantly or by whim—they must secure dictionary evidence.

Above all, let the students themselves spur offenders on to greater effort in spelling. If a kid becomes the class criminal because he reinstates a word on the list once it had been removed, he will be more careful next time; he may even learn to spell the word.

The goal of *Our Spelling Book* with blank pages is not unrealistic. It is comforting to know that in any average class no one word is likely to be universally misspelled. Group pressure from those who can spell "receive" or "environment" will soon correct those who write "recieve" and "enviroment" or "invironment."

Ask the students how they can teach each other to spell. Perhaps a close examination of the word is all that is needed. But let them devise the means for close examination. If they decide on some visual presentation—such as by overhead projector, fine. But let them handle the entire process. They may want to see the word large by opaque projector—let them prepare cards with the words written or printed in large size and with black or colored ink. If they are young enough, they may want to cut out huge alphabets and use a flannel board. If they are older, more sophisticated, or talented, they may decide to prepare slides or a filmstrip. If you are fortunate enough to possess the equipment, they might make a film or a video tape. Whatever they decide to do, let *them* do it, even if for the moment you do not see what they are trying to accomplish by their efforts.

The important thing is that whatever their activity, they are constantly concerned with words, and particularly with the words they have habitually misspelled.

You, as teacher, while letting the students manage the whole show, need not be merely a silent bystander. You can help by pointing out principles that help in spelling. (Don't mention rules!) You can show that the word "iron" occurs in "environment," that they would never spell the word for the chief officer of a state as "goveror," and that the n in "government" is as necessary as the n in "governor." Add bits of historical interest such as that the b in "doubt" was never pronounced but was put in to make the word conform to its supposed Latin ancestry in *dubitare* from which "dubious" does stem. On the other hand, the k in "knife" and the g in "gnaw" were at one time pronounced.

Have students find as many words as they can which will prove that silent letters have a use in the formation of derived words. Give them some examples:

	bomb	bombard	bombardier
	damn	damnation	damnatory
	contemn	contemner	
	column	columnar	columnist
	crumb	crumble	crumbliness
	solemn	solemnity	solemnize
			(but solemnness)
	limb	limbate	
but not	limb	limber	why not?

When they have figured the last example out, ask them if the same sort of reasoning applies to

comb   combination   combat   combustible

They may be surprised at the wealth of information about words that a good unabridged dictionary will provide them. The fact that none of these words bears any relation to "comb" might still serve to fix the notion of the silent *b* in students' minds.

SPELLING CAN BE GHOUGHMN

One good way to convince students that incorrect spelling at times can utterly obscure meaning is to present a short but familiar passage to them which has been typed with one hand out of position:

FIYR SCIRE ABD SEVEB TEARS AGI, IYR FATGERS BRIYGGT FIRTG IB TGUS CIBTUBEBT A BEW BATUIB CIBCEUVED UB KUBERTT ABD DEDUCATED TI TGE ORIOSUTUIB TGAT AKK NEB ARE CREATED EQYAK.

It may be argued that these resulting "words" are something other than spelling errors. But are they? Is the touch-typist who never looks at his keyboard or his typing as it emerges, but who carelessly positions his hand wrongly and types "niderb" when he certainly means "modern," any more or less a criminal that the junior who carelessly writes "modren" when he certainly means "modern"? Of course, the touch-typist, the first time a couple of his fingers collided,

SPELLING, PUNCTUATION, AND VOCABULARY

would realize that he was in error, and no such string as the above garbled sentence would be likely to occur.

But what of the student who types carelessly and then fails to proofread? Such errors are legion, yet we as teachers count them (perhaps rightfully) as spelling errors even though we know that no kid is going to spell "the" as "tje," "brother" as "vrother," or "fast" as "fqst." How many spelling mistakes are simply the failure to make the hand put down on paper what the mind knows?

In the introduction to this chapter, attention was called to the importance of getting students to realize that the sounds of English are represented by the characters of writing and not the other way around. Every good dictionary gives a listing of these representations. Instead of trying to follow the old procedure of making the student who says that /newmonia/ isn't in the dictionary refer to his listing and find that the sound /n/ may be spelled *pn*, give the class a problem in detectivism.

Shaw's spelling of "fish" as *ghoti* is old hat by now. Don't use it. Put

G H O U G H M N

on the board and offer a prize to the first one who can decipher *your* erratic spelling. You will no doubt have to explain that you used

GH	for	F	as in	rou*gh*
OU	for	U	as in	s*ou*thern
GH	silent		as in	thou*gh*
MN	for	N	as in	*mn*emonic

and that your word was

F U N

You may give a few more examples, but only a few. Let your students contrive the most unintelligible spellings for words they can and attempt to stump their classmates *and you* with them. They will learn what sounds are sometimes represented by what letters, and they will perhaps become convinced that standardized spellings are needed.

One more principle that can engender respect for English orthography is that there is no one-to-one relationship between words as they appear in print and words as they are spoken. Put on the board

H A R Y A

and ask students what it is and what it means. Unless they know what you are up to, you will get no reasonable response. But put "hello" in front of it and "today" after it

Hello, HARYA today?

and "harya" is immediately recognized as

how are you

but "harya" is no doubt a better mimicry of actual and hurried speech than is "how are you."

We do not speak in words as we write in words. Have students prove it to themselves. Let each of them write out a sentence and then read it with a full pause after each individually pronounced word. Then have them read as they normally would and next with increasing rapidity and verve. In our sentence, "Hello, how are you today?" notice how easily and quickly "how are you" becomes "harya."

As a clincher, present a passage of mixed spellings which mimic sometimes somewhat slovenly speech and sometimes dictionary constructed "words." Such a passage might be:

Watchadoon, whashyadune chuid?
Nuffinmush, weravin ghoughmn.
Djeetyet?
Uvkorus kneact.
Letticegyeetven.
Noffurewile, umwaten, weightun furmadad.
Warezeyat?
Idunno.

Ask students how happy they would be if everyone were permitted to spell like this when writing. But the above passage which translates thus:

"What are you doing, what are you doing, kid?"
(*ch* as in *ch*aracter, *ui* as in b*ui*ld)
"Nothing much, we are having fun."

"Did you eat yet?"
"Of course not." (*kn* as in *kn*ee, *ea* as in h*ea*rt, *ct* as in indi*ct*)
"Let us go eat, then."
"Not for a while. I am waiting, waiting for my Dad."
"Where is he at?" (HORRORS)
"I do not know."

can convince them that conformity to a standard is necessary to keep the channels of communication clear *when the speaker is not present* to furnish the clues needed for interpretation.

The spelling program which is successful must make students accept the responsibility for correct spelling and accept it willingly. A major reason for misspelling is that the writer does not know when he has erred. No one misspells intentionally except for the special effects of dialect or humor. But students can through involvement with the writing of others—their fellow students, newspapers, magazines, and books—gradually train themselves to see their own faults. What is required is a constant awareness rather than casual involvement.

Spelling becomes a matter of pride. The students—no, of course, not all of them—become determined that no fellow student is going to catch them in spelling errors. How the student actually learns to spell is entirely his own affair. The teacher can give all sorts of help, but only if it is wanted and is willingly and gratefully received. The student who wants and needs to learn to spell will devise an efficient means for teaching himself. We, as teachers, can only applaud and try to help hasten the process.

PUNCTUATION

Like spelling and vocabulary, the teaching of punctuation is nine-tenths a matter of motivation. If we can make students want to punctuate, they will learn. Everyone knows, or should know, that the worst possible way to accomplish the aim of acceptable (not correct) punctuation is "memorize a set of rules, then apply them." But rules can be useful. One technique which has on many occasions worked well is to mimeograph on a single sheet the most basic rules and give this list to students. Then ask them to investigate whatever they may be reading at the present time (not textbooks) and see how many violations of the rules they can find. Perhaps you might have a bulletin board headed "Criminal Punctuation" and your students serving as "policemen" charged with bringing in culprits.

Students enjoy this kind of activity because for one thing it allows them to exercise a sense of superiority. Their perspicacity, backed with their set of rules, permits them to assert authority over successful and famous authors. For another thing, it helps to destroy their belief that books and authors are infallible. Another advantage is that by reference to their punctuation lists and their search for violations, they are inductively learning the principles of punctuation. The resistance to the memorization of rules does not occur simply because the students have not been asked to memorize anything.

This activity will not be optimally helpful if it stops here. Don't let it! On a day when your best laid lesson plan goes awry—when students begin to be bored—quit whatever you are doing and announce, "Trial Day," or "Court is now in session."

Students no doubt will think you have lost your bananas and will inquire, "What trial?" "What court?"

You can then explain that it certainly is not fair to list all these famous books and authors as culprits without giving them a fair trial. The idea will probably catch on like wildfire. Let *them* organize their own court—select judge, jury, prosecutor, and defender. Let them determine procedure. Each author, standing indicted, is brought to trial on each of his individual offenses. A written record is kept. (Once more, spelling and vocabulary exhibit themselves.) The verdicts are recorded.

The culprits are guilty without doubt if your mimeographed sheet is taken as the law of the land. But the defense attorney for any one of your violators may wish to plead extenuating circumstances. The question then becomes, not has a law been broken (which it obviously has), but is the defendant guilty of not communicating in the most efficient manner possible?

It probably will come as no surprise to you to find that acquitals are more frequent than convictions. This fact should lead students to another important discovery, that punctuation by rule is not so successful as it might be.

Two things should come out of this activity. First, that the rules are good and necessary *some of the time*. Second, that the real purpose of punctuation is to ensure the most effective communication possible.

The rules are indeed useful and can serve as guides; but, in essence, just like the definitions in a dictionary, they stand only as a record of what majority of educated people do or have done in certain situations and under certain circumstances.

THE VARIABILITY OF PUNCTUATION

How does one punctuate the translation of Caesar's famous dispatch to the Roman Senate?

>VENI VIDI VICI

By strict rule it should be

>I came; I saw; I conquered.

But by another rule, which allows the semicolons separating short clauses to be supplanted by commas,

>I came, I saw, I conquered.

is acceptable. But is there anything wrong with

>I came — I saw — I conquered.

or with

>I came! I saw! I conquered!

Even under certain rather ludicrous circumstances

>I came. I saw. I conquered?

might be perfectly correct — rulewise.

Punctuation is a way of expressing in graphemes the suprasegmentals of English. (Here we go in jargon again.) What is really meant is that punctuation marks are intended for the most part to represent the pauses and emphases of naturally spoken English. There are rules and conventions (some of them pretty senseless) which do other things, of course, but if students can be led to make punctuation mirror careful conversation, much of the battle will be won.

The graphemic system of English is as much as anything a timesaving device. To prove it, put on the chalkboard a pure graphemic transcription of a sentence without breaks for words or for punctuation:

theenglishlanguageusesforbetterorforworseanalphabetmadeupofvowelsandconsonants

208 CREATIVE APPROACHES TO THE TEACHING OF ENGLISH: SECONDARY

Communication is just as possible from this passage as from:

The English language uses, for better or for worse, an alphabet made up of vowels and consonants.

But the transcription of the first sentence is simply not efficient; the unraveling of meaning consumes too much time.

In exactly the same way that we faulted the students' "Manifesto" (see p. 193) because it demanded too much time for translation into accepted and familiar spelling, so do we fault the unbroken graphemic string. No one (and James Joyce is no exception) has the right to demand that his reader expend such an amount of time to decipher his message.

GHOUGHMN WITH MRS. OLSEN

An excellent way to teach punctuation is to have students consider some television commercial with which they are all familiar—one which they can all quote. As they reel it off to you, put it on the chalkboard without capitalization or punctuation but with word divisions:

im mrs olsen i dont take shortcuts not with my cooking and especially not with my coffee

Let the class decide on the way marks should be put in to represent Mrs. Olsen's speech most accurately. (On spelling again, note that speech gives no clue as to whether "Olsen" or "Olson" is the correct spelling.) Students will discover, probably after much argument, that there are several ways by which the statement could be punctuated, none of them without logical defense.

I'm Mrs. Olsen; I don't take shortcuts, not with my cooking, and especially not with my coffee.

I'm Mrs. Olsen. I don't take shortcuts; not with my cooking and, especially, not with my coffee.

I'm Mrs. Olsen. I don't take shortcuts—not with my cooking—and especially, not with my coffee.

These are not the only possibilities, but they are enough. Be sure to point out that random punctuation, just putting in marks for appearance, does not work and can utterly obscure meaning.

I'm, Mrs. Olsen I, don't take; shortcuts not with my: cooking and, especially not, with my coffee.

Let students play around with other commercials and for that matter with anything they have heard but never seen in print. When they tire of this activity, ask them to construct short paragraphs in which their meaning is clearly conveyed *without the use of punctuation*. It is difficult but possible. From their struggle these writers will come to have a healthy admiration for the value of punctuation. They will also learn much about good sentence structure; they will learn to avoid ambiguities.

All that was said in the section on spelling about student editing and student publishing applies equally to punctuation. In languaging we are not studying theoretical ways and means of doing something at some theoretical future time which may or may not occur. We are studying the very activity we are engaged in at the present moment. We study the language as it emerges in our classroom, and we consider ways to improve our utterances for whatever immediate purpose we have in mind. And we know that one of our constant concerns is with *how* this evanescent structure of emerging speech can best be captured in the permanent structure of writing. Both spelling and punctuation are necessary components of writing.

PUNCTUATION TEST

It is great fun to give the following punctuation test[2] but not if you give it in the way a test is usually given. But don't. Make it oral, with everyone getting the same grade, or divide it among teams, with points for first solutions. And don't be surprised when students come up with answers differing from yours—they may well be right. The test as printed here has the intended punctuation inserted; the copies given to students would be devoid of marks.

---

[2] I cannot give credit for this test because I know not from whence it came. I have encountered it in many different forms over the years. The sentences in this version are primarily my own having been either newly constructed or paraphrased from the original.

TEST

Here are some pairs of sentences. The way in which each is punctuated determines its meaning. Punctuate the sentences in accordance with the directions printed below each pair.

1. A. Three boys kissed Mary all told.
   B. Three boys kissed Mary; all told.
      a) Punctuate to save Mary's reputation.
      b) Punctuate to show boys cannot be trusted.
2. A. Each year there are fifty-odd teachers in the school.
   B. Each year there are fifty odd teachers in the school.
      a) Punctuate to show approximation.
      b) Punctuate to reveal some student's opinion.
3. A. The teacher called the students names as they entered.
   B. The teacher called the students' names as they entered.
      a) Punctuate to get the teacher fired.
      b) Punctuate to show orderly procedure.
4. A. Harry, says Mary, is a hairy hulk of a football player.
   B. Harry says Mary is a hairy hulk of a football player.
      a) Punctuate in the realm of possibility.
      b) Punctuate to cause trouble between Mary and Harry.
5. A. In the graduation procession will be the principal carrying the class list and six board members.
   B. In the graduation procession will be the principal, carrying the class list, and six board members.
      a) Punctuate to make Superman of the principal.
      b) Punctuate to startle none of the parents.
6. A. Everyone I know drinks too much.
   B. Everyone, I know, drinks too much.
      a) Punctuate to indicate you need new friends.
      b) Punctuate to condemn an entire population.
7. A. The cafeteria will serve a half roasted turkey.
   B. The cafeteria will serve a half-roasted turkey.
      a) Punctuate so that you will enjoy lunch.
      b) Punctuate so that students may become ill.
8. A. FACULTY EATS CHICKEN, STUDENTS, BEANS
   B. FACULTY EATS CHICKEN; STUDENTS, BEANS
      a) Punctuate implying cannibalism.
      b) Punctuate protesting discrimination.
9. A. During rehearsals, the cast has coffee and rolls on the stage.
   B. During rehearsals, the cast has coffee, and rolls on the stage.

SPELLING, PUNCTUATION, AND VOCABULARY

   a) Punctuate to indicate perfectly normal procedure.
   b) Punctuate to show clownishness or poisoned coffee.
10. A. Mary left Harry, convinced he was no good.
    B. Mary left Harry convinced he was no good.
       a) Punctuate with Mary and Harry headed for the divorce court.
       b) Punctuate so that Harry sees the error of his ways.
11. A. Harry urged the election of capable student senators and representatives who would support him.
    B. Harry urged the election of capable student senators, and representatives who would support him.
       a) Punctuate to assure the school good government.
       b) Punctuate to cast reflection on both Harry and the representatives.
12. A. Mary, too, hastily voted for Harry.
    B. Mary too hastily voted for Harry.
       or
       Mary, too hastily, voted for Harry.
       a) Punctuate to make Mary one of a crowd of hurried voters.
       b) Punctuate so that Mary probably regretted her action.
13. A. POPULATION OF SCHOOL BROKEN DOWN BY CLASSES AND SEX
    B. POPULATION OF SCHOOL: BROKEN DOWN BY CLASSES AND SEX
       a) Punctuate this headline and cause a scandal.
       b) Punctuate so that no one will raise an eyebrow.
14. A. The romance of Mary and Harry ended happily.
    B. The romance of Mary and Harry ended, happily.
       a) Punctuate story-book fashion.
       b) Punctuate perhaps to please Mary's mother.
15. A. Why did Coach Jones begin his speech with this remark, "I am confident"?
    B. Why did coach Jones begin his speech with this remark, "I am confident?"
       a) Punctuate so that Coach Jones is confident.
       b) Punctuate so that there is some doubt about it.
16. A. A winning team knows its master.
    B. A winning team knows it's master.
       a) Punctuate in recognition of the coach.
       b) Punctuate warning other teams to watch out.
17. A. In the tournament, Harry must still play Larry, who tied Gary, and Jerry.

B. In the tournament, Harry must still play Larry, who tied Gary and Jerry.
   a) Punctuate so that Harry is now in the semi-finals.
   b) Punctuate so that Harry can be champion by winning one game.

VOCABULARY

"And so, to the land's last limit we come—and can no longer." Which is a poor paraphrastic way of robbing Alfred, Lord Tennyson, of a way to start this concluding section of a chapter on spelling, punctuation, and vocabulary. So much of what has been said about spelling especially (and punctuation to some extent) is equally applicable to vocabulary; therefore, this section will be rather short.

One important aspect of vocabulary building (and one which has much wider application than the rather limited use discussed here) is found in literary detectivism. Students are somehow stimulated to greater effort on their own, once they discover that textbooks and works of literature are not infallible. The discovery of errors in spelling, punctuation, grammar, and syntax in textbooks establishes a healthy skepticism and convinces students that such writing is not, after all, so perfect that they could never aspire to write equally well. Be prepared with a few examples of your own which you have found in their texts, and then set them at it, *not* as a separate activity, but as an additional something to look for while studying. Just as we are willing to interrupt whatever else we are doing when we encounter a word which needs attention, so are we willing to have study interrupted. Once students are able to carry on simultaneously the process of language and the process of languaging itself, a great stride has been taken in the direction of adult and critical reading.

A healthy interest of a group of teen-agers in the correctness of the language they read can go far toward the improvement of the language they use. The experience of grading the themes written by their peers helps to establish a valuable critical ability. They know that their fellow students are not infallible; it is a step toward wisdom when they discover that the printed word is not infallible either. Once students have developed a degree of proficiency in spotting errors while not neglecting study or reading for enjoyment, branch out. The language of the textbook is almost universally the language of strict adherence to rule. But what about the language of literature? Get them to examine selections from their anthology (if you are so unfortunate as to be stuck with one) or from their paperbacks (if you are in an enlightened school). They will soon discover that this writing is not always (perhaps not even *often*) according to rule.

That the procedure being advocated here is strikingly similar to the one discussed in the section on punctuation cannot be denied. In fact, the two should be carried on simultaneously—but the concern now is with words rather than with the forms of words and the forms of sentences.

Students will find few actual vocabulary errors; any author who has published has learned not to misuse words. But in addition to mechanical errors of spelling and punctuation, they may find words that typesetters or some other gremlins have changed. But, more importantly, they will discover new and strange usages which give words a power far beyond that of their ordinary and rather humdrum employment.

Your students will begin to draw certain important deductions, especially about fiction. The author sometimes writes to you as author—in which case he more or less follows textbook rules, or he writes to you as character—in which case he follows the rules of that particular character. Conscious misspelling, punctuation, and syntax may be helpful devices by which an author builds a character. What was correct when it was written may not be correct when it is read months, years, or generations later. Shakespeare could not pass the high school composition course under most contemporary teachers. Correct English could deal a death blow to literature.

The obvious example of author as author and author as character is found in a story containing dialogue, especially if the dialogue is attempting dialect. The author is assumed to be an educated, cosmopolitan man. He writes, as himself, with a certain degree of correctness, but he also writes *to* the character's degree of correctness:

> As I approached her dilapidated little shack, I saw Carola disappearing down the road. Nollie said, "Carola sayed he be goin tuh the store; he be right back."

The author speaks first, in the part of the passage before the first quotation mark. His English is standard. "Nollie said" is his and is correct for him. Nollie's "Carola sayed" is character speech and also correct, or at least appropriate, for the character. But we would not tolerate the author's use of the reversal

... Nollie sayed, "Carola said ... "

nor would we tolerate the peculiar "he be goin" for "she was going" as author speech although the failure to distinguish pronominal gender is common in many dialects. The substandard use of "be" for "was" is perfectly correct English—the only trouble is that this use disappeared from "standard" English 300 or 400 years ago.

There is no need to dwell on the fact that people often see what is in their minds rather than what is actually on the paper before them. Suppose one encounters this sentence in his reading, "Oil paint becomes permanent only *it if is* transferred to canvas." The transposition of words from the intended "if it is" to the meaningless "it if is" goes unnoticed by the proofreader because the mind interprets the three successive two letter morphemes in the only way in which they can *mean*. Neither "it if is" nor "is if it" means and "is it if" means only in a special context questioning the identify of a word. In like manner, a book with a mathematical slant written by C. N. Alberga (a real author's name, by the way) is apt to have the writer's name misread as C. N. Algebra, while a book on flying fishes by the same author would not suffer like misinterpretation.

What has all this to do with the teaching of vocabulary? Either nothing or a great deal. Nothing, in the sense that it does not add words to the students' store; a great deal in the sense that students need to know much about language and languaging before they can be stimulated to vocabulary building. They need to know that there are levels of appropriateness, that words can serve useful purposes while seemingly not conforming to rule. They need to know that rules are man-made, and that their application is by no means universal. They need to know that the sole purpose of an extensive vocabulary is to provide them with a better tool for communication—the immediate communication of everyday existence.

ALADDIN AND HIS WONDERFUL WORDS

The reader of this chapter is without doubt well aware that little has been said in it about teaching by games. This lack is not due to a belief that games are of little value—they are indeed of considerable value. But so much has been made of them that they can hardly be called creative approaches any longer.

Games are usually something the teacher has devised or collected and introduced into the classroom. Try a new approach. Ask your students to devise a game or a situation comedy or something else which can be used to teach *words* to pupils say three or four grades behind them in school.

"New words for old!" Try to trick Aladdin into giving up a valuable old word for a gaudy but worthless new one.

Silly, isn't it? But it might be fun, and even high schoolers might become quite involved in making up tallies of words for Aladdin and for his adversary, the Djinn. Much argument might ensue as to which words are precious and which are cheap. While so doing, students will be encountering words and perhaps for the first time judging them. They will learn that many times people who should know better become so fond of a cheap, tinselly word that they neglect the sound old word to the point that it atrophies.

Students need large vocabularies, but they need useful synonyms rather than erudite and esoteric ones. Perhaps their doctor might need "anorexia," but the kid who has mastered "loss of appetite" or "I ain't hongry" doesn't need it.

The blatantly obvious but often ignored key word in any consideration of vocabulary is *need*. There is no problem of motivation to learn when there exists a recognized need. What we must reach, if we are to be successful, is actual student need—not the imagined student need projected by teachers and educationists.

Put the proposition squarely before students. Tell them that your only concern is to help them learn words they need and can use daily. Then, let them decide what these words are.

As much as students are ordinarily opposed to vocabulary lists, such lists may have a value, especially if they are used in reverse. You might follow these steps:

1. Let each student prepare a list of from 10 to 15 words unfamiliar to him and of any kind whatsoever.
2. From this list they are going to determine which words, if any, deserve a place in their permanent vocabularies.
3. Each student copies the list on a card and carries it with him week-long.
4. During the week the students look for occurrences of the words in print or in speech.
5. At the end of the week, a tally is made.
6. Words not found are deemed of little worth.
7. Words with high scores are most likely already in the vocabularies of the majority of students.
8. Words with rather high frequency of occurrence may be worthy of addition to the permanent vocabulary.

9. A judgment is made.
   a) the word is a useful synonym for a common but overworked word.
   b) the word is useful in its own right.
10. The word, by decision, is added to the vocabulary.

Now the sneaky thing about this is that the words students think they have discarded are also added to their vocabularies. They can never again encounter one of these rejected words without recognizing that at one time they had a speaking acquaintance with it. Words which are completely understood but which are of infrequent use need not be memorized—spellings and certainty of meaning can be checked in a dictionary.

Words are like money. If you are frugal, you can get by with little. But it is much more fun to be able to spend lavishly, no matter whether you are spending real or verbal money—dimes and quarters or nouns and verbs. Unfortunately, there is no verbal slot machine where you can hit a vocabulary jackpot. (Have students make a game of it?)

Once students know that the words they are learning (and learning to spell) are words for use at the present time and for use lifelong, much resistance to vocabulary study will be removed.

REFERENCES

1. Algeo, John. "Why Johnny Can't Spell," *English Journal,* 54 (1965), 209–13.
2. Allen, Robert L.; Allen, Virginia French; and Shute, Margaret. *English Sounds and Their Spellings.* New York: Thomas Y. Crowell Company, 1966.
3. Anderson, Harold Homer (ed.). *Creativity and Its Cultivation.* New York: Harper and Brothers 1959.
4. Baughman, M. Dale (ed.). *101 Examples of Creative Teaching in the Junior High School.* Danville, Ill.: The Interstate Printers and Publishers, Inc., 1962.
5. Blau, Harold. "First Aid for Extremely Poor Spellers," *English Journal,* 55 (1966), 583–84.
6. Bolinger, Dwight. "The Evolution of Language: Courses, Forces, Sounds, and Spellings," Chapter 6 in *Aspects of Language.* New York: Harcourt, Brace & World Inc., 1968.
7. Brengelman, Frederick H. "Dialect and the Teaching of Spell-

ing," *Research in the Teaching of English,* 4, No. 2 (1970), 129-38.
8. _____. "Generative Phonology and the Teaching of Spelling," *English Journal,* 59 (1970), 1113-18.
9. Bugelski, B. R. *The Psychology of Learning.* New York: Holt, Rinehart & Winston, Inc., 1956.
10. Chall, Jeanne S. "What about Controlled Vocabulary?" *Reading for Effective Living.* Proceedings International Reading Association Conference, 3 (1958), 177-86.
11. Church, Frank C. "Stress-Terminal Patterns: Intonation Clues to Punctuation," *English Journal,* 56 (1967), 426-34.
12. Cole, Luella. *The Teacher's Handbook of Technical Vocabulary.* Bloomington, Ill.: Public School Publishing Company, 1940.
13. Dale, Edgar. "The Problem of Vocabulary in Reading," *Education Research Bulletin,* 35 (1956), 113-23.
14. Davis, A. L. (ed.). *Culture, Class, and Language Variety.* Urbana, Ill.: National Council of Teachers of English, 1972.
15. Dolch, E. W. "Vocabulary Development," *Elementary English,* 30 (1953), 70-75.
16. deBono, Edward. "Thinking Sideways," *Bell Telephone Magazine,* 48 No. 4 (1969), 26-32.
17. duSable, D. D. *Learning by Discovery: Rationale and Mystique.* Urbana, Ill.: University of Illinois, Bureau of Educational Research, 1961.
18. Eberhardt, W. "Discovery of Meaning—Childhood's Greatest Adventure," *Education Research Bulletin,* 24 (1945), 152-62.
19. Evertts, Eldonna L. (ed.). *English and Reading in a Changing World.* Urbana, Ill.: National Council of Teachers of English, 1972.
20. G. W., *Magazine, or Animadversions on the English Spelling* (1703). Los Angeles: The Augustan Reprint Society, Publication 70, 1958.
21. Gammon, Agnes L. "Comprehension of Words with Multiple Meanings," *California Journal of Educational Research,* 3 (1952), 228-32.
22. Getzels, Jacob W. *Creativity and Intelligence: Explorations with Gifted Students.* New York: John Wiley & Sons, Inc., 1962.
23. Goodman, Kenneth S. "Orthography in a Theory of Reading Instruction," *Elementary English,* 49 (1972), 1254-61.
24. Gordon, Alice Kaplan. *Games for Growth: Educational Games in the Classroom.* Palo Alto, Calif.: Science Research Associates, College Division, 1970.

25. Grommon, Alfred. "Preparing High School Students for College Composition," *California Journal of Secondary Education,* 28 (1953), 113-18.
26. Gunn, Agnella M., et al. "Creative Approaches to the Teaching of English," *Journal of Education* (Boston University School of Education), December 1964.
27. Haefner, R. "Casual Learning of Word Meanings," *Journal of Education Research,* 25 (1932), 267-77.
28. Hall, Robert A., Jr. *Sound and Spelling in English.* Philadelphia: Chilton Company, 1961.
29. Held, J. R. "Teaching Punctuation in the Ninth Grade by Means of Intonation Cues," *Research in the Teaching of English,* 3 (1969), 196-208.
30. Horn, Thomas D. "Some Issues in Learning to Spell," in Paul C. Burns and Leo M. Schell (eds.), *Elementary School Language Arts: Selected Readings.* Chicago: Rand McNally & Co., 1969.
31. _____. "Spelling," in R. L. Ebel (ed.), *Encyclopedia of Educational Research.* 4th ed.; New York: The Macmillian Company, 1969.
32. Hullfish, H. G., and Smith, P. *Reflective Thinking: The Method of Education.* New York: Dodd, Mead & Company, 1961.
33. Hunter, Elizabeth. *Encounter in the Classroom: New Ways of Teaching.* New York: Holt, Rinehart & Winston, Inc., 1972.
34. James, Henry Thomas and others. *The Schools and the Challenge of Innovation.* New York: McGraw-Hill Book Company, 1969.
35. Johnson, Lois J. "Proofreading—a Student Responsibility," *English Journal,* 56 (1967), 1323-24, 1332.
36. Kagan, Jerome (ed.). *Creativity & Learning* (The Dædalus Library). Boston: Houghton Mifflin Company, 1967.
37. Kirkman, A. J. "Command of Vocabulary among University Entrants," *Educational Research* (Britain), 9 (1967), 151-59.
38. Kyle, G. C. "A Core Vocabulary in the Language Arts," *Phi Delta Kappan,* 34 (1953), 231-34.
39. Laird, Charlton, "Down Giantwife: The Uses of Etymology," *English Journal,* 59 (1970), 1106-12.
40. Langer, J. H. "Vocabulary and Concept Development," *Journal of Reading,* 10 (1967), 448-56.
41. Lefcourt, Ann. "Spelling and the Dictionary," *Elementary English,* 49 (1972), 1228-32.
42. Lindsey, J. F. and Hick, S. D. "A Note on Teaching for Creativ-

ity," *California Journal of Educational Research*, 21 (1970), 35-42.
43. McCullough, Constance M. "An Inductive Approach to Word Analysis," *Education*, 75 (1955), 583-87.
44. Marshall, Sybil. *Adventures in Creative Education*. Oxford, Eng.: Pergamon Press Ltd., 1968.
45. Massialas, Byron G., and Zevin, Jack. *Creative Encounters in the Classroom: Teaching and Learning through Discovery*. New York: John Wiley & Sons, Inc., 1967.
46. Michael, William B. (ed.). *Teaching for Creative Endeavor: Bold New Venture*. Bloomington, Ind.: Indiana University Press, 1968.
47. Miles, I. W. "An Experiment in Vocabulary Building in High School," *School and Society*, 61 (1945), 285-86.
48. Mullen, William B. "Teaching Contextual Definition," *English Journal*, 54 (1965), 419-24.
49. National Council of Teachers of English, Curriculum Commission, *An Experience Curriculum in English*. New York: Appleton-Century, 1935.
50. National Council of Teachers of English, Commission on the English Curriculum, *The English Language Arts in the Secondary School*. New York: Appleton-Century-Crofts, 1956.
51. Olson, Dorothy C. "A Perfectly Normal Spelling Dilemma," *English Journal*, 58 (1969), 1220-22.
52. Petty, Walter T.; Herold, Curtis P.; and Stoll, Earlene. *The State of Knowledge about the Teaching of Vocabulary*. Sacramento State College, Report of Cooperative Research Project 3128, Contract OE-6-10-120 U.S. Office of Education. Urbana, Ill.: National Council of Teachers of English, 1968. (Contains complete and comprehensive bibliography.)
53. Quirk, Randolph and Smith, A. H. *The Teaching of English*. London: Oxford University Press, 1964.
54. Robertson, Stuart. *The Development of Modern English*, rev. by Frederick G. Cassidy. 2d ed.; Englewood Cliffs, N. J.: Prentice-Hall, Inc., 1954.
55. Sachs, H. J. "The Reading Method of Acquiring Vocabulary," *Journal of Education Research*, 18 (1928) 235-38.
56. Shaw, Harry. *Spell It Right*. New York: Barnes & Noble, Inc., 1961.
57. _____. *Punctuate It Right*. New York: Barnes & Noble, Inc., 1963.

58. Sherwin, J. S. *Four Problems in Teaching English.* Scranton, Pa.: International Textbook Company, 1969.
59. Shumsky, Abraham. *Creative Teaching in the Elementary School.* New York: Appleton-Century-Crofts, 1965.
60. Smith, B. Othanel and Ennis, Robert H. (eds.). *Language and Concepts in Education.* Chicago: Rand McNally & Company, 1961.
61. Smith, James A. "Spelling" in *Creative Teaching of the Language Arts in the Secondary School.* Boston: Allyn & Bacon, Inc., 1967.
62. Smith, Rodney Pennell. *Creativity in the English Program.* Champaign, Ill.: National Council of Teachers of English, 1970. (Bibliography)
63. Stevens, William J. "Obstacles to Spelling Reform," *English Journal,* 54 (1965), 85-90.
64. Summerfield, Geoffrey (ed.). *Creativity in English.* Champaign, Ill.: National Council of Teachers of English, 1968.
65. Wilkinson, Andrew. *The Foundations of Language.* New York: Oxford University Press, 1971.
66. Wolfe, Don M. *Creative Ways to Teach English, Grades 7-12.* 2d ed.; New York: Odyssey Press, 1966.

R. BAIRD SHUMAN
Duke University

6 Reading

Anyone who has taught school at any level for even a short period of time has undoubtedly become keenly aware within a few days that the teaching of reading is not a fenced off, exclusive area into which only the trained reading teacher may enter, but that every teacher must, in one way or another, be vitally concerned with being able to assist his students in learning to read effectively. Although, as Charles Fries points out (20, p. 114), "there are still more human languages that have no writing and reading by their native speakers than there are languages with such writing," the fact remains that in our world, literacy is demanded, and those who do not possess it are virtual cripples. Ours is a print-oriented society and to minimize the importance of being able to read and write would be dishonest.

Reading is the single most important subject taught in the elementary school, where most people learn to read; nevertheless, because of social promotion and other such factors, a not inconsiderable number of youngsters who enter secondary school are poor readers or nonreaders. The secondary school teacher, who has been trained to teach a specific subject, often has not had a single course in the teaching of reading; yet, despite this, if he is to reach his youngsters, he must become concerned with teaching them some of the rudiments of reading within his own subject area.

WHAT IS READING?

The definition of reading will vary greatly depending on who is doing the defining. William S. Gray insists that reading is more than a physical act and that it must be tied to meaning: "Any conception of reading that fails to include reflection, critical evaluation, and the clarification of meaning is inadequate. . . . reading is also a form of experience that modifies personality" (25, pp. 26-27). Obviously, this is a very broad, humanistic definition, probably too broad for most of today's reading experts to accept.

Gray's colleague in the developmental approach to the teaching of reading, Arthur I. Gates, defined reading as "not a simple mechanical skill: nor is it a narrow scholastic tool. . . . it is essentially a thoughtful process [which] can and should embrace all types of thinking, evaluating, judging, imagining, reasoning, and problem-solving" (22, p. 3). Again, the definition is very broad and all-inclusive, perhaps too broad and all-inclusive to be serviceable to the average secondary teacher whose immediate problem is that he has to present substantive material of a complex nature to students ranging in age from, in most cases, 13 to 18, some of whom have insufficient reading ability to be able to deal with the material that must be covered.

For most such teachers, Ruth Strang's definition would be serviceable: "Reading is many-sided. It is a visual task involving sensation and perception. Reading is a psychological process; it involves fusing symbols with their meanings to comprehend an author's thought. Reading is a complex and unique experience involving the organism as a whole. It is a pattern of activities which varies with the reader's purpose and the kind of material which he is reading" (51, p. 62). Implicit in this definition is the recognition that there is more than one purpose for reading. Some purposes will be narrow, others broad. Individual circumstances dictate what purpose is appropriate to a given situation.

THE RELATIONSHIP BETWEEN READING AND WRITING

The four major skills of communication are listening, speaking, reading, and writing. The first two of these skills are closely related and most people cannot learn to speak except through careful listening. However, reading and writing are not quite such compatible skills as listening and speaking. Maria Montessori recognized this early in her work with children: "Experience has taught me to distinguish clearly between *writing and reading,* and has shown me that the two acts *are not absolutely contemporaneous.* Contrary to the usually accepted idea, writing *precedes reading*" (39, p. 296). While most modern researchers in the field of reading are not quite so dogmatic in their statements as Montessori was in hers, they would freely admit that for some students, writing may, indeed, precede reading. It is important that the teacher bear this in mind, for the *writing* student is not always the *reading* student; however, it is not possible for the nonreader to compose originally in written form. At the secondary level, if a student copies from another student's paper and does so to the extent of copying the other student's punctuation and spelling errors and, possibly, even the other student's name, the teacher should immediately suspect that he is dealing with a nonreader or with a very weak reader.

James P. Soffietti correctly asserts that "*writing* is simply a way of recording language by means of visible marks [while] *reading* ... involves the reverse process, i.e., the responding to visual forms with vocal or subvocal ones" (38, p. 53). In a sense, then, reading and writing are, instead of being compatible processes, almost diametrically opposite processes. Briefly differentiated, writing is a process of encoding while reading is a process of decoding. The teacher who is unaware of this differentiation is likely to find it very difficult to understand how a student who can write may be unable to read.

HOW LARGE IS THE READING PROBLEM?

The rate of illiteracy in the United States has been variously reported. If illiteracy is defined as a total inability to read and write, few adult Americans can be said to be illiterate. Even those who cannot read well enough to comprehend the writing in a simple magazine can probably read traffic signs, comic books, and some newspaper advertisements. Most Americans are able to sign their names even though the writing ability of some may not extend much beyond this. But by this standard of literacy, all but 2 or 3 percent of our populace may be called literate.

One government study considered adults who had not completed the 4th grade of school to be functionally illiterate, and by that standard, 11 percent of our adult population was at that time—1953—considered illiterate (26, p. 37), although this group undoubtedly included numerous people who were functionally literate. When our government launched its "Right to Read" program early in the 1970s, it was estimated that "as many as 50 percent of our children are deficient in reading" (36, p. 18), and a survey conducted by Louis Harris for the National Reading Council indicated that "more than 18 million Americans over the age of sixteen lack the reading ability needed to survive in today's technological society" (36, p. 18).

J. N. Hook reports that in the 1960s, "a study of Michigan high schools revealed that about one third of the students did not read well enough to do the work expected in high school classes, and about two thirds of such students had not received any reading instruction designed to overcome their handicaps" (27, p. 78). Such a statement would not surprise the average high school teacher who every day encounters the frustrations and disappointments which reading disabilities cause their students.

Regardless of how one arrives at his statistics, reading problems loom large in our country. A colossal number of Americans are not sufficiently in possession of the basic skills of literacy to make the optimum use of their abilities in a society which places a tremendous—indeed, perhaps a disproportionate—value upon one's ability to read and write. The person who is lacking in literacy is severely handicapped both occupationally and socially. A large portion of the world of information lies outside his reach; and until he has mastered at least the rudiments of literacy, he will be living in an alien world.

THE SECONDARY SCHOOL ENGLISH TEACHER AND READING

Just as some administrators think that anyone who can speak English should be able to teach it, so do many administrators think that every secondary school English teacher is able to teach reading. And the administrator who has no teachers trained specifically in reading is probably correct in assuming that the English teacher is better able to help students with reading difficulties than most of his other teachers are. Like it or not, most secondary school English teachers will teach some reading, and a goodly number will be specifically assigned to teach in reading classes. In some schools, particularly in junior high schools in ghetto areas—to which, incidentally, many beginning teachers are assigned—all reading classes will be equally divided among the English teachers. In other such situations, an English teacher's assignment may be exclusively in reading. The school that has a reading specialist is as rare as it is fortunate.

In any case, many beginning English teachers have had no training in the teaching of reading and find themselves very much at sea when they are assigned one or more reading classes. But even the teacher who is not so assigned "becomes suddenly aware that she actually has freshmen, sophomores, juniors, and seniors who can't read—*really* can't read or read on such a low level that for the purposes of the class they might as well not read at all" (3, p. 884). Beth Allen goes on to say that such a situation "holds the added implication that [the English teacher is] the faculty member in the school who should 'do' something" about reading.

No pat solution exists to this problem. Everyone preparing to teach secondary English should be strongly advised to take a reading course as a necessary part of his training. Certainly the English teacher should want to know something about reading. In "The English Teacher: A Portrait," John Gerrietts lists among the qualifications of a good English teacher "Moderate knowledge of corrective and developmental reading techniques" and among the qualifications of a superior English teacher "A relatively thorough knowledge of corrective and developmental reading techniques" (53, p. 9).

Every secondary school should have available to teachers as many textbooks on the teaching of reading in the secondary school as possible. Minimally, every secondary school should have a subscription to the *Journal of Reading, The Reading Teacher, Reading Research Quarterly, Reading World,* and *Reading Improvement.* School districts would also be well advised to subsidize memberships in the International Reading Association for English teachers who spend 30 percent of their time or more teaching reading and to encourage such teachers to attend the annual convention of this important organization. It is unreasonable to expect the English teacher who belongs to the National Education Association and to the National Council of Teachers of English to pay out of his own pocket membership fees in the International Reading Association if his need for membership in this organization comes about because he is being required by his district to teach out of field.

RESOURCES FOR TEACHING READING

Among the books which secondary schools should have available to everyone who is teaching reading, the following are the most vitally important and practically useful:

Aukerman, Robert. *Reading in the Secondary School Classroom.* New York: McGraw-Hill Book Company, 1972.

Bamman, Henry A.; Hogan, Ursula; and Greene, Charles E. *Reading Instruction in the Secondary Schools.* New York: David McKay Co., Inc., 1961.

Berger, Allen and Hartig, Hugo. *The Reading Materials Handbook.* Oshkosh, Wis.: The Academia Press, 1969.

Early, Margaret (ed.). *Reading Instruction in Secondary Schools.* Newark, Dela.: International Reading Association, 1964.

Emery, Raymond C., and Houshower, Margaret B. *High Interest-Easy Reading for Junior and Senior High School Reluctant Readers.* Champaign, Ill.: National Council of Teachers of English, 1965.

Fader, Daniel, and McNeil, Elton B. *Hooked on Books.* New York: Berkley Publishing Corporation, 1968.

Fries, Charles C. *Linguistics and Reading.* New York: Holt, Rinehart & Winston, Inc., 1962.

Hafner, Lawrence E. *Improving Reading in Secondary Schools.* New York: The Macmillan Company, 1967.

Herber, Harold H. (ed.). *Developing Study Skills in Secondary Schools.* Newark, Dela.: International Reading Association, 1965.

———. *Teaching Reading in Content Areas.* Englewood Cliffs, N.J.: Prentice-Hall, Inc., 1970.

Hook, J. N. *The Teaching of High School English.* 4th ed.; New York: The Ronald Press Company, 1972.

Karlin, Robert. *Teaching Reading in High School.* Indianapolis: The Bobbs-Merrill Company, 1964.

Laffey, James L. (ed.). *Reading in the Content Areas.* Newark, Dela.: International Reading Association, 1972.

Marksheffel, Ned D. *Better Reading in the Secondary School.* New York: The Ronald Press Company, 1966.

Massey, Will J., and Moore, Virginia D. *Helping High School Students to Read Better.* New York: Holt, Rinehart & Winston, Inc., 1965.

Olson, Arthur V., and Ames, Wilbur S. (eds.). *Teaching Reading Skills in Secondary Schools: Readings.* Scranton, Pa.: International Textbook Company, 1970.

Penty, Ruth C. *Reading Ability and High School Dropouts.* New York: Teacher's College, Columbia University, 1956.

Pescosolido, John, and Gervase, Charles. *Reading Expectancy and Readability.* Dubuque, Ia.: Kendall/Hunt Publishing Company, 1971.

Robinson, H. Alan, and Rauch, Sidney J. (eds.). *Corrective Reading in the High School Program.* Newark, Dela.: International Reading Association, 1966.

Robinson, H. Alan, and Thomas, Ellen L. (eds.). *Fusing Reading Skills and Content*. Newark, Dela.: International Reading Association, 1969.
Sargent, Eileen E.; Huus, Helen; and Andressen, Oliver. *How to Read a Book*. Newark, Dela.: International Reading Association, 1970.
Spache, George D. *Good Reading for Disadvantaged Readers*. Champaign, Ill.: Garrard Publishing Company, 1970.
———. *Good Reading for Poor Readers*. 5th ed.; Champaign, Ill.: Garrard Publishing Company, 1970.
Shaw, Phillip B. *Effective Reading and Learning*. New York: Thomas Y. Crowell Company, 1956.
Simpson, Elizabeth A. *Helping High School Students Read Better*. Chicago: Science Research Associates, 1954.
Stewart, L. Jane; Heller, Frieda M.; and Alberty, Elsie J. *Improving Reading in the Junior High School*. New York: Appleton-Century-Crofts, 1957.
Squire, James R. *Responses of Adolescents While Reading Four Short Stories*. Champaign, Ill.: National Council of Teachers of English, 1964.
Weiss, M. Jerry (ed.). *Reading in the Secondary Schools*. New York: Odyssey Press, 1961.
Willard, Charles B. *Your Reading: A Book List for Junior High Schools*. New York: New American Library, Inc., 1966.

This basic library of about 30 books would cost under $250 and would serve the school and its reading teachers for years to come. It is a minimal collection but far exceeds that available in most secondary schools today.

ENTICING THE STUDENT TO READ

If the student is to be encouraged to learn how to read or to improve his poorly developed reading skills, he must be surrounded by attractive reading materials. In many cases, the student's home will suffer from a great dearth of reading material, and the people with whom the deficient reader customarily associates will not be enthusiastic readers. Therefore, at school he must be made to realize both the importance and joy of reading. It certainly would be helpful to him at this stage to see that his teacher reads and considers books to be important to him. Many students have, quite literally, never known anyone who likes to read; and when they find that a teacher to whom they relate well actually is excited about books, they may reach a turning point in their own enthusiasm for reading.

Few people read books after they have left school, yet most instruction in reading still involves the use of books. Perhaps better results would be achieved overall if teachers asked themselves one pertinent question: "What will most of my kids read when they leave school?" In most cases, people who are not compelled to read will read—aside from road signs, memos, and other such materials—newspapers, magazines, comic books, how-to-do-it books, catalogs, and other such utilitarian fare. Perhaps, then, the reading teacher would be approaching his task realistically and practically if he were to begin his instruction in reading by using the sorts of materials which his students are most likely to encounter when their formal educations have ended.

Where funds are available, it would be wise to have reading classes subscribe on a monthly basis to three or four newspapers. Each class should decide toward the end of each month which subscriptions to continue and which ones to permit to lapse. Classes might also enter magazine subscriptions—and, within the limits of good taste, students should decide to which magazines they wish to subscribe. Students should also be encouraged to bring in newspapers and magazines from home to be added to the class collection.

Students who learn to read newspapers comparatively are learning one of the most important lessons available to them. Reading classes might have a unit on the newspaper in which students learn to differentiate between fact and opinion, between biased reporting and straight reporting, between the headline and the whole story. They might, as a first lesson in comprehension, scan the classified ads looking for items they wish to buy or they might hold job interviews based on help-wanted ads in the newspaper. Norman C. Odom has used the newspaper with great success as a teaching medium in reading classes (40, pp. 475-76), and makes excellent suggestions about means of using the newspaper as a versatile device for reading instruction. Howard Decker also suggests ways of using the newspaper with deficient readers, and while space does not permit the inclusion of all 60 of his suggestions, it is worthwhile to note some of them:

Assign each student to find five words in the newspaper which he does not understand. Then each student should look up the words in a dictionary and use the words in original sentences.
Find numerous examples of abbreviations used in the newspaper (CIA, FHA, HAW, NATO, etc.). Have students circle these initials and then find the proper name for each set of initials.
Assign your students to turn to one particular section of the newspaper and make a list of the words used more frequently in that one section than in any other section of the newspaper.
... tell your students to read the Sunday edition of the newspaper and make a

list of the differences they notice between the Sunday paper and the weekday issues.

Choose a dozen or so news stories and clip the headlines off. Then challenge your students—particularly slow readers—to match the stories with the correct headlines.

Assign the class to read the comic strips for ten or fifteen minutes and then conduct a class discussion of the types of humor: slapstick, wit, irony, satire, sight jokes, puns, etc. (13, p. 269).

Certainly the student who is able to visit a newspaper and to see how an issue is put together will have much more zest for reading a paper, so a class trip to the local newspaper would be an appropriate activity for students in a reading class. It would also be desirable to have a newspaper reporter or feature writer come to the school to talk with reading classes about his job.

THE USE OF MAGAZINES

When students are permitted to order magazines which interest them, teachers should decide in advance not to be disappointed if they do not order *Harper's, Atlantic Monthly, Saturday Review, Time, Newsweek,* or *National Geographic.* Rather, if the class is typical, it will enter subscriptions to magazines like *Ebony, MAD, Sports Illustrated, Hot Rod, True Confessions, Popular Science, Popular Mechanics,* and assorted movie magazines and comic books. The teacher must remember that in dealing with severely disabled readers, it is more important to get the student to read than to impose controls upon what he reads. Once the student is enthusiastic about reading, the teacher can begin to help him develop taste in reading; but for the time, the student should be encouraged to read what interests him. In doing so, he will very likely be reading at his own level, and this is all to the good.

One inventive teacher whose students' problems included "bilingualism, emotional blocks, poor starts in reading, and other disabilities," found that her students, who ranged in age from 15 to 19 and in reading level from 2nd to 6th grade, responded most enthusiastically to *MAD* because they could "relate to the 'now' things dealt with" in it and because "of the boost in self-esteem they gain from seeing adults portrayed unflatteringly and teenagers shown as the more reasonable species." This teacher, rather than trying to change her students' tastes, recognized that "the reading of *MAD* in the classroom may be approached from many angles; reading skills, social and behavior attitudes, or just pleasure reading," and she went on to use the magazine as an effective teaching device, emphasizing the use of satire in the publication. She reported, "The use of *MAD* is excellent for improving reading skills, because it uses something basic to the learning of reading, and that is pictorialism. Coupled with the mastery of phonetic patterns, children first learn to read by building a 'sight word' vocabulary from pictorial representation. . . . they can build vocabulary by associating words with pictures in the magazine" (45, pp. 266-67).

Comic books, while admittedly infraliterary, have similar advantages for the disabled reader. They can provide a base from which students are eventually able to work toward reading more difficult materials, and certainly there is no doubt about the popularity of comic books among teen-agers of all reading levels. Most junior high school students, good readers and poor, spend more than half of their disposable income on this single reading item, and they do so with little encouragement or direction from their elders.

A CLASSROOM PAPERBACK LIBRARY

Every secondary school English classroom should have a paperback library of at least 250 books. Certainly the classroom in which reading is to be taught should have even a larger collection than this. Most adults, if they read books at all, read paperbacks. Therefore, teen-agers who find reading difficult should be encouraged to read paperbacks rather than being forced to read from weighty anthologies which are heavy and uncomfortable to hold.

Paperback libraries can be built gradually, largely through contributions of used books from the community. In all instances, the teacher will have to use good judgment in selecting appropriate books for a classroom library. Excellent suggestions of books appropriate to different age and ability levels are easily available in Dwight Burton's *Literature Study in the High Schools* (9), with which most English teachers are familiar. CeCelia Algra and James Fillbrandt also provide helpful insights into adolescent reading interests in "Book Selection Patterns among High School Students" (2).

Sometimes book wholesalers can be persuaded to contribute single copies of paperback books to classroom libraries, and often secondhand book stores are willing to sell used paperbacks in quantity at much reduced prices. One teacher kept a constant flow of paperbacks moving through her classroom by making a felt wall hanging with 12 large pockets sewn onto it. She put a popular paperback book in each of the pockets and told her students that they could take and keep any book they wished to, but that they had to replace it with another book. This technique was amazingly successful and generated considerable enthusiasm for reading among youngsters who had previously been rather apathetic.

Teachers will also find that their colleagues are usually willing to contribute used paperback books and magazines to classroom libraries, and normally a thank-you note listing the books and magazines contributed will make the gift qualify as a tax deductible item provided that the note is written on school stationery.

Joan Dobson contends that every school should have available for circulation among the student body a minimum of eight books per student. She recommends the purchase of large quantities of paperbacks: "The cost of new paperbacks with a 20 percent discount allowed by the local paperback distributor averages 60 cents per book: thus the total cost for a 2,400 volume library would be $1,440.00. Most communities could help to offset initial cost by donations of good used paperbacks." Ms. Dobson goes on to say that "One of the virtues of the paperback is that its low price allows stocking of the currently most popular books in multiple copies" (15, p. 1136).

The English teacher, particularly one who teaches reading, will find that the annual *Paperbound Book Guide for High Schools* which is published by the R. R. Bowker Company, 1180 Avenue of the Americas, New York City 10036 and is distributed free of charge, is a useful resource. The same company publishes the much more comprehensive *Paperbound Books in Print* which appears in nine monthly issues and three cumulative volumes each year. An annual subscription to it costs $23.50.

FREE READING MATERIALS

The teacher should explore all possible sources of obtaining free material for use in the classroom. Most states have a *Driver's Handbook* which one studies before taking the test for a driving license. Teen-agers are particularly enthusiastic about trying to read a book which is of such practical and immediate value to them, and copies are generally available from the State Department of Motor Vehicles free of charge.

Catalogs of automotive equipment, hi-fi equipment, farming equipment, and sports equipment are easily available without cost, and their interest level among students is high. Chambers of commerce are generous in distributing materials about their regions, and large mail-order houses regularly issue catalogs of general merchandise. The teacher who comes to know his students' hobbies will be able to obtain free reading materials related to these hobbies if he is resourceful. Students should be encouraged to send for free materials on their own, for they are more likely to read material which comes through the mail addressed to them personally than to read material which someone else provides for them. Many students almost never receive mail and are quite thrilled to discover that a postal card sent to the right place with a legible return address and an intelligible request will bring them material containing information which they can use. They will exert every effort to read such material when they receive it.

TYPES OF READING PROBLEMS

The secondary school student who is unable to read or who is reading far below grade level may be suffering from dyslexia which is caused by mixed dominance—a right-handed, left-eyed child or vice versa. The teacher should suspect this problem and seek professional help for the child who shows symptoms of it. The problem generally cannot be dealt with effectively by an untrained person. A child may be dyslectic if he has great trouble reading and if he makes numerous reversals in his writing—writing the letter *S* or the letter *R* backwards (Ƨ or Я), copying a simple word like *the* as *hte*. This child, when trying to read aloud, may frequently reverse words. He usually will not be a nonreader, but will be a very inefficient reader. The teacher wishing to know more about dyslexia should read Wagner's book on the subject (55).

If one were to follow any random group of 30 youngsters through the first eight years of school and if each child in the group were exposed to essentially the same teaching procedures, he would find that some of the youngsters would be reading above grade level, some approximately at grade level, some far below grade level, and one or two not at all. The individuals within any group of children exposed to the same basic education will develop differently, largely because of outside influences and differences in native ability.

Charles Fries writes quite erroneously, "Learning to read ... is *not* a process of learning new or other language signals than those the child has already learned. The language signals are all the same. The difference lies in the medium through which the physical stimuli make contact with his nervous system" (20, p. xv). For the black child or the child from a non-English-speaking background, Fries' contention simply is not true. Even for the child accustomed to hearing relatively standard English spoken, the written word represents a new dialect, for spoken and written English are two separate, though related, entities. For the child who has grown up in an atmosphere in which little standard English is heard, the written word is twice removed from his experience, and his reading problems are intensified most significantly by this fact.

William Labov, in writing about the difficulties which ghetto youngsters have in learning to read, contends that "the chief difficulty which we can now identify, therefore, is not so much in the dialect differences themselves as in the ignorance of those differences. If the teacher believes that the students' sound system matches his own, he is apt to teach reading in terms of the 'sounds' of letters.... The teacher would certainly profit from knowing at the outset ... which sound distinctions are actually made by the students and which are not" (31, p. 43).

It has not been until very recently that linguists have had any comprehensive view of the grammar and structure of black English, which is a distinct dialect of English. J. L. Dillard has recently demonstrated that black English assumes a word order closely resembling that of West African languages (14), and that, while not making a clear distinction between the present and past tenses, it does differentiate clearly between continuous and momentary action. The black dialect will also tend to omit the double pluralization in a word like *themselves,* which in typical black dialect will come out *themself* and, while sounding ungrammatical, will be perfectly clear in meaning.

Dillard and his frequent collaborator, William A. Stewart, president of the Education Study Center in Washington, urge that black children be taught to read their own dialect before they are confronted with books in standard English. To this end, the Education Study Center has produced three experimental reading books in which black English is accompanied by parallel versions in standard

English. The theory behind these texts is that once the child learns to read the dialect he is accustomed to hearing spoken about him, he will be better able to make the transition to reading standard English.

Some linguists have suggested similarly that, as an aid to beginning readers, "a more uniform symbol system [replace] our traditional orthography . . . [in order to] reduce the amount of frustration and failure that children experience when they first encounter the written page. The assumption is that if we build the confidence of young readers in their ability to 'crack a writing code,' they can more easily learn . . . how to crack the conventional code" (41, p. 181).

When Kenneth Johnson was teaching in the Watts section of Los Angeles, he had his students produce a play which they tape recorded. The dialogue was in their usual dialect. After the play was on tape, Johnson transcribed and reproduced it in mimeographed form. He then said to his students, "This is a great play, but whitey wouldn't understand it. Why don't we translate it?" The students did this and produced a parallel version which they presented; and from this experience, they gained a practical understanding of dialectal differences without having had any value judgments about language forced upon them.

Some teen-agers are what might be termed *phoney nonreaders*. Fader relates the story of Wentworth, a typical phoney nonreader. Wentworth attended a junior high school where most of his teachers had written him off as unteachable. He was alleged to be unable to read. Fader, having gained Wentworth's confidence, was surprised to find that Wentworth indeed could read and often did so on his own. He asked Wentworth about this and received the following answer: "Sure I can read. . . . I been able to read ever since I can remember. But I ain't never gonna let *them* know, on accoun' of iff'n I do I'm gonna have to read all that crap they got" (18, p. 22). Many youngsters who are turned off by school feign ignorance, sometimes to get attention, sometimes to show contempt. Many such youngsters are bright, but have never experienced anything but defeat and humiliation from authority figures (teachers) who are culturally alien to them.

Some youngsters who cannot read have eye problems; in most schools, each student's vision and hearing are checked annually. Where this is not the case, the teacher might arrange through the principal to have eye examinations for those students who are unable to read. If a student is diagnosed as having a visual defect but cannot afford to buy corrective lenses, the guidance counsellor should be notified so that he may attempt to aid the student in getting the needed glasses. Also, the teacher or counsellor might get in touch with New Eyes for the Needy, Inc., Short Hills, New Jersey 07078. This nonprofit organization provides glasses for qualified people who cannot afford them.

READING TESTS

In most schools, teachers will have available to them the cumulative record of each child he is teaching. This record will generally contain both IQ and reading test scores. Very often the teacher will attempt to review the cumulative records for all of his students within the first few weeks of school. Herein, perhaps, lurks a danger, for test scores do not tell the whole story about a youngster. Yet, many teachers, seeing that a child has a low IQ and has consistently scored far below grade level on reading tests, tend to lower their expectations for the child in question, thereby perhaps helping to perpetuate the cycle of defeat and nonachievement which has characterized the youngster's whole educational history.

Albert J. Harris acknowledges that "standardized tests of reading ability are especially valuable for making comparisons among pupil populations and for tracing growth in research studies." But he goes on to warn teachers that "because they show how a child compares with other children rather than exactly what he can do with specific kinds of reading materials, standardized tests are somewhat less useful for instructional guidance than has often been assumed" (17, p. 6).

The teacher who wishes to get some general notion of his students' reading ability may find the *San Diego Quick Assessment* a useful tool. This test consists of 11 lists of 10 graded words drawn from basal readers and the Thorndike list. The student is asked to read through the list aloud. When he misses no more than one word at a given grade level, he can be expected to read independently at that level. When he misses two, this is his indicated instructional level. When he misses three or more, the material at this grade level will be too difficult for him (32, pp. 305–7).

If the teacher has a relatively accurate IQ score for a student, he can get a general indication of the level at which the student should be able to read by using the following equation:

$$\text{Numbers of years spent in school} \times \frac{IQ}{100} + 1$$

Therefore, a child with an IQ of 120 who is entering the 10th grade might be expected to be reading at the 11.8 grade level, whereas a similar child with an IQ of 90 would be expected to read at the 9.1 level (7, pp. 92-95).

It must be emphasized here that no one test gives a total indication of a student's reading ability. Many factors must enter into any determination of what may reasonably be expected of a student with a reading handicap.

One of the best diagnostic techniques a teacher can use is the so-called *cloze procedure*. The teacher can easily construct this test himself. He merely selects typical 200-300 word passages from books which his students are actually using, and reproduces these passages, omitting every 10th word. Every blank should be of the same size so that no clues are given about the length of the missing words. It is also important that the ideas contained in the selected passages are related. The student is asked to fill in the missing words. If, on several of these tests, his score averages below 40 percent, the material is too difficult for him (8, pp. 429-36). This technique is particularly useful for assessing the student's ability to read with comprehension books in content areas.

Literally hundreds of standardized reading tests are available to teachers. Karlin points out (28, pp. 93-94) that although these tests give teachers helpful indications of his students' reading abilities, they suffer from numerous weaknesses. Many of them are too narrow in scope. For example, they usually include a section on vocabulary, but they often do not attempt to measure a student's ability to deal with multiple meanings of words, using contextual clues. Most do not measure small units of growth, therefore are not sufficiently accurate in what they tell. They do not provide any way of interpreting incorrect responses, so that the teacher cannot be sure whether the student failed to know the meaning of a given word or whether he was unable to read the word. The standardized test can in no way duplicate typical reading conditions nor can it test on pages of continuous material since, by its very nature and form it deals with isolated bits of reading materials.

Over and above this, some students do not test well. Some, who might read with good speed and comprehension materials for which they have immediate use — books on how to modify automobiles, for example — will do poorly on standardized reading tests merely because of the nature of the reading selections found in them.

Therefore, the teacher must be cautioned to use the standardized reading test with judgment and to regard its results as possible indications of a student's ability, but not, certainly, as the final word.

FREQUENTLY USED STANDARDIZED TESTS

The following are the tests most frequently available to teachers and most often used by school districts:

Comprehensive Test of Basic Skills (CTBS), California Test Bureau, Del Monte Research Park, Monterey, California 93940.
Iowa Test of Basic Skills (ITBS), Houghton Mifflin Company, Educational Division, 110 Tremont Street, Boston, Massachusetts 02107.
Iowa Test of Educational Development (ITED), Science Research Associates, Inc., 259 East Erie Street, Chicago, Illinois 60611.
Metropolitan Achievement Tests (MAT), Harcourt Brace Jovanovich, Inc., 757 Third Avenue, New York City 10017.
Sequential Tests of Educational Progress (STEP), Educational Testing Service, 20 Nassau Street, Princeton, New Jersey 08540.
SRA Achievement Series, Science Research Associates, Inc., 259 East Erie Street, Chicago, Illinois 60611.
Stanford Achievement Tests (SAT), Harcourt Brace Jovanovich, Inc., 757 Third Avenue, New York City 10017.
Tests of Academic Progress (TAP), Houghton Mifflin Company, Educational Division, 110 Tremont Street, Boston, Massachusetts 02107.

Also in common use are the *California Reading Test, Cooperative Reading Comprehension Test, Davis Reading Test, Gates Reading Survey, Iowa Silent Reading Tests, Kelley-Greene Reading Comprehension Test, Nelson-Denny Reading Test,* and *Spitzer Study Skills Test.* In most secondary schools, the guidance counsellor or the district supervisor in reading can inform teachers of which tests are available.

APPROACHES TO THE TEACHING OF READING

It might almost be said that there are as many approaches to the teaching of reading as there are teachers of reading. John Manning lists four basic approaches (4, pp. 413–15): developmental, synthetic, language immersion, and eclectic. Carl Wallen lists six (56, p. 454): basal, phonic, linguistic, programmed, individualized, and language experience. But for our purposes, probably Karlin's division is most appropriate, for the average English teacher who is called upon to teach reading will be most concerned with the three approaches which he lists (28, pp. 20-21): developmental, corrective, and remedial.

The English teacher has always been concerned to some extent with the first two of these approaches and, through the years, has become increasingly concerned with the third, which is closely related to the other two. In fact, Karlin contends that "if there is any difference between developmental and remedial instruction, it is a difference in degree and not kind" (28, p. 21).

Developmental reading is concerned with bringing the student step by step from the earliest and simplest reading skills—word recognition, for example—to the point that he can employ the most demanding reading skills, such as interpretation, appreciation of style, and recognition of literary devices. Karlin lists six areas in developmental reading in their order of difficulty: (1) word recognition; (2) meanings; (3) study skills; (4) flexibility; (5) appreciation; and (6) interests (28, p. 19).

The Sub-Committee on Maturity in Reading of the Regional Commission on Interrelationships of Secondary Schools, Colleges, and Professional Schools in 1959 presented a broader list of reading abilities in ascending order of difficulty and complexity: (1) interest in books and reading; (2) independence in attacking words; (3) interpretation of vocabulary in context; (4) expansion of vocabulary through semantic variations; (5) adjustment of rate and method to the purpose of materials; (6) desire to read both intensively and extensively; (7) ability to read critically; (8) awareness of the creative aspects of reading; (9) capacity to distinguish between fact and propaganda; (10) recognition and appreciation of literary allusions and figurative language; and (11) sensitivity to the author's style and intent (43). Certainly these are valid ends toward which every English teacher works whether he be teaching reading *per se* or literature.

Developmental reading instruction is based largely upon readiness and upon the sequential development of a reading program which will lead logically and step by step from one level of difficulty to the next. Curriculum guides in literature are usually sequentially developed so that each item in the guide will provide a foundation for a broader understanding of works occurring later in the guide. Every English teacher is familiar with this approach. The only word of caution that need be uttered here is that which would remind the teacher that not every student is ready to tackle a given reading assignment at a given time, so that options must be available if instruction is to be individualized in such a way as to suit the needs of the students in the best manner possible.

Corrective reading is essentially remedial reading; however, it takes place in the regular classroom and is taught as individual students require it by the regular teacher. Corrective reading instruction works well with students who, basically, are able to read and whose chief problems come from adjusting to a new style of writing or to a new vocabulary. However, as Beth Allen quite rightly asserts, "the true nonreader is almost impossible to help in the regular classroom because of the embarrassing attention it focuses on his deficiency before his classmates—persons whose good opinions he usually prizes above almost anything else in school. The solution is to find about thirty minutes a day to work with him privately" (3, p. 885).

This may be all well and good if, out of the 100-130 students the average teacher deals with each day, there is only one nonreader. But even if this is the case, a problem still exists, for teachers do not have 30 extra minutes each day which coincide with the 30 minutes that the nonreading student has free. If the teacher has an aide, as many English teachers now do, either the teacher or the aide can work with nonreaders. Failing this, the teacher may, through the Future Teachers Association in the school, find a competent student to help tutor the nonreader.

More secondary school students will be retarded readers than nonreaders, even in ghetto schools, so the major thrust of corrective reading instruction must be in the direction of the retarded readers. In many cases, retarded readers can be enlisted to help teach nonreaders, and in doing so may begin to overcome some of their own reading handicaps (21; 35, pp. 221-25). Indeed, in one experiment in which college freshmen tutored primary school youngsters on a one-to-one basis, the test results at the end of one semester indicated that those being tutored had advanced an average of 1.1 years in instructional level while the average tutor had advanced 2.4 years (35, p. 223).

One teacher has found that remedial reading students work better in pairs than alone. She writes that "two working together can be especially important in easing the blow to the self-image" that comes from being a severely retarded reader. She continues, "The tension built up from the learning situation itself may also be eased when one has a partner" (11, pp. 110-11). The main thrust of what she says in the article is that the disabled reader will be self-conscious in his difference from his friends, but that if he is paired with someone with like problems, he will feel more a part of the class and will relate better to the total group.

Cohn has observed that "when two students are involved in such a program, their interaction can relieve anger and hostility, ease tension, elevate the self-image, and stimulate learning through competition" (11, p. 112).

Most remedial reading instruction is reserved for students reading two or more years below grade level and is ideally offered by people who have had some specific training in the teaching of reading. The English teacher in a situation in which he must teach remedial reading should take course work in the teaching of reading as soon as possible and state departments of education must be made to realize that many teachers working toward graduate certificates in the teaching of English will profit much more from taking two or three reading courses than they will from taking graduate level courses in 18th-century British literature or in Middle English philology. As important as the substantive area is to teachers, no amount of competence in it will make it possible for them to teach literature to nonreaders.

ESTABLISHING PRIORITIES

Many teachers, undoubtedly impelled by the worthiest of motives, put so much emphasis upon their subject matter that they lose sight of the fact that schools are for students. It is understandable that a teacher feels a responsibility to cover a given amount of material in a course. However, the teacher who insists on teaching the substance of the course whether or not it has meaning and value to the majority of students in the class needs to reassess his priorities.

The new teacher is often intimidated by the curriculum guide for a given grade level and feels that the most important job that he has is to cover the minimal standards set down by such a guide for a given year. This is a worthy ambition, perhaps; however, no guide is perfect nor can any guide take into account the actual situations which a teacher will meet daily in the classroom.

If the guide calls for the teaching of *Julius Caesar* in the 10th grade, for example, the teacher would do well to defer the teaching of this classic until he knows whether or not his students are capable of reading it with understanding, for if they cannot read with understanding, they can never read with enthusiasm; and the literary component of the English curriculum must be directed toward helping students to develop an appreciation of and enthusiam for literature. This is what the teaching of literature is all about. The English class has provided the student with very little if, upon leaving school and ending his formal education, he never wants to read another book. And the easiest way to turn a student away from voluntary reading is to make his reading experience in school a defeating one.

The teacher of high school students with reading disabilities must heed the words of people like Beth Allen if they are ever to have any impact upon their students: "The student has to want to learn and to believe that he can learn, and by the time students have come this far without learning to read, they probably don't believe they can learn and they have to be lured, oftentimes, into wanting to" (3, p. 887).

If the English teacher is faced with a class in which there is a preponderance of disabled readers, his first, most obvious task—despite anything that a curriculum guide or an English supervisor might suggest—is to work with his students on their learning problems. Most administrators and supervisors are sufficiently aware of the severity of reading problems that, if consulted, they will be very supportive of a teacher who bends the curriculum to meet this immediate and pressing need.

WHO ARE YOUR STUDENTS?

Many teachers fail to meet the most pressing needs of their students because they labor under the delusion that some set of vague academic standards must be upheld. To such teachers, the 9th- or 10th- or 11th-grade curriculum is set and the student who cannot adapt to the curriculum is obviously below standard and must be penalized. It would never occur to such a teacher that failing grades might reflect a deficiency in his teaching techniques rather than a failure on the part of the failing student.

Such a teacher is the spiritual product of another age, a member of a vanishing breed; but until the breed vanishes, it can wreak havoc in the lives of many students. One who teaches in today's schools must remember one basic fact about today's school population: Nearly every citizen of the United States attends school minimally until age 16.

At the turn of the century, all but about 10 percent of the

population left school at the end of the 8th grade. That minority which went on to secondary school would, in all probability, continue to college. High school graduation requirements and college entrance requirements were identical. The secondary school population was academically oriented. Ninth graders could read and write reasonably well, for those who couldn't never got to be 9th graders.

Today, high school is available to everyone and there is little place in our society for those who have not completed high school. But in order to accommodate a drastically different sort of student body, schools have had to change significantly—as they indeed have—and teachers have had to accept the idea of dealing with students in those areas of instruction in which they most need help.

Today's teacher will be continually unhappy and frustrated if he places his subject before his students in importance. Everyone wishes that he might be able to count on the fact that all secondary school students are able to read; but since they are not, the teacher must adjust his philosophy of what he is doing to meet the actual needs of his students. If they cannot read effectively within his content area, then he has little choice but to concentrate on their reading problems first and on their mastery of the content area second, at least at the beginning. This is not to say that he should ignore his content area completely; however, until students are able to read effectively in it, he must provide options which will involve them in the content area without their being forced to read extensively in it. Films, filmstrips, cassettes, video tape, phonograph records and other such materials are often available and may be used first in place of extensive readings and later as a supplement to them. Teacher lectures are another valuable supplement in some cases, although at the secondary level, these should be informal and should not normally occupy an entire class period. They should be used to generate discussion from which can grow an enthusiasm for the subject matter under consideration.

It is of the utmost importance that the teacher always remember that the 15- or 16-year-old disabled reader is, despite his reading disability, approaching maturity and must be dealt with on a mature level. If he is brought to the point of dealing with mature ideas, he may be brought to the point of realizing more fully than ever before the importance of reading as a tool. If, realizing this, he is still unable to overcome his disability, then the teacher's task comes to be that of teaching him how to function best in spite of his disability—how to look to sources other than written ones for ideas, how to reason, how to develop his memory, and how to be sensitive to all that is around him.

FILMS AND THE DISABLED READER

When she came to the English department at Lillis High School in Kansas City, Sister Bede Sullivan found that reading deficiencies represented the greatest single teaching problem in the entire school. Undaunted by what she found at Lillis, Sister Bede launched a schoolwide film program which was to receive national recognition and which was to bring large numbers of barely literate students to a mature understanding of many of the literary and artistic techniques used in making films.

Sister Bede arranged to have a feature film shown to the entire school every Monday morning and the same film shown again every Friday after three day's classroom discussion of it. This meant that the normal schedule of the school had to be altered to permit two two-hour film viewing periods each week; but most of the teachers at Lillis felt that this disruption in the schedule was a small price to pay for the results that were ultimately obtained.

The total English program centered around the film for the week and, as the term went on, the films progressively became more artistically complex. Reading was encouraged, but those who had severe reading problems were still actively involved in the discussions which the films generated in their classes (52).

Because of the expense of renting regular feature films, a program of this sort must receive schoolwide support, and not all schools have the need for such a program. However, schools in which the majority of students are reading significantly below grade level might find the results of such a program highly rewarding.

Besides Sister Bede's fine book, the most helpful sources for the teacher interested in using films as a part of the literature program and as a possible springboard to reading are the National Council of Teachers of English-sponsored *The Motion Picture and the Teaching of English* (46), Arthur Knight's *The Liveliest Art* (29) which chronicles the first half-century of movie making, John Culkins' *Film Study in the High School* (12), and *Film: The Creative Eye* (50) and *Film Study and the English Teacher* (49), both by David Sohn.

SELF-CONTAINED READING-ORIENTED SECONDARY CLASSES

The Sewanhaka (New York) Central High School District, a close suburb of New York City serving 12,000 secondary school students, sought a solution to the problem of dealing with a small number of its students with average or better intelligence who had such severe reading problems that they could not meet the reading demands of even the "modified" curriculum. The school district realized that the future of these students was bleak, indeed, because a 10th grader reading at the 6th- or 7th-grade level, even with specialized remedial reading instruction is not likely to approach grade level in his reading in a year's time. The major problem was that the student with a really severe reading handicap, even if he were making tremendous progress in his reading class, would have to face the constant and demoralizing frustration of being unable to handle the reading assignments in his other classes.

The district decided that what it needed for its extremely handicapped readers was a reading-oriented, self-contained secondary classroom. However, numerous problems stood in the way of accomplishing this. To begin with, the cost would be high. Second, if the emphasis were on reading, how could the course content be preserved to the satisfaction of accrediting agencies? Third, there was the problem of finding a teacher who was trained in reading, but could work within the substantive areas that needed to be covered as well. Besides these problems, the planners had to consider how students accustomed to three years of departmentalized instruction would react to working within a framework in which there was only one teacher. And finally, parents had to be sold on the idea of having their youngsters pulled from conventional senior high school classes and put into a situation involving this novel format.

The financial problem was solved when Title I, ESEA provided federal funds so that the district could set up a 10th grade, self-contained classroom. The program was designated SCALE, an acronym for *S*elf-*C*ontained *A*cademic *L*earning *E*nvironment.

A soundproof room was found for the class to meet in, and it was equipped with carrels which had projection readers in them. High interest/low readability books in various subject areas were gathered, with special attention being given to the fact that their content was roughly parallel to that of the texts being used in regular classes.

Twelve students were enrolled in the program for which the teacher was Mrs. Virginia Whitener, a certified science teacher with a background of social casework and with credentials in the teaching of reading. The 10th-grade students selected for the program were either failing or marginal in academic achievement, had average or better intelligence, and had reading scores far below grade level. The average IQ was 106. The mean reading score was 6.7. One pupil with an IQ of 114 was reading at the 6.2 level, a full five years below what might have been expected of him.

Of the 12 students selected for SCALE, 11 had made scores on the California Test of Personality which indicated social maladjustment. Most had very poor self-images and tended to be antisocial. Previous teachers had categorized both them and their parents as apathetic. The students came mostly from large families of the lower middle-class economic group. Before being admitted to the program, both the students and at least one of their parents were interviewed. The first meeting with parents was in the evening and was attended by at least one parent for each child, the SCALE teacher, the principal of the school, the Title I director, and the reading/English supervisor. Additional meetings with parents were held as the program proceeded.

The emphasis of the SCALE classes was on reading, but during the four periods that the class met each day, the basic academic areas were also covered. Students spent the remainder of each day in regular elective classes so that they did not lose touch with the total school program, and the teacher spent the remainder of each day working individually with SCALE students, visiting their homes, and preparing materials for them.

The results of the program were highly gratifying. Most of the students approached grade level in reading and, through the course of the program, made a much better social adjustment than they had previously achieved (16).

Not every school can institute a program such as that described here; however, modifications of such a program may be possible, particularly in districts where teacher aides are available and can be assigned to work with youngsters who need special help. A good aide, working under the direction of a qualified teacher, can provide the individualized instruction which severely handicapped readers require.

THE SUSTAINED SILENT READING PROGRAM

One of the most obvious problems that deficient readers have is that they mouth each word. Their lips move when they read and, even when a dozen of them are all concentrating on reading to themselves, noise will arise in the classroom as they pronounce subvocally or, sometimes, quite vocally the words that they see. It is not unusual in a reading classroom to see a group of students working conscientiously on their reading and to hear a steady hum in the room as they pronounce words to themselves.

If students are ever to become sufficiently proficient in reading that they can use the skill well, they must learn to read silently. One can categorically say that the reader who pronounces words as he reads cannot read with sufficient speed to meet the reading demands which are placed upon him in his academic classes.

Robert A. McCracken, the director of the Reading Center at Western Washington State College, has experimented most successfully with a program first developed by Lyman C. Hunt, Jr., of the University of Vermont and originally designated *Uninterrupted Sustained Silent Reading*. Because the acronym USSR was somewhat suspect in the early sixties, when the program was being tested, the first word was dropped and the program was referred to as the SSR Program.

McCracken reports on this program and on his use of it (34). It must be remembered that McCracken is working with highly motivated college students who come to him voluntarily because they have reading problems, and it was essentially with this type of student that Hunt had worked earlier. The program, as McCracken spells it out, is probably too rigid for use with a broad range of secondary school students. However, with some adaptations, the secondary teacher may be able to use it with selected students. The great virtue of the program is that much of it can be run by paraprofessionals.

McCracken lists six rules which must be rigidly enforced if the program is to work:

1. *Each student must read silently.* McCracken would not be above threatening students who do not do this. The teacher must convince the students of his seriousness about the business of silent reading.
2. *The teacher reads.* He brings to class something which he wishes to read, and he reads it. He permits no interruption. He sets the example for good reading practices and proves by his example that reading is important to him.
3. *Each student selects a single book, magazine, or newspaper to read.* If he does not know what to select, the teacher assigns him a book for the day. Then on the next day, he probably will choose his own. He is not permitted to switch his reading materials once the period has begun.
4. *A timer is used.* A simple egg timer with a bell should be set, initially for five or ten minutes, which is a sufficient period for a deficient reader to sustain silent reading at first. A wall clock should not be used because

some poor readers will become clock watchers. The timer is set, the classroom becomes quiet, and everyone reads. When the bell rings, the instructor says, "Good. You sustained your reading today for ten minutes. Continue reading silently if you wish."
5. *There are absolutely no reports or records of any kind.* As the students become more proficient in silent reading, discussions of books and written work relating to the reading might be a *natural* outcome; but initially, the only requirement should be silent reading.
6. *Begin with whole classes or larger groups of students heterogeneously grouped.* This is a very interesting aspect of the Hunt method. It is felt that in small groups, students will feel free to talk among themselves, but that in large groups, students will maintain the silence upon which the success of the program depends. Since the periods of sustained silent reading are short to begin with, the expectation that the class will be completely silent during the timed period is not unreasonable.

It might be noted that a junior high school teacher whose students had great trouble in learning to read silently used an adaptation of the Hunt method, but added to it one creative practice of her own. She provided chewing gum for everyone in class at the beginning of the timed period and said that everyone might chew, but that he had to chew with his mouth closed. In a school where gum chewing was prohibited, this relaxation of the rule—which was sanctioned by the principal, incidentally—gave students a good feeling about their reading class.

THE READING CLASSROOM

The weaknesses and limitations of the formalized classroom have been convincingly chronicled by Silberman in *Crisis in the Classroom* (48), by Postman and Weingartner in *Teaching as a Subversive Activity* (42), by Kohl in *The Open Classroom* (30), and by numerous other writers who have a vital concern with education. In view of what the Dramer study (16) indicated about the social adjustment problems of those with severe reading handicaps, it certainly is apparent that the secondary school reading classroom must not be a formal or forbidding place. If it is to serve its purpose most effectively, it must be the sort of room which students look forward to coming into.

The individual teacher can do much to create the atmosphere requisite for reading instruction. With a little help from the school administration, still more can be done.

The teacher who works with youngsters in the teaching of reading must ask himself at the outset two basic questions:

1. What does the average person read?
2. Where does the average person do his reading?

The first question has already been partially answered earlier in this chapter. The average adult reads few books, some magazines, some newspapers, many sets of directions telling how to do things, and many road signs, billboards, and other such printed media. Therefore, the reading classroom should abound in the sorts of materials which the average person normally encounters in his reading. The walls should have posters on them, bulletin boards should have cartoons and other word-oriented pictorial material displayed on them, and a broad range of books, magazines, and newspapers should be easily available. In the reading classroom, students should never want for things to read.

In answer to the second question, one must acknowledge that little reading, if any, takes place under conditions simulating those of the library or the formal classroom. People read on trains and buses, in noisy offices, draped over an easy chair at home with music or the television playing in the background, propped up in bed just before sleep comes on, sprawled on the floor, or in any other number of contorted positions, usually with noise of one sort or another very near at hand.

Therefore, if the teacher is really concerned with helping the student to develop the reading skills which he will need to use for the rest of his life, he had better pay some heed to simulating the conditions under which his students are likely to do their reading.

The first step is probably to push back to the perimeters of the room all movable furniture so that there is open space to work with. Teachers might then encourage students to bring to school shag rugs, cushions, or used furniture so that the classroom look can be done away with or at least minimized. It would be helpful to have two library-type tables with chairs to be used when students are doing artwork or group work, both of which should be encouraged in the reading classroom. The classroom should have a phonograph or cassette player so that music can be played during reading periods. The music will minimize other noises which might prove distracting to the weak reader.

Students should be invited to bring to the classroom plants, aquariums, or other items which will make them feel more nearly a part of the class. And to whatever extent is possible and feasible, there should be freedom of movement within the classroom—students should be able to sharpen pencils, talk with other students, and move around generally without having to ask permission (1). It may take time to achieve the sort of climate within which this is possible, but the teacher must constantly strive to achieve this climate, for without it many of the basic factors contributing to a student's inability to read will continue to exist and to impede his progress toward being able to read well. Also, it must be remembered that often the poor reader has a short attention span, so to expect him to sit quietly in one place and read for an entire class period is unreasonable. The freer the atmosphere in which he is permitted to operate, the more likely it is that his reading skills will improve.

MUSIC AND THE DEFICIENT READER

Music may serve a vital function in the reading classroom other than that of merely providing a background which will minimize other distracting noises. At the secondary level particularly, the interests of the slow reader must be capitalized upon if progress in reading is to be made. Also, in analyzing the processes by which people come to be able to read, one begins to appreciate that word clusters or word groups are important—more so than individual words, if one is to increase his speed in reading.

Two Arizona State University reading specialists experimented with using the metronome as a reading aid with 400 elementary, secondary and college students (19). They hypothesized that one major reason that students make errors in oral reading—and probably in silent reading as well—is that they overreach their present perceptual span; that is, they tend to jump ahead in their reading before having sufficiently decoded the group of words on which they first fixed.

Fazio and McDonald began by setting the metronome for 40 clicks a minute, the lowest possible calibration. They had each student read two-or three-word phrases aloud for each click of the metronome. He could not go on to the next phrase until the metronome had clicked, so he had no motivation to overreach. The effect of this experiment as applied to oral reading was that it caused the student to learn something about how to group words.

When the experiment was extended to include silent reading, the "student would read a phrase per click in order to condition himself in reacting to words as thought units" (19, p. 290). By growing accustomed to the metronomic method of reading, students began to read phrases rather than single words. Once students became accustomed to the slow (40 click per minute) metronomic rate, they could increase the rate and thereby, in gradual steps, increase their reading speed.

The experimenters suggest that "the remedial teacher can use the metronome in a game to develop sight vocabulary. In this game the metronome is set at a pace of about forty clicks per minute. At each click the teacher flashes a word for the student to recognize before the next click. This has proved a motivational device in getting students to practice instant recognition of words" (19, p. 291).

The researchers found the metronomic technique to be particularly useful with "high school students who made much greater gains than college students with similar selections from Baker's *Reading Skills*" (19, p. 291). The use of the metronome helped students to establish for themselves in a very natural way a feeling for the rhythms of English.

In Winston Salem, North Carolina, an athletic coach, Royal Lancaster, conjectured, "I do everything I do in rhythm, so I wondered if using the rhythm of music could help pupils who stumble and stutter when they read, who read so jerkily the reading has little or no meaning for them" (24, p. 24). Lancaster, a skilled guitarist, arranged to meet with a special class of slow readers during his planning period each Friday. He had each member in the group teach something or do something which had to do with reading. One student might teach the lyrics of a popular song. Another might read a story into a tape recorder. Another might review and discuss a song that the group had learned at its last meeting.

The coach used the opportunity not only to help students learn to read better mechanically, but also to bring them to a better understanding of literary elements, without which they would not be likely to develop into mature readers. For example, in reviewing the song "Games People Play," special attention was given to difficult words and poetic expressions: "What kind of games do people play? What does 'ivory tower' mean?" (24, p. 24). Lancaster also asked for an interpretation of the feelings evoked by some of the songs.

This group's regular English teacher found that youngsters looked forward to the Friday sessions with the coach. She found that students who had had considerable trouble with reading gained assurance when they were able to sing songs with refrains. Reading the refrain, while a type of drill, is relatively painless to the student; and through the repetition of a refrain, the student could come to recognize words.

The students involved in this special group were thought by their regular teacher to have gained from it a great deal of self-esteem and confidence. She also thought that they had learned important lessons about rhythm in reading; students who had never been able to read from a page with much expression were able to sing with expression and ultimately were able to transfer this ability to their oral readings. The students also built vocabulary through learning the lyrics to songs which appealed to them.

Essentially the technique used here was simple and is available to anyone in any school. The reason that the technique succeeded was that the students felt that someone whom they respected had a real interest in them and was willing to work with them on something which they really thought mattered.

Still another approach to the teaching of reading through the use of music is reported by Don L. Wulffson, who worked with severely retarded readers at San Fernando High School in Los Angeles (57). Wulffson tells of one 15-year-old Mexican American boy who was asked to read aloud the following paragraph: "I'm going to become a naturalist which is what I wanted to be before I met Clifford in the fourth grade. Nancy says it's foolish to think that being a naturalist is sissy." Wulffson transcribed as accurately as he could what the boy actually read to him: "I'm going to become a *newspaper whether* is what I wanted to be before I *must complete* in the *forest ranger. Once soon it fish* to *catch at* being a *newspaper* is *things*."

Working with this level of retardation, Wulffson sought any means he could devise to entice his students to work on learning how to read. He began by providing each student with the lyrics of a popular song which he would then play for them on the phonograph. The student would follow along as the record played, in essence reading to himself as the record reinforced his activity by providing the words for him. Thus, with this sort of reinforcement, the student came to recognize words and to learn them.

Wulffson points out that often "the student with a reading disability is frustrated and bored with the reading materials with which he ordinarily has to work. In my classroom I have not yet found a student who is reluctant to *listen* to and *read* the lyric of a song" (57, p. 180).

Wulffson suggests that discussion and writing activities related to the lyrics be introduced. He also suggests having the students "draw a picture representing the lyric content. Having the students draw allows them to show their reading comprehension in a way they enjoy and with a facility they do not experience with the written word" (57, p. 180).

Using a variation of the *cloze technique* (see p. 236), Wulffson provided students with lyrics from which words, and later phrases, were omitted. He supplied the missing words and phrases at the bottom of the paper and asked his students to fill in the blank spaces appropriately. This simple exercise helped students to develop a sensitivity to word relationships as well as to reading.

Again, without elaborate materials or equipment, an imaginative teacher has found a viable means of working with students toward a solution to their reading problems. Capitalizing on student interests and demonstrating a sincere concern for his students, Wulffson was able to make headway with them. Other teachers, probably using more conventional materials, had obviously not been able to reach these students through the years, for their reading problems had persisted.

USING THE SCHOOL LIBRARY

Probably English teachers and reading teachers have no greater allies in most schools than school librarians. It is quite usual for English students to spend one class period every week or two in the school library as a group, and it is particularly important that slower readers come to know the library and the resources which it can offer.

Fundamentally, Loban, Ryan, and Squire suggest that "for most pupils, the important knowledge to be gained is how titles are arranged in the card catalog; how books are arranged on the shelves; and how dictionaries, encyclopedias, and any reference books in the library may be found and used. The *Readers' Guide, World Almanac,* and atlases deserve special attention" (33, p. 217). It must also be noted that students cannot function in the library if they do not know the alphabet well. Therefore, as a preliminary step to visiting the library, it would be well for the teacher to obtain from the librarian 500 or 600 surplus catalog cards and to give each student in the class 20 or 25 cards to alphabetize. Students who cannot perform this task — and in classes of slow readers, there will be many such — need to be instructed in the alphabet, as rudimentary as such a procedure may appear to be at the secondary level.

At this point, also, students should be made aware of how to use resource books. Many of them will now know the difference between a table of contents and an index and will not have much conception of how or when to use either.

As a classroom exercise, the teacher should obtain a set of books with a fairly extensive index and with a well-developed table of contents—it would probably be well to borrow a set of history books for this purpose. The books should be distributed along with about 10 factual questions which will require the student to use both the index and the table of contents: "What period in history followed the Civil War? When was Benjamin Harrison President of the United States? Who was elected President of the United States in the election of 1860?, etc." If students are severely handicapped in reading, they might work in groups of four or five to answer these questions.

The next step would be for the class to go to the library for a period. At the beginning of the period, everyone would be given a separate task to perform—one student would be asked to find the name, height, and architect of the tallest building in the world. Another would be asked to find out how many marriages took place in a given state in a given year. Another would be asked when and by whom the Department of Agriculture was established and who was its first Secretary. Each student would be expected to report not only his answer, but also on his source, indicating how he went about finding his answer and telling which books he consulted that did not provide the answer before he discovered the book that did.

As well as encouraging students to go to the library and use it as frequently as possible, the teacher might ask the librarian to come into the classroom occasionally to discuss books with students. One high school librarian tells of going into a classroom, armed with a half dozen or so books, to discuss a topic. Since the school was about to observe Negro History Week and Brotherhood Week, the librarian in question decided to create the most relaxed atmosphere possible and then to begin talking about "Discrimination."

She began by saying, "We are in someone's living room . . . and we are expecting another guest. The guest is an Englishman. What do you think he will look like?" After the students had responded and produced a stereotypical Englishman much resembling Anthony Eden, the librarian said, "Oh, I'm sorry I made a mistake. I do not expect an Englishman at all. I am really expecting an Italian. What kind of man do you expect now?" And she went on to get the students to describe all sorts of other people in like manner. Then she asked what Americans are like, and was told, not surprisingly, "Oh, we are all different." She then got the students to realize that this is the case because we know Americans from first hand, but we know people from nations we have not visited from various fragments of information we have gathered about them (44, pp. 550-51).

She used this technique as a springboard to get the students to look into some foreign magazines like *Soviet Life* and to read some books about foreign cultures. Through exploring a topic with the students she was working with, this librarian introduced them to some of the important things that can be discovered by reading and left them with an invitation to come to the library and let her introduce them to books about things that they might find of interest.

Joan Dobson tells of how a paperback library was set up in a corner of the regular library in the junior-senior high school with which she works in Hanover, New Hampshire. "Attractive book covers are just one of our lures to reading. The paperback library area itself is unusually inviting: there are six small round tables, each surrounded by five brightly colored moulded chairs. Two floral print butterfly chairs and six basket chairs remain vacant while a student stretches out on the wall-to-wall carpeting to really enjoy his book. Lighting is good. The area is relatively free of external traffic" (15, p. 1136). It is vital that some corner of the library be set up for informal reading. Even better than this, some schools might follow the lead of New Haven, Connecticut, where the public schools are establishing reading lounges with comfortable chairs and with paperback bookstores nearby (27, p. 113).

Finally, the reading teacher might persuade the librarian to check out to the classroom a variety of books so that a classroom library, which would change every few weeks, might be established. The purpose of the school library is not to hoard books, but to put as many as possible in the hands of potential readers. Reluctant readers would be a bit more likely to use books which are part of the classroom collection than to go independently to the library to find and check out a book, since most reluctant readers have not yet formed the habit of going to the library voluntarily.

MULTIPLE PHASE ELECTIVES IN READING

In recent years, many high schools have done away with conventional semester-long or year-long English classes and have replaced the former required English courses with electives which in most cases are nongraded but in many cases are phased according to difficulty. Sometimes the elective course runs for the entire semester, but more often the offering is for 9 or 12 weeks and carries credit of either one fourth or one third of a Carnegie unit. In most cases students are assured of having a balanced English curriculum because they are required to have minimally one writing course, one grammar course, and one literature course in each year's sequence (47, pp. 31-37).

One of the early phase elective programs was begun as a United States Office of Education Project at Trenton High School in Trenton, Michigan. The original proposal was made in 1966 and a pilot program was begun in the spring of the following year. By the fall of 1967, the entire English curriculum went over to this system and the project, designated APEX, an acronym for Appropriate Placement for Excellence in English, became the model for many other school districts which desired to work into an elective English program (54).

The original APEX program differed from many similar programs which followed it in that the courses, while elective, ran for an entire semester of 18 weeks.

The APEX program offered only one course specifically in basic reading, an 18-week course entitled "Basic Reading Skills," which was offered at the phase 1-2 level (the phases in the program ranging from 1 to 5 in ascending order of difficulty). The course was to include instruction in various types of reading, specifically in (1) skimming, (2) careful reading, (3) reflective reading, (4) rereading, (5) recreational reading, and (6) oral reading.

The *Gates Diagnostic Reading Test* was given at the beginning of the course to determine where the student stood, and graded reading materials were used throughout the course, including a substantial amount of SRA materials.

At phase 5, a course entitled "Advanced Reading Techniques" was offered. This course was designed to help the superior student bring his reading ability to the highest level possible for him and was concerned both with improving reading speed and level of comprehension. As in the basic course, initial diagnostic tests were given and early in the course tachistoscopic training was offered. The course stressed many of the skills which the student might be expected to use in college, particularly note-taking, the development of good study habits, skimming, and scanning.

Multiple elective programs have come a long way since these early beginnings even though only a few years have elapsed. Many schools have gone over to multiple elective programs in all subject areas. Beginning with the 1972-73 school year, for example, Maury High School in Norfolk, Virginia, is offering nine-week electives in all areas. In this situation, most English offerings will provide nonreading options for those who do not read well. The curriculum will also include courses in speed reading, developmental reading, and study skills (37). Courses such as "Perusing Periodicals" and "How Does a Poem Say?" will also be intimately involved with the development of reading skills, although they will not be taught by the reading teacher as such.

In neighboring Chesapeake, Virginia, beginning in the fall of 1973, the senior high school will be offering 91 elective courses in English, each to run for nine weeks. Each student is required to select one course each in literature, writing, oral communication, and language study each year (10). The reading courses are counted among the literature offerings and fill a literature requirement. Four courses are offered specifically in reading: "Free Reads (Individualizing Reading)," which is designed for the student, regardless of ability, who does not like to read; "Reading for Efficiency," a course designed for the college-bound student who has mastered the basics of reading but wishes to increase his speed and comprehension; "Between the Lines (Critical Reading)," a course for the student of average or above-average ability who wishes to develop "the ability to evaluate reading materials and the ability to understand the implied meaning of reading materials" (10, p. 6); and "Read (Reading Improvement)," a highly individualized course "utilizing multi-level materials geared to meet the needs of the student whose basic skills of word analysis and paragraph comprehension are not adequate to meet his needs" (10, p. 6).

Besides these courses specifically in reading, Chesapeake will offer courses entitled "Modern Magazine," "Printer's Ink (Reading the Newspaper)," "The Comic and the Cartoon," and "Nuts and Bolts (Literary Terms and Devices)," all of which will focus quite extensively on the development of reading techniques, as will the course entitled "In the Mood (Oral Interpretation of Literature)," which is being offered under the courses in Oral Communication (10, p. 12).

Multiple elective programs are on the increase and they offer the sort of flexibility which will permit maximal use of those teachers in a school who are specifically trained in reading. Where multiple elective programs are not feasible, probably schools should attempt to hire at least one well-trained reading teacher who would set up a reading clinic in the school to be available to all students. If one is working in a situation in which conventional scheduling is used, it is apparent that usually there just are not enough reading teachers to go around. Ways must be devised to make each reading teacher serve as many students as possible.

A READING PROGRAM TAKES TO THE ROAD

The Southern Columbia Area School District of Catawissa, Pennsylvania, with the help of Title I funds, met its problem of not being able to offer reading instruction to all who needed it by outfitting a truck as a reading clinic and sending it around, on a regular schedule, from school to school within the district. The reading teacher was able to serve large numbers of students through the use of this "Readmobile."

Karen Gates, the teacher in this program, relates, "We read books about cars, make-up, and fashion. We even use Charlie Brown paperbacks for those who react positively to comic strips. In short, we aim to use the right book for the right child at the right time" (23, p. 90). It is gratifying to note that of the 40 senior high school students involved in this program, 29 were able to return to the regular classroom in one year.

HELPING TO SHAPE STUDENT ATTITUDES TOWARD READING

Robert Aukerman complains that "dissection of literary works identify setting, tone, characterization, theme, subtheme, conflict, climax, figurative language, alliteration, denouement, and genre—this sort of thing has bored generations of adolescents who should rather have been excited by literature. Apparently, the ability to identify the technical aspects of literature is an important objective for the teacher but a disastrous one for the student" (6, p. 138). As strong a statement as this is, it is not an overstatement of what actually exists in many English classrooms.

Richard Alm, the editor of *English Journal,* places the responsibility for student indifference to literature squarely on the English teacher. He writes, "The change in our students' attitude toward books—from wonder to jadedness—is in part our doing" (5, p. 263), and he goes on to list five factors which often lead to this jadedness.

Alm contends, first of all, that we often select the wrong books for students to read. In a survey which he conducted in 400 communities, Alm found that the most commonly taught works in our high schools and junior high schools were the same titles that were most commonly taught in secondary schools around 1900: *Julius Caesar, Macbeth, Silas Marner, A Tale of Two Cities, Hamlet, The Scarlet Letter, Idylls of the King, Merchant of Venice, The Odyssey,* and *Ivanhoe.* The situation has improved somewhat since Alm's study was published in 1963, but reading lists and approaches to literature are still antiquated in many places.

Alm cautions that we sometimes expect too much of our students, demanding more of them than they can give. The teacher fresh from college sometimes has forgotten what it is like to be a high school sophomore or junior. Also, many teachers who teach a book to an entire class expect more or less uniform reactions, and sometimes demand such reactions on examinations, yet we all know that the same book may mean many things to many readers.

Teachers often get in the way of a book. Sometimes the best means of teaching is for the teacher to be as inconspicuous as possible; but not all teachers have yet learned this. Alm very correctly notes that the "literary artist tries to communicate directly to his readers, but often we teach as if what the writer has to say must be strained through our consciousness" (5, p. 264).

Finally, Alm alleges that some teachers make such matters as "the author's life, the milieu in which he wrote, the surface characteristics of the work" (5, p. 264) more important than the work itself. The effects of the New Criticism are coming to be felt increasingly by English teachers at all levels, but many still find greater security in discussing details ancillary to a work of literature than in trying to lead a discussion of the work itself. Perhaps English teachers would be wise—certainly, they would be more effective—if they were to follow Postman and Weingartner's advice and limit themselves "to three declarative sentences per class and 15 interrogatives" (42, p. 138). Most teachers talk far too much.

The teaching of reading is a means to a very important end—the end that the student will be able to proceed independently into the exciting world of ideas which can be his through reading. The reading teacher has no more important task than that of working toward building an attitude that will impel the student to want to read. Once this has been accomplished, many of the problems facing the poor reader will begin to disappear, and the student will be on his way to full membership in a society which places an immense importance upon literacy.

REFERENCES

1. Adams, Anne H., and Shuman, R. Baird. "Sinning to Build an Atmosphere for Secondary School Reading," *Journal of Reading,* 16 (1972-73), 20-24.
2. Algra, CeCelia, and Fillbrandt, James. "Book Selection Patterns among High School Students," *Journal of Reading,* 14 (1970-71), 157-62.
3. Allen, Beth. "Poor and Non-Readers in the Secondary School: A Teacher's Dilemma," *English Journal,* 57 (1968), 884-88.
4. Allen, Dwight W., and Seifman, Eli (eds.). *The Teacher's Handbook.* Glenview, Ill.: Scott, Foresman and Company, 1971.
5. Alm, Richard S. "Goose Flesh and Glimpses of Glory," *English Journal,* 52 (1963), 262-68.
6. Aukerman, Robert C. *Reading in the Secondary School Classroom.* New York: McGraw-Hill Book Company, 1972.
7. Bond, Guy, and Tinker, Miles. *Reading Difficulties: Their Diagnosis and Correction.* 2d ed.; New York: Appleton-Century-Crofts, 1967.
8. Bormuth, John R. "The Cloze Readability Procedure," *Elementary English,* 65 (1968), 429-36.
9. Burton, Dwight. *Literature Study in the High Schools.* 3d ed.; New York: Holt, Rinehart & Winston, Inc., 1970.
10. Chesapeake Public Schools. "Suggested Elective English Courses." Chesapeake, Va.: Chesapeake Public Schools, 1972. Mimeographed.
11. Cohn, Maxine D. "Pairing of Remedial Students," *Journal of Reading,* 14 (1970-71), 109-12.
12. Culkin, John. *Film Study in the High School.* Bronx, N.Y.: Fordham Film Study Center, Fordham University, 1965.
13. Decker, Howard R. "Five Dozen Ideas for Teaching the Newspaper Unit," *English Journal,* 59 (1970), 268-72.
14. Dillard, J. L. *Black English: Its History and Usage in the United States.* New York: Random House, Inc., 1972.
15. Dobson, Joan L. "Whoever Heard of James Fenimore Cooper?" *English Journal,* 59 (1970), 1135-37, 1153.

16. Dramer, Dan. "Self-Contained Reading-Oriented Classes in Secondary Schools," *Journal of Reading,* 14 (1970-71), 365-68, 425.
17. Evertts, Eldonna L. (ed.). *Aspects of Reading.* Champaign, Ill.: National Council of Teachers of English, 1970.
18. Fader, Daniel. *The Naked Children.* New York: The Macmillan Company, 1971.
19. Fazio, Gene S., and McDonald, Thomas. "Using a Metronome in Reading Class," *Journal of Reading,* 13 (1969-70), 289-91.
20. Fries, Charles C. *Linguistics and Reading.* New York: Holt, Rinehart & Winston, Inc., 1962.
21. Gartner, Allen; Kohler, Mary; and Reissman, Frank. *Children Teach Children: Learning by Teaching.* New York: Harper & Row, Publishers, 1971.
22. Gates, Arthur I. "The Nature of the Reading Process," *Reading in the Elementary School,* Part II of *The Forty-eighth Yearbook of the National Society for the Study of Education.* Chicago: University of Chicago Press, 1949.
23. Gates, Karen M. "A Readmobile Takes to the Road," *Journal of Reading,* 14 (1970-71), 89-93.
24. Gibbs, Mary Ellen. "The Coach Teaches Reading through Music," *Journal of Reading,* 14 (1970-71), 23-25.
25. Gray, William S. *The Teaching of Reading: A Second Report,* Part I of *The Thirty-sixth Yearbook of the National Society for the Study of Education.* Bloomington, Ind.: Public School Publishing Company, 1937.
26. _____. "How Well Do Adults Read?" *Adult Reading,* Part II of *The Fifty-fifth Yearbook of the National Society for the Study of Education.* Chicago: University of Chicago Press, 1956.
27. Hook, J. N. *The Teaching of High School English.* 4th ed.; New York: The Ronald Press Company, 1972.
28. Karlin, Robert. *Teaching Reading in High School.* 2d ed.; Indianapolis: The Bobbs-Merrill Company, Inc., 1972.
29. Knight, Arthur. *The Liveliest Art.* New York: The New American Library, Inc., 1957.
30. Kohl, Herbert. *The Open Classroom.* New York: Random House, Inc., 1969.
31. Labov, William. *The Study of Nonstandard English.* Champaign, Ill.: National Council of Teachers of English, 1970.
32. LaPray, Margaret, and Ross, Ramon. "The Graded Word List:

Quick Gauge of Reading Ability," *Journal of Reading*, 12 (1968-69), 305-7.
33. Loban, Walter; Ryan, Margaret; and Squire, James R. *Teaching Language and Literature*. New York: Harcourt, Brace & World, Inc., 1961.
34. McCracken, Robert A. "Initiating Sustained Silent Reading," *Journal of Reading*, 14 (1970-71), 521-25, 582-83.
35. McWhorter, Kathleen T., and Levy, Jean. "The Influence of a Tutorial Program upon Tutors," *Journal of Reading*, 14 (1970-71), 221-25.
36. Martin, John Henry, and Harrison, Charles H. *Free to Learn: Unlocking and Ungrading American Education*. Englewood Cliffs, N. J.: Prentice-Hall, Inc., 1972.
37. Maury High School. "Student Curriculum Guide, 1972-73" Norfolk, Va.: Maury High School, 1972. Mimeographed.
38. Mazurkiewicz, Albert J. (ed.). *New Perspectives in Reading Instruction*. 2d ed.; New York: Pitman Publishing Company, 1968.
39. Montessori, Maria. *The Montessori Method*. New York: Schocken Books, 1964.
40. Odom, Norman C. "A Dozen Assignments from the Newspapers," *Journal of Reading*, 14 (1970-71), 475-76.
41. Postman, Neil, and Weingartner, Charles. *Linguistics*. New York: Dell Publishing Company, 1966.
42. _____. *Teaching as a Subversive Activity*. New York: Delacourt Press, 1969.
43. *Report of the Sub-Committee on Maturity in Reading, Regional Commission on Interrelationships of Secondary Schools, Colleges and Professional Schools*. Pittsburgh: University of Pittsburgh, Coordinated Education Center, 1959.
44. Ryder, Sarah. "The Librarian Goes to the Classroom," *English Journal*, 54 (1965), 550-51.
45. Sanders, Betty. "*MAD* Magazine in the Remedial English Class," *English Journal*, 59 (1970), 266-67, 272.
46. Sheridan, Marion C.; Owen, Harold H., Jr.; Macrorie, Ken; and Marcus, Fred. *The Motion Picture and the Teaching of English*. New York: Appleton-Century-Crofts, 1965.
47. Shuman, R. Baird. "The Rotating Unit Approach to the Teaching of English," in Howard C. Zimmerman (ed.). *Educational Comment: Ideal Designs for English Programs*. Toledo, Ohio: University of Toledo, 1968, 31-37.

48. Silberman, Charles E. *Crisis in the Classroom.* New York: Random House, Inc., 1970.
49. Sohn, David A. *Film Study and the English Teacher.* Bloomington, Ind.: Field Services, Indiana University Audio Visual Center, 1968.
50. _____. *Film: The Creative Eye.* Dayton, Ohio: George A. Pflaum, 1970.
51. Strang, Ruth; McCullough, Constance M.; and Traxler, Arthur E; (eds.). *Problems in the Improvement of Reading.* 2d ed.; New York: McGraw-Hill Book Company, Inc., 1955.
52. Sullivan, Sister Bede. *Movies: Universal Language: Film Study in High School.* Notre Dame, Ind.: Fides Publishers, 1967.
53. Tate, Gary (ed.). *Reflections on High School English.* Tulsa, Okla.: University of Tulsa, 1966.
54. Trenton Public Schools. *Project APEX: Appropriate Placement for Excellence in English.* 3d ed.; Trenton, Mich.: Trenton Public Schools, 1968.
55. Wagner, Rudolph E. *Dyslexia and Your Child.* New York: Harper & Row Publishers, 1971.
56. Wallen, Carl J. *Competency in Teaching Reading.* Chicago: Science Research Associates, Inc., 1972.
57. Wulffson, Don L. "Music to Teach Reading," *Journal of Reading,* 14 (1970-71), 179-82.

Index of Names

Adams, Herbert, 76
Adams, Vernon, 111, 112
Adland, David, 58, 59
Adler, Richard, 143
Albee, Edward, 40, 75, 76
Alberga, C. N., 214
Albert, Richard N., 71
Algra, CeCelia, 230
Allen, Beth, 225, 239, 241
Allen, June, 116
Allen, Robert, 119
Alm, Richard S., 257
Ames, Wilbur, 18
Andrews, Tom, 70
Applebee, Roger K., 3, 7
Aristotle, 153
Ash, Irvin O., 105
Asker, William, 105
Aukerman, Robert, 257
Austell, Jan, 70

Bacon, Wallace, 6
Baldwin, James, 72
Balzac, Honoré, 138
Barbig, Evelyn, 144
Barnes, Douglas, 58, 91
Barnfield, Gabriel, 44
Bateman, D. R., 106
Beach, Richard, 21, 22
Beckett, Samuel, 75, 76, 77
Bergeron, David, 86
Bernstein, Abraham, 16
Blondino, Lawrence, 170, 171
Breed, Paul F., 52
Breen, Robert, 6
Briggs, Thomas H., 105
Britton, James N., 139
Brooke, Charlotte, 113
Bruner, Jerome, 104–105

Buck, Pearl, 16
Burke, Kenneth, 2, 3, 6
Burton, Dwight, 5, 20, 22, 39, 42, 56, 230

Caesar, Julius, 70
Caldwell, Erskine, 85
Cameron, Kenneth, 57
Camp, Gerald, 69
Camus, Albert, 77
Carlsen, G. Robert, 4, 9, 20, 22, 29
Caxton, William, 191
Church, Joseph, 2
Cohen, Helen Louise, 55
Cohn, Maxine D., 240
Conant, James B., ix
Conway, Frances, 140
Cooper, Charles, 14
Cote-Merow, Janet, 117
Cox, Catherine, 138
Crouse, Russell, 85
Culkin, John, 243
Cummings, E. E., 108

Decker, Howard, 228
DeMott, Benjamin, 58
Derrick, Clarence, 141, 142
Dillard, James L., 125, 126, 154, 233
Dixon, John, 10, 11, 12, 13, 14, 16, 33
Dobson, Joan, 231, 254
Dodds, Barbara S., 22
Doughty, Peter, 121
Downs, Robert, 146–147
Dramer, D., 247
Drucker, Peter F., 101
Duke, Charles R., xi, 39–100
Dunsany, Lord, 30

INDEX OF NAMES

Ediger, Marlow, 164
Esslin, Martin, 75, 77
Evans, Bertrand, 9
Evans, Don, 87
Evans, Verda, 31

Fader, Daniel, 3, 22, 25, 234
Farrell, Edmund J., 128, 161
Fazio, Gene S., 249
Fillbrandt, James, 230
Fillmore, Charles, 102, 128
Fisher, John H., 1
Flanigan, Michael, 23, 24, 25, 26
Fort, Keith, 33
Francis, W. Nelson, 103, 111
Fries, Charles, 221, 233
Frost, Joe L., 137
Frye, Northrup, 8, 9

Gates, Arthur I., 222
Gates, Karen, 257
Geller, Robert, 76
Genet, Jean, 75
Gerrietts, John, 225
Getzels, Jacob W., 136, 137
Giardino, Thomas F., 33
Goldsmith, Oliver, 40
Gray, William S., 222
Guffin, Jan A., xii, xiii, 133–185
Guilford, J. P., 136

Hackett, Vicki, 117, 118, 121
Halliday, M. A. K., 102, 128
Hardy, Thomas, 27
Harris, Albert J., 235
Harris, Louis, 224
Harris, Roland J., 105
Hawthorne, Nathaniel, 86
Heine, Heinrich, 138
Hemingway, Ernest, 108
Heyman, Ken, 24
Hipple, Theodore W., ix
Hoetker, James, 50, 84
Homer, 23, 29
Hook, J. N., 6, 8, 9, 10, 13, 106, 109, 224
Howe, Alan, 81
Hoyt, Franklyn, 105
Huftel, Sheila, 24
Hughes, Carol, 127
Hunt, Lyman C., Jr., 246, 247

Ionesco, Eugene, 50, 57, 77

Jackson, Philip W., 136, 137
Jenkins, William, 139

Johnson, Falk S., 106
Johnson, Kenneth R., 125, 234
Joki, Virginia, 9
Joos, Martin, 139
Joseph, Stephen, 169
Josephs, Lois, 57
Joyce, James, 208
Judy, Stephen, 175

Kaleheim, Lee, 57
Karlin, Robert, 236, 237, 238
Keyser, Samuel Jay, 105, 122, 123
Kirkegaard, Sören, 77
Kirkland, Jack, 85
Knight, Arthur, 243
Koch, Kenneth, 140, 169, 176
Kohl, Herbert, 247
Kuhns, William, 33

Labov, William, 233
Lacampagne, Robert, 144
Laird, Charlton, 128
Lamb, Sydney J., 102, 128
Lancaster, Royal, 250
Lass, Abraham, 52
Lee, Janice, 106
Lehner, Andreas, 25
Lester, Mark, 106
Lindsay, Howard, 85
Loban, Walter, 21, 41, 85, 252
Lueders, Edward, 134
Lynch, James, 9

McCracken, Robert A., 246
McCrimmon, James M., 175
McCullers, Carson, 24
McDaniel, Ernest, 142
McDonald, Thomas, 249
MacLeish, Archibald, 57
McNeil, Elton B., 22
Macrorie, Ken, 175
Major, Clarence, 73
Malmstrom, Jean, 106
Mandel, Barrett John, 17
Manning, John, 237
Mapes, Elizabeth, 86
Marckwardt, Albert, 102
Matthews, Dorothy, 60
Mead, Margaret, 24
Meadows, Robert, 31, 32, 87
Mearnes, Hughes, 169
Mellon, John C., 106
Mersand, Joseph, 40, 52
Miller, Arthur, 24, 40, 57, 72, 80, 86

INDEX OF NAMES

Miller, James E. Jr., 8
Miller, Victor, 89
Moffett, James, 16, 41, 58, 91, 103, 120, 149
Molière. See Poquelin, Jean Baptiste
Montessori, Maria, 222, 223
Moreton, Edward John. See Dunsany, Lord
Morrisey, Jane, 123–124
Mueller, Richard, 67
Muller, Herbert J., 10, 148

Nelson, Jack, 88
Newton, Sir Isaac, 138
Nold, Ellen, 86

Odom, Norman C., 228
O'Donnell, Roy C., 106
O'Keefe, Patrick A., 32
Olson, Arthur, 18
O'Neal, Robert, 22
O'Neill, Eugene, 40, 57
Ornstein, Robert, 71
Osborne, John, 75
Osterweis, Rollyn, 141
Owen, Wilfred, 29

Pearce, John, 121
Peluso, Joseph L., 42
Perkins, Flossie L., 22
Pietras, Thomas, 142
Pike, Kenneth L., 101, 128
Pinter, Harold, 75, 76
Pluckrose, Henry, 179
Plutarch, 70
Polanski, Roman, 69
Pooley, Robert C., 108, 109
Poquelin, Jean Baptiste, 138
Postman, Neil, 30, 81, 82, 102, 105, 107, 117, 177, 186, 247
Poteet, G. Howard, 33
Probst, Robert E., xi, 1–38
Purves, Alan C., 21, 22, 26, 27, 29

Quintilian, 153

Rabkin, Gerald, 52
Ransom, John Crowe, 9
Reed, Henry, 29
Reising, Robert W., xii, 101–132
Richards, Bertrand F., xii, xiii, xiv, 186–220
Roberts, Paul, 153
Robinson, Barry, 40
Robinson, Nora, 105

Rogers, Carl, 136
Rosenberg, Arnold J., 15
Rosenblatt, Louise, 1, 2, 5, 7, 10, 11, 17
Rowland, G. Thomas, 137
Ryan, Margaret, 21, 252

Sand, Ole, 143
Sapir, Edward, 128
Sargon, Miriam Goldstein, 118
Saroyan, William, 24
Sassoon, Siegfried, 29
Sattler, Donald, 106
Sauer, Gay, 77
Schools, Leo, 96
Schreiber, Morris, 71
Sears, Donald A., 112
Serling, Rod, 80
Seymour Dorothy Z., 125
Shakespeare, William, ix, xi, 39, 40, 43, 56, 63–71, 80, 213
Shaw, George Bernard, 40, 70, 203
Sheehan, Peter J., 41–42, 75
Shuman, R. Baird, xii, xiv, 19, 144, 164, 165, 172, 221–262
Shuy, Roger W., 128
Silberman, Charles E., 247
Simons, Herbert D., 125
Sledd, James, 104, 111
Smith, George, 77
Smith, Rosemary, 105
Soffietti, James F., 223
Sohn, David, 243
Southey, Robert, 29
Sparks, Merla, 15
Squire, James R., 3, 7, 10, 21, 252
Steichen, Edward, 92
Stein, Gertrude, 182
Steinberg, Charles S., 82
Stewart, William A., 126, 233
Strang, Ruth, 222
Strom, Robert, 137, 139
Sublett, Henry L., Jr., 164, 165
Sullivan, Sister Bede, 243
Sweet, Bruce, 87

Tate, Allan, 9
Tennyson, Alfred Lord, 212
Terman, Lewis, 136
Thornton, Geoffrey, 121
Tickton, Sidney, 177
Tiedt, Iris M., 22, 114, 115
Tiedt, Sidney W., 22
Torrance, E. Paul, 136, 137
Turner, Darwin, 72

Wagner, Rudolph E., 232
Wallen, Carl, 237
Ward, Douglas Turner, 71
Weber, J. Sherwood, 22
Weingartner, Charles, 30, 102, 105, 186, 247
Welland, Denis, 24
West, William W., 104, 106, 118, 119, 120
White, Charles, 89
White, Marian E., 22

Whitehead, Frank, 21
Whitener, Virginia, 244
Willard, Charles B., 22
Wilson, Jean, 22
Wilson, Kenneth G., 102
Winner, Edward C., 25
Wolf, Mary, 89
Wulffson, Don L., 251–252

Zeffirelli, Franco, 69–70
Zidonis, F. J., 106

Index of Titles

"After Blenheim," 29
Ah! Wilderness, 51
All My Sons, 24, 57
Andersonville Trial, The, 81
Androcles and the Lion, 81
"Annotated Guide to Audiovisual Materials for Teaching Shakespeare, An," 71
Annotated List of Recordings in the Language Arts with Supplement, An, 71
Approach to Teaching Usage, An, 126
Arthur Miller, 24
Arthur Miller: The Burning Glass, 24

Bald Soprano, The, 51, 57
Behind the Camera, 33
Black English, 126
Blues for Mr. Charlie, 72
Book of Job, 57
"Book Selection Patterns among High School Students," 230
Books and the Teen-Age Reader, 4
Books for You, 4
Books That Changed America, 146–147
Books That Changed the World, 147

Chairs, The, 51
College English, 47
Commentaries (Caesar's), 70
Compleat Guide to Film Study, The, 33
Creative Power, 169
Creative Themes, 179
Creative Youth, 169
Crisis in the Classroom, 247

"Criteria for Developing and Evaluating Curriculum Guides," 107
Crucible, The, 24, 51, 86

Death of a Salesman, 24
Deciding the Future: A Forecast of Responsibilities of Secondary Teachers of English, 1970-2000, A. D., 128
Dialects of English, The, 107
Diary of Anne Frank, The, 86
Dictionary of Afro-American Slang, 73
Discovering American Dialects, 128
Discovering Your Language, 117
"Does It Matter?," 29
Domains in Language and Composition Series, 107
Dramatic Criticism Index, 52
"Dulce et Decorum Est," 29

Elementary English, 115
Emperor Jones, The, 57
Enemy of the People, 51
"Enemy, The," 16
English Journal, 15, 47
"English Teacher: A Portrait, The," 225
"Exploring the Grading Process with Students," 143

Family, 24
Family of Man, The, 92, 141
Film Study and the English Teacher, 243
Film Study in the High School, 243
Film: The Creative Eye, 243
First Churchills, The, 82

INDEX OF TITLES

Five Clocks, The, 139
Four Views of Caesar, 70

Gates Diagnostic Reading Test, 255
Gideon, 82
Growth through English, 10
Guide for Appropriate Usage, 126

Hamlet, 6, 70, 81
High Interest—Easy Reading for Junior and Senior High School Students, 4
High School English Instruction Today, 3
History of the English Language, A, 107
Hooked on Books, 3, 25
Human Comedy, The, 24
Hundred and First, The, 57

Idylls of the King, 258
Iliad, The, 23, 29
Illinois Schools Journal, 164
Index to Plays with Suggestions for Teaching, 52
"Individual Reading: Report of the Committee on Extensive Reading," 25
INTERACTION, 120
Ivanhoe, 258

J. B., 57
Jane Eyre, 82
Journal of Reading, 225
Jude the Obscure, 82
Julius Caesar, 67, 81, 240

Language in Use, 121, 122
Language of Advertising, The, 107
Language of Man Series, 107
Last of the Mohicans, 81
Leader, The, 77
Life with Father, 85
Linguistics: A Revolution in Teaching, 102, 105
Literature and the Reader, 22
Literature as Exploration, 11
Literature Study in High Schools, 230
Liveliest Art, The, 243

Macbeth, 7, 51, 69, 70
MAD, 229, 230
"Man He Killed, The," 27, 29, 30
Man Series, 18

Match Play, The, 57
Me Nobody Knows: Children's Voices from the Ghetto, The, 169
Meaning of Language, 107
Measure for Measure: The Tenth Report of the Committee on Classroom Practices, 143
Media and Methods, 81
Member of the Wedding, The, 24
Merchant of Venice, 258
Milestones of the Drama, 55
Moby Dick, 6, 18
Motion Picture and the Teaching of English, The, 243
Much Ado About Nothing, 82

"Naming of Parts," 29
Newsweek, 81

Odyssey, The, 258
Oh Dad, Poor Dad, Mama's Hung You in the Closet and I'm Feeling So Sad, 84
Olson's Reading Interest Inventory, 18
"On Teaching Drama," 52
Open Classroom, The, 247
Overcoat, The, 81

Paperbound Book Guide for High Schools, 231
Paperback Books in Print, 231
Pere Goriot, 81
Plays Recommended for High Schools, 52
Possessed, The, 81
Pride and Prejudice, 18

Raisin in the Sun, A, 51, 85
Ralph Roister Doister, 40
Ransom of Red Chief, The, 81-82
Readers' Guide to Periodical Literature, 252
"Reading a Play: An Essay for Students," 84
Reading Improvement, 225
Reading Research Quarterly, 225
Reading Skills, 250
Reading Teacher, The, 225
Reading World, 225
Reflections, Essays on Modern Theatre, 75
Response to Literature, 10
Romeo and Juliet, 69, 70

INDEX OF TITLES

Scarlet Letter, The, 86
Self-Instructional Orientation for Teachers, 112
Shakespeare in the Classroom, 71
She Stoops to Conquer, 40
Ship of Dreams, The, 85
Short Introduction to English Grammar, 111
Silas Marner, ix, 7
Six Wives of Henry VIII, 82
Snow Goose, The, 82
Soviet Life, 254
Street Rod, 25
Structure of American English, The, 111
Student-Centered Language Arts Curriculum: Grades K-13 A, 58, 120
Students as Audiences, 50
Students' Guide to 50 American Plays, 52

Tale of Two Cities, A, 258
Tartuffe, 51
Teaching as a Subversive Activity, 186, 247
Teaching English in Secondary Schools, ix

Television and the Teaching of English, 81
Telling Writing, 175
Time Magazine, 74, 81
"To Be Read," 175
To Be Young, Gifted and Black, 81
Tobacco Road, 85
"Two Bottles of Relish, The," 30
TV Guide, 81

Understanding Body Language, 107
Unrequired Reading, 22
Uptaught, 175
Uses of English, The, 10

View from the Bridge, A, 57

Waiting for Godot, 76, 77
Walden, 159
West Side Story, 69
Where Do You Stand on Linguistics?, 112
Wishes, Lies, and Dreams, 140, 169
World Almanac, 252
Wuthering Heights, 25

General Index

Absurdist plays for use in secondary schools, 77–78
Academic theater, 49
Activities in teaching drama, 83–89
Adolescent reading interests, three major periods, 20
Advanced Placement Tests, 142
Airport game, 89–90
Alphabet, English, 189
Alphabet, teaching of, 252
American Theatre Association (ATA), 49, 52
Anglo-American Conference on the Teaching of English (Dartmouth), 10–14, 17, 23, 27, 43, 58, 91, 136, 148
Anthologies of black drama, 74
APEX, 255
Audio-visual resources for Shakespearean drama, 69–71

Background to Shakespearean drama, 66–68
Barrington (Illinois) High School, 88–89
Basic library in reading, 226–227
Bible, impact on dramatic literature, 57
Bibliography, Shakespearean, 68–69
Black drama, 71–74
Black English, 124–126, 233
Black plays suitable for secondary schools, 73–74
Books, free distribution of, 25

California Test of Personality, 245
CEEB Writing Sample, 142
Characteristics of absurdist drama, 75

Characteristics of teleplays, 79–80
Chesapeake (Virginia) Public Schools 256
Cinquain, 161
Classroom atmosphere, 14–17
Classroom library, 230–231, 254
Classroom movies, 32
Cloze procedure, 236, 252
Comic books, 230
Committee on Curriculum Bulletins, 107
Committee on Extensive Reading, 25
Communication, oral, 43
Community theater, 48
Competition, model of, xi, 15
Composition constituents, 153
Composition, spelling and, 197–200
Composition texts, criticism of, 149
Conservational grammar, 116–117
Conventions of Shakespearean drama, 64
Coöperation, model of, xi, 15, 16
Corrective reading, 239
Creative dramatics, 91–97
Creative dramatics, values of, 91
Creative expression, factors inhibitive to, 137
Creativity, 136–138

Dartmouth Conference, see Anglo-American Conference on the Teaching of English (Dartmouth), 10–14, 17, 23, 27, 43, 58, 91, 136, 148
Deep structures, 115, 116
Detective story, teaching of, 31
Developmental reading, 238
Dialects, xii, 124–126, 233
Dictations, 156

GENERAL INDEX

Dionysian ritual, 95
Drama, xi, 39–100
Drama and the language curriculum, 91
Drama, approaches to teaching, 55–60
Drama, black, xi, 71–74
Drama, contemporary, 56
Drama differentiated from other genres, 59
Drama, 18th century, 56
Drama, Elizabethan, 56
Drama, Greek, 55, 95
Drama, medieval, 55
Drama, 19th century, 56
Drama, objectives for teaching, 42
Drama, resources for teaching, 44–47
Drama, special types of, 63–83
Drama, student-centered, 91
Drama, teaching of, 39–100
Drama, television, xi, 79–83
Dramatics, creative, xi, 91–97
Duologues, 95

Editing, 198
Education Study Center, 233
Educational Laboratory Theatre Project, 50, 51, 52
Electives in reading, 254–257
English teachers, responsibilities of, ix
Euclid (Ohio) English Demonstration Center, 112
Evaluation of writing, 141–143
Existential questions in absurdist drama, 76

Field research in grammar, 126–128
Film, literature and, 32
Film making, 32
Film study, 33
Film, uses in teaching reading, 243
Film, uses in teaching writing, 179–181
Films of Shakespearean plays, 69–71
Fluency in writing, 153–156
Free writing, 156

General Composition Test, 142
Generative writing, 174–177
Genre approach to teaching drama, 59–60
Grading student writing, 188
Grammar, xii, 69–91

Grammar and improvement of writing, 105–106
Grammar, conservational, 116–117
Grammar, inquiry method, 122–124
Grammar, resources for teaching, 109–111
Grammar, teaching of, 69–91
Graphemes, 188, 192
Graphemic system, 187
Great drama, guide for determining, 52
Great English Vowel Shift, 191
Group editing, 199
Group work in writing, 165–169
Guidelines for teaching black drama, 72

Haiku, 161
Hallmark Hall of Fame, 82
Historical approach to teaching drama, 55
Hollywood Television Theatre, 82
Homework, 162–165

Illiteracy, rate of in U.S., 223
Improvisation, 90, 93, 95–96
In-service programs in grammar, 111–112
Individual reading, 23–26
Interest inventory, 19
International Reading Association, 225

Journals, 157–160

Kinesthetics, 113

Language, Elizabethan, 66
Language of writing, the, 150–153
Language, role of in Shakespearean drama, 64–65
Language study, xiii
Languaging, 186
Lifeboat situation, 96–97
Lillis High School (Kansas City), 243
Literary works, selection of, 18–22
Literature and film, 31–33
Literature and writing, 33–34, 145–148
Literature, approaches to the teaching of, 9, 10, 12
Literature as experience, 1, 4, 11
Literature, discussion of, 26
Literature, teaching of, 1–38

Magazines, use in reading classes, 229–230
Masterpiece Theatre, 82
Maury High School (Norfolk, Virginia), 256
Mercury Players, the, 88
Metronome and reading, the, 249–250
Multiple phase electives in reading, 254–255
Music and the deficient reader, 248, 249–252
Music and the teaching of reading, 248, 249–252
Music, use of in English classes, 179, 248, 249–252

National Council of Teachers of English, 1, 47, 71, 128, 143, 161, 225, 243
National Education Association, 143, 225
National Educational Television Network, the (NET), 82
National Reading Council, 224
National Study of High School English Programs, 3, 7, 11
Naturalistic approach to writing, 175
NET Playhouse, 82
Network Standard Dialect, 126
New Criticism, the, 258
New critics, 10
New Eyes for the Needy, Inc., 235
Newspapers and the teaching of reading, 228
Norman Conquest, 190
North Carolina Department of Public Instruction, 126

Oral communication, 43
Orthography, English, 190
Ottawa (Illinois) High School, 111

Pantomime, 93–95
Paperback library, 230–231
Periodical resources in drama, 47–48
Phonemes, 192
Phonemic system, 187
Phonetic alphabet, 190
Phonetic spelling, 190
Play selection, 52–53
Plays, grouping of, 57
Plays suitable for classroom study, 53–55

Poetry, 2
Poor fluency, signals of, 155
Princeton (New Jersey) High School, 87
Princeton High School Repertory Program, 87
Printing press, 190–191
Projects, group, 29
Projects, individual, 29
Provincetown Players, the, 88
Public Broadcasting System (PBS), 82
Punctuation, 205–212
Punctuation, teaching of, 205–212
Punctuation test, 209–212

Reading, 3, 221–262
Reading, approaches to teaching, 237–240
Reading, corrective, 239
Reading defined, 222
Reading, developmental, 238
Reading, individual, 23–26
Reading interests, adolescent, 4
Reading materials, free, 231–232
Reading, motivation, 3
Reading plays, 83
Reading Problems, types of, 232–235
Reading, relationship to writing, 222–232
Reading, remedial, 239, 240
Reading, resources for teaching, 226–227
Reading, teaching of, 221–262
Reading tests, 235–237
Recordings of Shakespearean plays, 69–71
Reference materials on teaching absurdist drama, 77–78
Remedial reading, 239, 240
Repertory Company, the, 88
Resources for teaching drama, 44–47, 96–97
Resources for teaching grammar, 109–111
Resources for teaching reading, 226–227
Resources for teaching writing, 181–182
Response, individual, 27
Revision, 172–174
Right to Read Program, 224

GENERAL INDEX

San Diego Quick Assessment, 235
Scholastic Aptitude Test, 142
School library, 252–254
Self-contained reading-oriented secondary classes, 243–245
Self-instructional materials in grammar for teachers, 112–113
Sequence in grammar, 108–109
Sequence in writing, 174
Sequential approach to teaching drama, 56
Sestina, 161
Sewanhaka (New York) Central High School District, 243–244
Shakespearean drama, 63–71
Shakespearean language, 64–65
Silent letters, 201–202
Silly syntax game, 120
Slow learner, the, 138–141
Social development approach in teaching drama, 58–59
Song lyrics and reading, 251
Sound narratives, 178
Sources for teaching teleplays, 83
Sources in creative dramatics, 96
Sources of teleplays, 82–83
Southern Columbia Area School District (Catawissa, Pennsylvania), 257
Speech and the language curriculum, 91
Spelling, 186–204
Spelling and composition, 197–200
Spelling, phonetic, xiii
Spelling, teaching of, 186–204
Standardized reading tests, 237
Standardized tests in writing, 141–142
STEP test, 141
Student grading of writing, 171
Student profiles, 169–172
Study Group on Response to Literature, 12, 23
Subject-Predicate game, 117
Suprasegmentals, 207
Sustained Silent Reading Program, 245–247
Symbolizing process, 2

Tape recorder, use in grading compositions, 178
Tape recorder, use in writing classes, 178
Teaching approaches to Shakespearean drama, 68-69
Teaching load in English, ix
Technology and writing, 177–181
Television adaptations of literary works, 81
Television and classroom experience in drama, 81–82
Television drama, 79–83
Television, use of, 31
Textbook English, 188
Theater of the Absurd, 74–78
Thematic approach to the teaching of drama, 57–58
Thematizing, 2
Timed dictations, 156
Transformations, grammatical, 115–116
Trenton (Michigan) High School, 255
Tyrone Guthrie Theatre, the, 52

Uninterrupted Sustained Silent Reading Program, 246

Videotape, uses in teaching writing, 178
Vietnamese War, 29
Vocabulary, 212–216
Vocabulary, teaching of, 212–216

Word-class game, 117, 121
Writing, 133–185
Writing and literature, 33–34
Writing assignments, 161–162
Writing assignments, long-term, 162
Writing clinics, 16
Writing, creative, xii
Writing, expository, xii
Writing, generative, 174–177
Writing, literature and, 33–34, 145–148

THE BOOK MANUFACTURE

Creative Approaches to the Teaching of English: Secondary was composed in linofilm at Allied Typesetting, Dexter, Michigan, and was printed and bound at Napco Graphic Arts, Inc., New Berlin, Wisconsin. Cover design was by William A. Norman. The type is Times Roman with Spartan display.